Praise for Key Questions fo

Key Questions for Educational Leaders is a terrific book. The multiple and diverse authors invite readers to consider and reconsider the complexities of leading schools for liberal democratic societies. *Key Questions for Educational Leaders* should become standard fare in educational leadership circles and well beyond. -**Catherine A. Lugg, Professor of Education, Rutgers University, U.S.A.**

This is a most welcome book. The editors have performed an excellent service by bringing together into a single volume a first rate range of contributors. People with interesting and important insights into the key issues confronting educational leaders today. Too often today the emphasis is on looking for quick and easy answers - rather than facing up to the hard questions that face school leaders. What is education for? Who should decide and how it is possible to develop education systems that are democratic, culturally responsive and inspiring for all? This book provides important responses to these questions - I hope it is widely read by students, scholars and school leaders. -**Professor Howard Stevenson, Director of Research, School of Education, University of Nottingham, U.K.**

Key Questions for Educational Leaders presents a comprehensive collection of leadership research. It is a great resource to critically interrogate educational leadership to inform your leadership practice. -**Rob Nairn; Executive Director Australian Secondary Principals' Association.**

Both theoretically sound and practical, *Key Questions for Educational Leaders* is a stunning compilation of essays that span across important epistemological tensions often ignored in the literature on leadership studies. The volume is absolutely a gem for inspiring dialogue within both the classroom and larger community regarding critical concerns vital to a critical praxis of social justice—one not only committed to emancipatory ideals but also to genuinely transforming the world for the better. -**Antonia Darder, Leavey Endowed Chair of Ethics and Moral Leadership, Loyola Marymount University, U.S.A.**

Whether you're an aspiring leader, a newly-appointed one, an established/ experienced school leader or even a consultant one, there's something in

Key Questions for Educational Leaders for you. The book could be used to build capacity, to create confidence, to pose hard questions, to challenge or just to generate curiosity. Extensive bibliographies accompanying the articles can be used for additional reading or further research. In short – a gem! - **Clive Byrne, Director, National Association of Principals and Deputy Principals, & President, European School Heads Association.**

The editors have assembled an impressive array of internationally recognized scholars and practitioners to offer helpful perspectives on the interface between the best of what we know about effective school leadership and impactful change through critical social justice and equity lenses. **Robert L. Jarvis, Ph.D., Director of K-12 Outreach and Equity Leadership Initiatives, Penn Center for Educational Leadership, Graduate School of Education, University of Pennsylvania, U.S.A.**

It would be hard to imagine a key question in educational leadership the forty plus outstanding international scholars and practitioners have not raised in this small but hyper charged volume. The range and depth in this concise and readable book is a real accomplishment ensuring that copies will be widely used and much quoted. Bravo! -**Fenwick W. English, R. Wendell Eaves Senior Distinguished Professor of Educational Leadership, School of Education, University of North Carolina at Chapel Hill, U.S.A.**

Griffiths and Portelli open the doors to the most essential questions in educational leadership. More importantly, they and their colleagues carry us around in these rooms helping us gather the knowledge and know how to make the world a better place for students and for those who educate and care for them. -**Joseph F. Murphy, the Frank W. Mayborn Chair of Education and Associate Dean at Peabody College of Education of Vanderbilt University, U.S.A.**

Encapsulated are responses to key questions that are relevant to both everyday practitioners and educational researchers yet largely ignored in mainstream leadership texts and professional development programs. -**Jill Blackmore, Alfred Deakin Professor, Deakin University, Australia.**

If you are looking for ten things to do to make you a 'successful leader' you won't find them here. This book goes way beyond these kind of quick fix, transferable 'solutions' to school leadership. It problematizes core issues starting with the purpose of education itself. It is an excellent overview of some of the most critical perspectives and writers in the field and provides a very strong lead-in to a more meaningful and transformative study of leadership. Congratulations on this fine collection. **-Gerry Mac Ruairc, Senior Lecturer, Director PDES/M.Ed (Leadership), Chair of Teaching and Learning, School of Education, University College Dublin, Ireland.**

The various sections are scholarly and professionally relevant and provide a clear and academically rigorous outline of the key themes and issues in each of the topics covered providing a rich resource that will be of value for many years to come. I have pleasure in strongly recommending this text as a significant and innovative resource for educationalists with an interest in the full range of educational leadership scholarship. **-John West-Burnham, Professor of Educational Leadership, St Mary's University, Twickenham, London, U.K.**

If you want to understand the complexities, including the contradictions and tensions of educational leadership, read this book! Darrin Griffiths and John Portelli have done a superb job of bringing together a group of authors whose chapters will engage the reader in reflecting and interrogating their own educational practices of leadership, while at the same time keeping the focus on having learners in schools have a better experience than has historically been the case. **-Blye Frank, Professor & Dean, Faculty of Education, University of British Columbia, Canada.**

This book is a wonderful resource for educational leaders and leadership preparation programs. It is exciting to see new work from some of the most influential researchers in our field writing about many of the most important educational questions of our time. **-Linda Skrla, Professor and Department Chair, Educational Administration and Leadership, Benerd School of Education, University of the Pacific.**

Griffiths and Portelli have brought together a vibrant collection of international scholars. The organization of content of the book allows us an opportunity to wrestle with some of the most important questions regarding educational leadership. **-Dr. George Theoharis, Chair – Department of Teaching and Leadership, Syracuse University, U.S.A.**

This book provides a refreshing and comprehensive approach to educational leadership, bringing together essays by leading academics from across the world. -**David Egan, Professor of Welsh Education Policy, Director, Wales Centre for Equity in Education, University of Wales Trinity St. David, U.K.**

Reading *Key Questions for Educational Leaders* felt like standing without an umbrella in an education philosophy and educational equity downpour. The contributors—among the most compelling educational practitioner-scholars in the world—did not waste a single syllable. They shed every hint of scholarly pretension and pelted me, in the most pleasing possible way, with a barrage of brief but deeply engaging meditations a range of critical leadership questions. I came out fairly drenched, but also rejuvenated and newly equipped to think about leadership and educational equity in sophisticated, transformative ways. I can't wait to use this book in my classes and professional development work with educational leaders. – **Paul Gorski, Associate Professor in New Century College and a Research Fellow in the Center for the Advancement of Well-Being, George Mason University, U.S.A.**

John P. Portelli and Darrin Griffiths have brought together a wealth of practical ideas for a critical, engaged and inclusive leadership that goes far beyond formulas for mere management of education. -**Ratna Ghosh, James McGill Professor and William C. Macdonald Professor of Education at McGill University, Montreal, Canada.**

This edited book is a must read for aspiring and experienced educational leaders, and for those who prepare them. *Key Questions for Educational Leaders* provides rich, in-depth perspectives on the most critical educational and societal topics of the day, with a clear emphasis on social justice and educational equity. Those who lead schools in the 21st century will benefit from these authors and the expansive wisdom they provide. -**Casey D. Cobb, Associate Dean and Professor, Neag School of Education U.S.A., & Editor, Educational Administration Quarterly**.

Griffiths and Portelli have compiled a most engaging and informative book on leadership. These multiple perspectives on the various facets of leadership, provide an important contribution to the current discussions on leadership, and will be a significant resource for all educators. -**Lynn Butler-Kisber, Professor of Education, McGill University, Montreal, Canada.**

Key Questions
for
Educational Leaders

Key Questions
for
Educational Leaders

Darrin Griffiths and John P. Portelli
Editors

Word & Deed Publishing Incorporated & Edphil Books
1860 Appleby Line, Suite #778
Burlington, Ontario, Canada, L7L 7H7

Copy Editing: Ruth Bradley-St-Cyr (Bradley-St-Cyr & Associates, ruthbear@sympatico.ca)
Cover Design by Marcin Koziello contact.grafire@gmail.com
Interior design by Jim Bisakowski – www.bookdesign.ca
Website design by Global Village Design - globalvillageweb.ca

ISBN 978-0-9918626-1-0

Word & Deed Publishing Incorporated & Edphil Books
1860 Appleby Line, Suite #778
Burlington, Ontario, Canada, L7L 7H7
(Toll Free) 1-866-601-1213
Visit us at
www.wordanddeedpublishing.com

Dedication

I would like to acknowledge the difference that Brian Gurnham, my grade six and seven teacher in Beaconsfield, Quebec, made in my life. A superb teacher and person, Brian was a major reason why I went into teaching.

I want to dedicate this book to my brother-in-law Terry Herald, who is battling cancer with courage, integrity and faith.

Darrin

To the memory of my parents, Paul and Lily, who through their humility, spirituality, and example taught me immensely about educational leadership.

John

Acknowledgements

This collection has been in preparation for almost two years. A collection of this size would not have been possible without the support of a variety of people. We sincerely thank the contributors who have responded to our invitation and provided superb insights into the complex nature of educational leadership. We also thank Ruth Bradley-St-Cyr, the copy editor, for her fine editing, and Jim Bisakowski for his excellent interior design work.

Contents

Praise i

Dedication ix

Acknowledgements. x

Foreword xvii
    John P. Portelli and Darrin Griffiths

PART I
What Is the Purpose of Education?

William Ayers 3

Pierre Wilbert Orelus 4

John Roberts 6

Carolyn M. Shields 7

1. **What and Whose Knowledge in Schools Is Most Worthwhile?** . 9
    Ronald G. Sultana, University of Malta, Malta

2. **What Do We Know and How Do We Want to Be Known?** . . 17
    Helen M. Gunter, University of Manchester, U.K.

3. **What Are Seven Important Questions about Leadership?** . . . 23
    John MacBeath Cambridge University, U.K.

4. **Why Is the Issue of Indoctrination Important for Educational Leadership?** 31
    Charlene Tan, Nanyang Technological Institute, and
    Hairon Salleh, Nanyang Technological Institute, Singapore

5. **What Is the Relationship between Authority and Educational Leadership?** 35
    Nicholas C. Burbules, University of Illinois, Urbana–Champaign, U.S.A.

---

6. Why Is the Issue of Accountability Important for Educational
   Leaders? 39
   Fei Wang, The University of British Columbia, Canada

7. How Does Critical Thinking Support Educational Leaders? . 45
   Shirley R. Steinberg, University of Calgary, Canada

8. Why Should School Leaders Take Equity Seriously
   in Their Work? 49
   Awad Ibrahim, University of Ottawa, Canada

9. What Does Racism Have to Do with School Leadership? . . . 55
   Daniel D. Spikes, Iowa State University, U.S.A., and
   Mark A. Gooden, The University of Texas at Austin, U.S.A.

10. Why Should School Principals Think about Social Class? . . . 67
    Pat Thomson, The University of Nottingham, U.K.

11. How Can Educational Leaders Support Sexual and Gender
    Minority (SGM) Students in Our Schools? 73
    André P. Grace, University of Alberta, Canada

Part II
What Is Education Leadership?

Pierre Wilbert Orelus *81*
John Roberts *82*
Carolyn M. Shields *83*
William Ayers *84*

12. What Is Democratic Leadership? 85
    Philip A. Woods, University of Hertfordshire, U.K.

13. What Is Ethical Educational Leadership? 91
    Joan Poliner Shapiro, Temple University, U.S.A.

14. What Is Anti-Racist Educational Leadership? 99
    George J. Sefa Dei, OISE, University of Toronto, Canada

15. What Is Advocacy Leadership? 105
    Gary L. Anderson, NYU Steinhardt, U.S.A.

16. What Is Inclusive Leadership? 111
    James Ryan, OISE, University of Toronto, Canada.

17. What Is Feminist Leadership? 117
    Margaret Grogan, Chapman University, California, U.S.A.

18. What Is Culturally Proficient Leadership? 123
    Raymond D. Terrell, Miami University, U.S.A., and
    Randall B. Lindsey, California State University, Los Angeles, U.S.A

19. What Is Social Justice Leadership? 131
    Ira Bogotch, Florida Atlantic University, U.S.A.

20. What is Spiritual Leadership? 137
    Njoki Wane, OISE, University of Toronto, Canada

21. What Is Rural School Leadership? 145
    Jeanne L. Surface, University of Nebraska at Omaha, U.S.A. and
    Paul Theobald, Buena Vista University, U.S.A.

22. What Is Distributed Leadership? 151
    John B. Diamond, University of Wisconsin, U.S.A.

23. What Is Urban School Leadership? 157
    Coleen M. Scully-Stewart, OISE, University of Toronto, Canada

Part III
What Is a Good School?

John Roberts *169*
Carolyn M. Shields *170*
William Ayers *171*
Pierre Wilbert Orelus *172*

24. **How Does Educational Leadership Influence**
    Student Learning? 173
    Jacky Lumby, University of Southampton, U.K.

25. **How Has the Increase in Standardized Testing Impacted**
    Educational Leadership? .179
    Wayne Au, University of Washington Bothell, U.S.A.

26. **What Is the Importance of Critical Self-Reflection for**
    Educational Leaders? 185
    Victoria Handford, Thompson Rivers University, British Columbia,
    Canada

27. **How Should Student Voice Impact Educational Leaders?** . . .189
    Lawrence Angus, Federation University, Australia

28. **Why Is Inquiry Crucial to Educational Leadership?** 193
    Heesoon Bai, Simon Fraser University, Canada

29. **Why Is Open-Mindedness Important for**
    Educational Leaders? 197
    Douglas J. Simpson, Texas Christian University, U.S.A., and
    D. Mike Sacken, Texas Christian University, U.S.A.

30. **How Are Educational Leadership and Deficit Thinking**
    Connected? 201
    Kristin Shawn Huggins, Washington State University, U.S.A.

31. How Do Educational Leadership and Leadership Development Impact Student Achievement?. 207
Scott Lowrey, Elementary School Principal, Hamilton, Ontario, Canada

32. What Should Educational Leadership Programs Look Like? .213
Darrin Griffiths, Niagara University, U.S.A.

Part IV
What Is Student Achievement?

Carolyn M. Shields *221*
William Ayers *222*
Pierre Wilbert Orelus *223*
John Roberts *224*

33. What Are the Fundamental Tensions in Educational Leadership between Tests and Curiosity? 225
Lejf Moos, Aarhus University, Denmark

34. How Can Educational Leadership Support Student Engagement?. 229
John P. Portelli, OISE, University of Toronto, Canada

35. What Does Every Principal of Indigenous Students Need to Know? 235
Jason Price, University of Victoria, Canada, and
Nick Claxton, University of Victoria, Canada

36. How Can Educational Leaders Promote Mental Health in Schools? 241
Dana Carsley, McGill University, Canada, and
Nancy L. Heath, McGill University, Canada

37. Why Do Educational Leaders Need to be Concerned About "Dropouts"? 251
John Smyth, School of Education and Professional Development, University of Huddersfield, U.K.

38. What Factors Are Associated with Educator Leader Burnout?255
Kathryn Whitaker, University of Northern Colorado, U.S.A.

39. How Can Educational Leaders Contend with the Political Aspects of Their Role? 261
Sue Winton, York University, Canada, and Katina Pollock, Western University, Canada

40. How Can Educational Leaders Support Parent Engagement in Schools? 267
Herveen Singh, OISE, University of Toronto, Canada, and Jeewan Chanicka, Principal, Toronto, Canada

41. Why Should Educational Leaders Be Concerned with Special Education? 275
Susan C. Bon, University of South Carolina, U.S.A.

42. How Can Leaders Support Urban Teachers amidst the Pressures of Neoliberal Education Reforms? 281
Tricia M. Kress, The University of Massachusetts Boston, U.S.A.

Afterword 287
Darrin Griffiths and John P. Portelli

Contributors 289

About the Editors. 303

Foreword

John P. Portelli and Darrin Griffiths

W hy another book on educational leadership? Let us briefly explain our conceptualization with a couple of anecdotes.

When one of the co-editors was hired into the educational administration programme at Canada's leading institution (which rightfully prides itself on being one of the best in the world), an emeritus professor welcomed him with the following words: "Welcome to the programme. So you are one of our last hires who is not really in educational administration since you do work in philosophy." A rather odd way to welcome a new colleague, notwithstanding the honesty reflecting the state of the field in the late 1990s. Eventually ethical issues in educational leadership (thanks to the work of scholars like William Foster (1986) and Robert Starratt (1991)) became accepted and part of mainstream work in the field. However, some five or six years ago, another colleague gave a keynote address at a school board leadership conference pronouncing that educational leadership and equity have nothing to do with each other: apparently, according to this colleague, equity issues in educational leadership are not really issues central to educational leadership. Such an ideologically loaded pronouncement from a colleague who had argued for neutrality and objectivity in education was shocking. Several scholars (William Foster (1986), James Ryan (2006), and Carolyn Shields (2013) among others) had already argued, forcefully and convincingly, that equity and educational leadership go hand in hand. In fact, we believe that one cannot really have genuine and full-fledged educational leadership without a serious consideration of ethics, equity, and social justice issues and concerns. In our view, the pronouncement of our colleague would amount to stating that heart disease issues are not central to medicine.

We take the impetus from such anecdotes to note clearly that educational leadership is not an abstraction existing in a vacuum, cut off from central human predicaments involving ethical, social justice, and equity concerns. Neither is educational leadership located in a charismatic person who urges people to follow him or her, claiming that the best interests of the followers are central. Ultimately, educational leadership is a very human construct that consists of relationships among human beings struggling to achieve their aims. As such, educational leadership cannot exist without being involved with and concerned about ethical and equity issues and aims. How can an intrinsically human endeavor not be directly and inalienably concerned with the lived experience that forms a crucial part of our human predicament? We are after all *human* beings and not gods nor robots! Genuine educational leadership means being concerned about having ethically justified, equitable, socially just human relationships. But such matters are indeed controversial, hence the nature of "good practices" and "good conceptualizations" of educational leadership are still contested. This should not deter us since it is usually the case with all human matters since we are "unfinished beings" (Freire, 1998).

From our perspective, those involved in educational leadership must be concerned about both theoretical and practical matters; both are equally important. Just as Pablo Neruda, the Chilean Nobel prize winner, reminded us, it does not make sense to ask which of our two hands is most important when we clap; we need both. The same holds true for the relationship between theory and practice; there must be a symbiotic relationship between the two. Such a relationship also represents a certain ideological or political stance in education: neither theory nor practice should be a slave to the other; neither should be considered second-class; both are required to solve the human predicament. All of us involved in educational leadership, whether in universities, colleges, schools, or other institutions, must be involved in both theory and practice. Without theory, practice is blind; without practice, theory is sterile. Indeed, as we continue to analyze our human experiences in educational leadership, we realize that ultimately our work always intrinsically and simultaneously involves both theoretical and practical aspects. To reiterate a Deweyan maxim: doing is a form of thinking, and thinking is a form of doing.

As one would expect, in the theory and practice of educational leadership we find a variety of stances and suggestions for improvement. Although we believe that genuine and ethically acceptable educational leadership seriously and robustly tackles issues of equity and social justice (race, ethnicity, gender, sexuality, social class, religious beliefs, and so on), the essays in this collection deal with a variety of issues central to educational leadership. Their authors also represent a variety of positions: some similar to each other, others quite different.

So let us come back to the question we raised at the beginning: why another book on educational leadership? This book offers concise, clear, well-argued essays on issues central to educational leadership by scholars from different parts of the English-speaking world who have thought in depth about their topics. Each essay is guided by a straightforward question that those in educational leadership should address, both theoretically and practically.

The book identifies major issues in educational leadership and presents its positions based on research and experience. Our hope is that the book will assist current and prospective educational leaders, and anyone else interested in the vital pursuit of education, in the continuous journey of improving our thinking and actions. The aim of any educational leadership should be to make the student experience genuinely educational and meaningful, fair and equitable, enriching and socially just. Such a journey deserves meaningful discussions that take a variety of perspectives into account, and that is exactly what this book is meant to provide.

References

Foster, W. (1986). *Paradigms and Promises: New Approaches to Educational Administration*. Amherst, NY: Prometheus Books.

Freire, P. (1998). *Pedagogy of Freedom: Ethics, Democracy, and Civic Courage*. New York: Rowman & Littlefield Publ. Inc.

Ryan, J. (2006). *Inclusive Leadership*. San Francisco, CA: Jossey-Bass.

Shields, C. (2013). *Transformative Leadership in Education: Equitable Change in an Uncertain and Complex World*. New York: Routledge.

Starratt, R. J. (1991) Building an Ethical School: A Theory for Practice in Educational Leadership, *Educational Administration Quarterly*, 27 (2): 155-202.

PART I

What Is the Purpose of Education?

What Is the Purpose of Education?

William Ayers

The 1948 United Nations Universal Declaration of Human Rights pronounced education a fundamental human right: "Everyone has the right to education [which] shall be directed to the full development of the human personality and to the strengthening of respect for human rights and fundamental freedoms."

Schools reflect and reveal the communities they serve: a kingdom teaches allegiance to the crown while a theocracy preaches faithfulness and piety. Any outsider could learn a lot about a society simply by peeking into its classrooms — the old South Africa had beautiful palaces of learning for whites, and overcrowded, ill-equipped classes for blacks: apartheid schools mirrored apartheid society perfectly.

Education for free people is powered by a fragile and precious ideal: *every human being is of infinite and incalculable value*. Each of us is born deserving recognition and respect, equal in dignity and rights, endowed with reason and conscience and agency.

The purpose of education in a democracy is thoroughly social and radically individual: to achieve the fullest development of each — given the tremendous range of ability and the delicious stew of backgrounds and points-of-origin — as the necessary condition for the full development of the entire community, and, conversely, to realize the fullest development of all as essential for the full development of each.

What Is the Purpose of Education?

Pierre Wilbert Orelus

Various views, at times conflicting, about what *is* or what *should be* the purpose of education often emerge in heated educational and political debates. One's social class, intellectual formation, existential experience, and ideology often influence these views. One's view about the purpose of education might stem from one's colonial or colonized mentality: that students ought to be taught the canon, including dominant Western cultural and religious values, beliefs, and languages.

One's viewpoint about the purpose of education might be shaped by academic and personal experiences with, and professional observations of the type of citizens the school system produces. Such experiences and observations often lead to conflicting views. While for some the purpose of education might be to prepare students for the labour force, for others it may be to spark intellectual curiosity while at the same time challenging students to think more deeply and more critically about educational, political, and socio-economic issues affecting their lives and those of their fellow human beings. Still for those influenced by dominant Western ideology, the purpose of education might be to transform the "savage" into the civilized by teaching great moral and ethical values, among other myths.

Generally, individuals express or support views about the purpose of education that seem to serve their interests. For instance, individuals from lower socio-economic backgrounds might see education as a tool to help them improve their position in society. Similarly, someone from a privileged economic background might see education as a way to gain more economic and political power and higher social status.

In addition to the professional and academic formation students receive in school and the moral values they are taught, they should be inspired to become rebellious and fearless thinkers ideologically, intellectually, and philosophically. They should also be politically well equipped to read critically and understand our complex world — a world where the gap between the privileged and the poor seems to be widening every day. At the same time, students should also be inspired to be compassionate, loving, and responsible citizens prepared to serve humanity. Achieving such ambitious goals would require an inclusive, progressive, and humanistic education.

In short, schools that effectively and sufficiently prepare students to become successful academically, intellectually, and professionally are often labelled as good schools. Those that fail to do so are usually stigmatized as bad schools, regardless of the root causes of such failure. These root causes include unequal distribution of resources and other forms of inequity often race- and class- based. Some of these "bad schools" are sometimes closed by the government, usually at the expense of those from poor socio-economic backgrounds.

What Is the Purpose of Education?

John Roberts

Aboriginal education must transcend books and classrooms; it must reach far beyond teaching Aboriginal students ways to survive in a non-Aboriginal world. Most important is a return to the "old ways" in which spirituality and respect for the environment are stressed as essential components of the Aboriginal worldview.

An essential purpose of education is to revive the teachings of the Elders, which help to explain the bond between Aboriginal people and the land, as well as illustrating how balancing the ecosystem is critical to the health of the environment. An education system managed and implemented by Aboriginal people, based on improving self-esteem and creating enhanced self-awareness, is the only way to provide a supportive learning environment for students.

These teachings, along with educational strategies relying on Native learning and teaching styles, increased exposure to Aboriginal languages, and the incorporation of Native customs and experiences, will enable Aboriginal children both to succeed in a non-Aboriginal world and to create a culturally relevant educational environment.

What Is the Purpose of Education?

Carolyn M. Shields

Traditionally, institutions offering formal education have multiple purposes including socialization, custodial functions, individual development, economic development, and preparation for citizenship. In a democratic society, I believe the latter to be the most important. For any democracy to succeed, it is necessary to have a well-educated population — a large group of caring, thoughtful, and critical citizens who live in a relationship of mutual benefit.

The question might be reframed as this: What is education's role in the preparation of people ready to participate fully in civil society? First, education must help citizens to understand who they are in terms of their socio-cultural roots, for it is important to acknowledge that the present cannot be understood apart from either the past or the future. Hence, a good education helps students to listen carefully, learn multiple versions of reality, accept multiple perspectives, develop positive and caring relationships, deal with ambiguity and change, and be able to understand others' viewpoints, without necessarily achieving agreement. Education must prepare each individual to express his or her opinion without suppressing the right of others to do the same. Perhaps most importantly, education must help each individual strive to reach his or her full potential while at the same time recognizing our interdependence — we are our brother's keeper.

Chapter 1

What and Whose Knowledge in Schools Is Most Worthwhile?

Ronald G. Sultana

What we set out to teach in schools — the "intended curriculum"[1] — is necessarily a *selection* from a wide array of knowledge, skills, and values. Given the sheer amount and range of humanity's recorded historical experience as a species, this is inevitable; one cannot teach the next generations "everything." Indeed, the current mantra in education systems everywhere is that what matters most is to teach students *how* to learn (i.e. "metacognition"); they are encouraged to be purposeful, skilful, reflexive, and self-directed in a life-long and life-wide search for information, knowledge, and (hopefully) wisdom.

The obvious question that follows is this: If the intended curriculum is a selection from what is known, *who* makes this selection, for *what purpose*, and with which *consequences*? Certainly, such a selection is hardly, if ever, arbitrary (Apple, 1993). Curriculum specialists deploy their skills and theoretical understanding in making choices according to such criteria as "developmental age" and (presumed) cognitive "ability" of the targeted students, for instance. They also work within the set parameters

---

1. This must be distinguished from the "enacted" (or delivered) and "received" curriculum.

suggested (or imposed) by those who engage their services. Such parameters can vary from the (apparently) most innocuous to the most wilfully malign, but they are always ideological, i.e. they convey messages that set out to shape and equip citizens in particular ways, for hoped-for ends. They also subtly and not so subtly state *which* knowledge, and *whose* knowledge, matters.

A few examples will help make these points more clearly. Take that seemingly untouchable curricular monster, Mathematics, for instance. Curricula worldwide determine that this is an IMPORTANT subject, and they signal this in many ways:

All students must study it (i.e., it is not an optional or elective subject)

Compared to other curricular areas, it occupies several slots in the weekly K–12 timetable (it therefore enjoys a privileged place in the political economy of the curriculum)

In many countries, failure to achieve the required standard in Math excludes students from a variety of post-compulsory and higher educational pathways that lead to the more lucrative jobs in the labour market, and to comfortable lifestyles and life chances.

The stern warning "Let no one ignorant of Mathematics enter here" has been hung over many an institution ever since it was first displayed over Plato's academy two-and-a-half thousand years ago. The problem is that many of the claims made in favour of Math are highly suspect and arbitrary to some; the discipline only engages and exercises a particular range of intellectual and cognitive skills, many of which — some claim — are hardly ever needed or mobilized in everyday contemporary living. And as the adherents to the movement that has come to be known as "critical mathematics" have argued (e.g., Stinson, Bidwell, & Powell, 2012), the Math taught in schools is often the expression of the highly specialized and esoteric knowledge of an inner circle of subject specialists. As such, it ends up functioning as an instrument legitimizing exclusion of large groups of students, often identifiable by their social background. Instead, those critical of traditional Mathematics make a case for an inclusive and empowering "mathematicity" based on Freirian principles of critical literacy that enables students to read and de-code the world they live in

— deploying mathematical skills to engage with social, economic, cultural, and political issues and with actions for social change.

Whether we agree or not with such a critique, the example of "critical mathematics" powerfully reiterates the questions we have asked ourselves at the outset. Choices as to what to teach are made by powerful individuals or groups who determine what is worth knowing. In Malta, "somebody" (singular and/or plural) made a decision that the turgid, formally remote, often unfathomable verses of the national poet (an unmarried Catholic priest with a morbid fixation on his mother) are preferred as a curricular diet to the often politically astute, lively, cutting, interactive vernacular songs bred in the crucible of working class lives. In Ireland, Lebanon, Kosovo, and Israel/Palestine, "somebody" made a decision as to how the conflict that led to so much bloodshed would be represented in the history textbooks, *if at all*.[2] In Africa, Canada, Latin America, Morocco, Australia, and wherever we find Aboriginal peoples, "somebody" made a decision that "modern" Western curricular subjects are more valuable than the indigenous knowledge distilling centuries of experience rooted in particular ecological contexts and communities. Some educational systems value work-related skills and include vocational subjects and technological literacy in their compulsory curricula. Other systems do not, or do so in ways that reinforce the perception that such "practical" subjects are inferior to "academic" subjects, reproducing the age-old divide between brains and brawn.

What we choose to value as knowledge, how we value it, and what we choose to leave out, are all highly important decisions and choices with all sorts of effects and consequences. Politically, of course, and in relation to the formation of tomorrow's citizens, what individuals and groups know (in terms of the classic three-fold combination of "savoir," "savoir faire," and "savoir être"), as well as what they do *not* get to know, has important implications for the kind of society and the sorts of social relations developed. But curricular decisions and choices have pedagogical implications as well: *what* students are taught affects the extent of their *learning* (and motivation to learn) and hence the relative levels of

---

2. The so-called "null curriculum," or what is left out in the selection made by curriculum designers, is often as telling as what is included, if not more.

educational *achievement* (Yates, 2009). Students who reject the diet of classical literature and music that curriculum specialists decide should be a compulsory part of their educational experience might nevertheless engage with popular forms of literature and expressive arts. Teachers who struggle against the grain to teach formal Mathematics might be more successful in teaching "mathematicity" applied to addressing real-world problems that connect with students' everyday lives and experiences. Youngsters might more readily appreciate the value of history, as well as the problematic nature of narratives, if they collect and try to make sense of the life stories of people in their community, rather than reading about the lives of kings and queens, and knights and knaves from a remote, bygone era.

That concern with connecting with students' "frameworks of relevance" — what one could refer to as "social knowledge" — is one important and compelling side of the curriculum debate, i.e., the consideration of what should count as worthwhile knowledge. There is, however, another side. A simple but not simplistic way of stating this is to make a distinction between "the knowledge of the powerful" on the one hand, and "powerful knowledge" on the other (Young, 2008). In other words, while this chapter has thus far highlighted how powerful groups (based on privileges of class, gender, race, religious conviction, and so on) determine what should be included in a community's "canon" of "knowledge," there is another argument to be made that responds to these questions: Do all types and forms of knowledge have equal (epistemological) status? Is teaching Marley (Bob) as "objectively" enriching as teaching Mozart (Amadeus)? Is exposing students to Shakespeare as educationally legitimate as taking them to the town's production of a festive pantomime? How do we navigate between the poles of an *absolutist* conception of knowledge ("*this* is what matters") and a *relativist* one ("all knowledge is of *equal* worth") — what Nash (2004) refers to as the "necessary" and the "arbitrary"?[3] As McPhail (2013) puts it, should we go "for the canon or for the kids"?

There are at least two ways of addressing such important questions. The first was suggested by the Italian political philosopher Antonio Gramsci, who argued that the "subaltern" should have access to the knowledge produced and valued by the powerful. A case in point in late 19th and early 20th century Italy would have been prowess in speaking and writing Latin. The possession of such a "positional good" theoretically would enable the groups excluded from power to break into the social, cultural, and economic realms of the privileged. The curriculum was thus an aspect of "the war of position" that gave the working class access to the power needed to bring about social change.

The second way of addressing the curriculum problems identified in this chapter draws on Social Realist perspectives and claims that there are objective, non-positivistic criteria for discriminating between more and less powerful bodies of knowledge, helping us decide what should be included in curricula and what knowledge citizens are *entitled* to have. The more powerful knowledges — *disciplinary knowledge* — are powerful because of the *manner* in which they have been produced, and indeed it is crucial that learners understand and master these forms of knowledge production.[4] This includes an understanding of knowledge that is "historically produced through collective procedures within which critique is a constitutive principle" (Moore, 2013, p. 348). To continue quoting Moore, "The powerful are so not because they arbitrarily impose their knowledge/culture as 'powerful knowledge/culture,' but because they enjoy privileged access to the knowledge/culture that is powerful in its own right" (p. 350).

---

3. Nash (2004), for instance, confutes some of the claims made in favour of alternative mathematics by asking whether it might not be the case that official "mathematics in the strict sense provides knowledge about the real structure of the physical universe and in that sense is, for the most practical reasons, the intellectual birthright of all" (p. 609).

4. Disciplinary knowledge is "propaedeutic," a way of introducing students to important learning paths that in themselves have no limit, even if most students will choose not to go very far along such paths.

To conclude: therefore, while pedagogically it does make sense to engage learners' knowledge constructed experientially in their relations and interactions of everyday life, the school curriculum, for both political and epistemological reasons, needs to go well beyond that. It needs to "enhance" everyday knowledge by helping learners engage with the knowledge produced by disciplines that have a validity outside the particular historical and cultural standpoints and interests from which they have emerged. Failure to do so denies groups of students (often identifiable by their social class and ethnic affiliations) access to the structuring principles of disciplinary knowledge, and hence "to the world of concepts, theoretical explanation and understanding" (Lourie & Rata, 2014, 32).

In addressing these matters, epistemological considerations are intertwined with social, educational, and justice issues. In thinking about the curriculum, educational leaders might wish to endorse the view that "for knowledge to have the potential to be experienced by students as fulfilling and also to enable them to act in and on the social and physical worlds in ways that change the world for the better, it matters not only that that knowledge is not oppressive but also that it is rigorous and capable of withstanding as much criticism as possible" (Gewirtz & Cribb, 2009, pp. 120–121). As Lourie & Rata note, both disciplinary knowledge and social knowledge are important, and each plays a valuable role. While the latter is grounded in personal experience within a socio-cultural group, providing a sense of identity and belonging, the former "disturbs that common sense understanding of the world. It provides the means for doubt, criticism and judgement — intellectual tools that change individuals and change the world" (2014, p. 33).

References

Apple, M.W. (1993). The politics of official knowledge: Does a National Curriculum make sense? *Teachers' College Record, 95*(2), 222–241.

Gewirtz, S., & Cribb, A. (2009). *Understanding education: A sociological perspective.* Cambridge: Polity Press.

Lourie, N., & Rata, E. (2014). A critique of the role of culture in Maori education. *British Journal of Sociology of Education, 35*(1), 19–36.

McPhail, G. (2013). The canon or the kids: Teachers and the recontextualization of classical and popular music in the secondary school curriculum. *Research Studies in Music Education, 35*(1), 7–20.

Moore, R. (2013). Social Realism and the problem of knowledge in the sociology of education. *British Journal of Sociology of Education, 34*(3), 333–353.

Nash, R. (2004). Can the arbitrary and the necessary be reconciled? Scientific realism and the school curriculum. *Journal of Curriculum Studies, 36*(5), 605–623.

Stinson, D., Bidwell, C., & Powell, G. (2012). Critical pedagogy and teaching Mathematics for social justice. *International Journal of Critical Pedagogy, 4*(1), 76–94.

Yates, L. (2009). From curriculum to pedagogy and back again: Knowledge, the person and the changing world. *Pedagogy, Culture & Society, 17*(1), 17–28.

Young, M.F.D. (2008). *Bringing knowledge back in: From social constructivism to social realism in the sociology of education.* London: Routledge.

What Do We Know and How Do We Want to Be Known?

Helen M. Gunter

When you next attend a session about leaders, leading, and leadership in education, ask yourself, what knowledge is being used? What ways of knowing are being promoted? And, who are the knowers who present themselves as "in the know"? I raise this because I spend my working life reading official policy texts, commissioned reports, and attending sessions for educational professionals who are leaders. What is obvious is that clear and significant statements are made with no citations to support the claims being made, or at best restricted citations. The same information seems to flow around the globe, with the same names and books being promoted. Presentation slides have the same messages, with metaphors of birds flying in formation in order to illustrate the issue of being in the lead, and letting others take over through "distributed leadership." Furthermore, having been "trained" myself, I am concluding that leadership cannot really be trained. Yes, you can be prepared, but much of what is presented as leadership training is actually a proxy with an emphasis on management and doing the job in a predetermined way. This is what Jill Blackmore, Pat Thomson, and I (2014) have called the *Transnational Leadership Package* (TLP), where leaders doing leading and exercising leadership are rendered local deliverers of reforms determined by those at a distance from the classroom: "the TLP provides a kind of (largely) Anglocentric policy IKEA flat pack of policy 'levers' that will produce the actions and effects that count in national elections and international testing." It also enables a modernist gloss because "while modern but cheap, it is worth 'buying into' largely because to be seen as different is risky" (p. xi).

If you ask the questions I opened with to the people or documents in front of you, then you will probably find that the knowledge being promoted as a solution for problems you are told the school must solve is highly functional and sometimes normative. What I mean by this is that the aim is to remove the dysfunctions, where the claims may not be evidence based but "we" are exhorted to do it anyway, otherwise children will be disadvantaged. The forms of knowledge and knowing tend to be a concoction of personal beliefs, reform-complicit models, together with "meta-analysis and effectiveness studies, whose impressive statistical manipulations mostly boil down to saying that if you want to improve students' learning then you have to focus on how teaching and classroom practice can 'deliver' higher outcome standards" (Blackmore et al., 2014). Some researchers have taken on guru status in promoting their model whether transformational or invitational or sustainable or distributed or servant or... some other word. Leadership is a global industry worth billions, with knowledge flows and product promotion travelling around the world. This is seductive because the professional and the organization are always put into a deficit context; there is something wrong with us that requires us to be made over with a new identity with the language, posture, and endless emotional intelligence of leadership (Gunter & Thomson 2009). This is usually inflected with futuring because the professional and the organization need to break with the past, seeking a modernizing narrative about how globalized best practice can be delivered locally (Gunter & Thomson 2010).

Addressing the questions I opened with requires the professional to investigate the nature of professional work seriously, and discover what professionals want that work to be labelled. If classroom activity is teaching and learning, then why do we not just focus on the teacher with a respect for that role? The same can be applied to headteacher or principal: if the person's work is to develop the curriculum, the pedagogy, and set the direction for the school, then why do we have to adopt a seemingly normal label that in reality is a means by which identity is captured. What I mean is that education as a public good is rendered private in the ambitions of the leader, the performance of the leader, and enables public education as a service to be commodified ready for colonization by markets, or even replaced by new "independent" providers. Try not using the labels "leader," "leading," and "leadership" for a week; you will notice that it does not help you or others to do your job. Furthermore, it will enable you to recognize who is using this language and to ask "Why?"

Going beyond these questions enables the professional to access a range of resources. For example, the work we have done at Manchester demonstrates a number of key points. First, what is regarded as worth knowing is more a power question than an empirical one. Exchanges on leadership are based on staking a claim for recognition, and importantly selling your expertise, skills, and effective models. There is little that is new (Gunter 2012). Second, a range of resources is not engaged with because they are based on the idea that the professional is knowledgeable and has a social justice agenda. Our work on distributed leadership raises some interesting questions about why critical and socially critical research is missing, not least because it sees leadership as a resource that all can access rather than the property of some all-powerful being singled out through the virtue of title, pay, and acclaim (Gunter, Hall, & Bragg, 2013). Third, how professionals discursively construct leaders, leading, and leadership is about enabling the school to present a unified front for those who judge, grade, and reward/punish performance (Hall, Gunter, & Bragg, 2012). Fourth, there are approaches to research that demonstrate that knowledge is a co-construction, where gurus switch off their electronic presentation systems and get their hands dirty working on the problems that schools can tackle rather than being forced to solve. Partnerships between schools and higher education enable interesting and productive forms of scholarly activism, where educational matters can be confronted (Gunter, Hall, & Mills, 2014).

Reflecting on alternative questions enables educational professionals to stand back and look at what is happening. I have recently shown trends in education policy in England that suggest a shift towards totalitarianism. Qualified teachers are increasingly surplus to requirements, children may not be educated because their genes determine whether they can benefit from it, and seeking to debate matters about teaching and learning is regarded as disloyal to those working hard to improve standards (Gunter 2014). Indeed the former UK Secretary of State, Michael Gove, responded to a letter published in a national newspaper regarding changes to the curriculum, and signed by 200 professors of education (including myself), as "enemies of promise" who act like a Marxist "blob" pursuing their ideological interests. Central to the privatization of education is to position schools of education in universities as unsafe places to train teachers, consequently people are being appointed to teach without teaching qualifications. While this gagging and marginalization of researchers is generally regarded as ludicrous, it speaks to the generation of fear as a disciplinary process. The issue is not what was said, but that it could be said. The questions I have suggested you ask may therefore be dangerous, but if we begin on the basis that these questions are enduring ones that will outlive ministers of education and ourselves then we can focus on our contribution as a resource. Silence is not an option.

Acknowledgements

The ideas in this paper are based on three funded research projects: 1) ESRC (RES-000-23-1192) *Knowledge Production in Educational Leadership* (£99,000); 2) ESRC (RES-000-22-3610) *Distributed leadership and the social practices of school organisation in England* (£96,361); 3) British Academy (SG121698) *Consultancy and Knowledge Production in Education Project*. I am grateful to Professor David Hall and Colin Mills for their support, and to all those professionals who have participated in the projects.

References

Blackmore, J., Gunter, H.M., & Thomson, P. (2014). Foreword. In H.M. Gunter (Ed.), *Educational leadership and Hannah Arendt* (pp. xx–xx). Abingdon, UK: Routledge.

Gunter, H.M. (2012) *Leadership and the reform of education*. Bristol, UK: The Policy Press.

Gunter, H.M. (2014) *Educational leadership and Hannah Arendt*. Abingdon, UK: Routledge.

Gunter, H.M., Hall, D., & Bragg, J. (2013). Distributed leadership: A study in knowledge production. *Educational Leadership, Management and Administration, 41*(5), 556–581.

Gunter, H.M., Hall, D., & Mills, C. (Eds.). (2014). *Education policy research: Design and practice at a time of rapid reform*. London: Bloomsbury.

Gunter, H.M., & Thomson, P. (2009). The makeover: A new logic in leadership development in England? *Educational Review, 61*(4), 469–483.

Gunter, H.M., & Thomson, P. (2010). Life on Mars: Headteachers before the National College. *Journal of Educational Administration and History, 42*(3), 203–222.

Hall, D., Gunter, H.M., & Bragg, J. (2012). Leadership, new public management and the re-modeling and regulation of teacher identities. *International Journal of Leadership in Education, 16*(2), 173–190.

Chapter 3

What Are Seven Important Questions about Leadership?

John MacBeath

S even is, of course, the mythical number, so six or eight questions would simply not do. Seven days in the week, seven colours in the rainbow, Seven Wonders of the World, and as we know, our world was created in seven days (well, six with the seventh for a well-deserved rest). So in each of the following seven questions on leadership, there is a subversive intent - to revisit deeply embedded assumptions about leadership, but also to argue that subversion is what effective leaders do, challenging inert ideas, asking uncomfortable questions, and refusing to accept the status quo.

What Is Your Understanding of Leadership and Where Does It Come from?

Having just read the word "leadership" what images and associations does that term invoke? Where in our development from naive childhood to disingenuous adulthood did we first encounter the term, and how did it relate to our own personal and social experience? To what extent is our understanding of that idea related to a particular social or institutional context? Does it only come into play in situations that require a measure of followership? Do we tend to think of leadership in terms of individuals?

In 2001, McKinsey embarked on a "war for talent" (Michaels, Handfield-Jones, & Axelrod 2001). This was premised on the assumption that the leadership talent existed as a commodity somewhere and had to be found, captured, and imported to effect institutional change. Aggressive recruitment, premised on the maxim that "talented leaders create great organisations," failed to recognize the limiting conception of what "talent" is and where it resides. Malcolm Gladwell's rejoinder to the McKinsey premise was that "great organisations create talented leaders" (2002, p32).

While the McKinsey thesis is premised on the qualities of the individual, the Gladwell thesis looks to the organizational context that may promote or inhibit opportunities for an emergent, and possibly shared capacity.

What Is Your Leadership Status in the Organization?

If you belong to a formal organization such as a school, how do you define yourself to others, and to yourself? The "I am" response probably says as much about the organization as about you: I am *just* a teacher? *Chief* Executive? *Middle* manager? We have become inured to living in hierarchies that define our role, our freedom of initiative (or "wiggle room"), and constrain our sense of agency.

In 1990, Peter Senge coined the term "organizational learning disabilities" to describe the seven ways in which individual or collective intelligence could be constrained and diminished by convention and status. The first he described as "I am my position," a captive view of self and others which, Senge argued, was disabling of both the individual and the organization.

The seventh — the myth of the management team — was disabling of the organization when management protected itself from the threat of appearing uncertain or ignorant in the face of collective inquiry, resulting in "skilled incompetence" ("people who are incredibly proficient at keeping themselves from learning") (2006, p.25)

What Forms of Leadership Do You Exercise on a Daily Basis?

If you are a teacher, or *just* a teacher, it is impossible to avoid leading others. This may apply most obviously to children but in the day-to-day and moment-to-moment of school life, teachers exercise judgements on behalf of their colleagues, take responsibility for others, and direct, persuade, or support in a myriad of ways. Consider the following scenarios:

- On a school outing, a pupil accidently falls into a river. Who takes the initiative to organize a rescue or jumps in to save him?
- In the staff room, a teacher sitting alone while others share their "war stories" is in apparent distress. Who notices and goes over to offer support?

Teachers as leaders, as agents of change, is an idea that sits uneasily within increasingly top-down managerialist cultures and the growing institutional power distance between those who lead and those who follow. Ann Liebermann has written extensively about the clash between teachers who aspire to lead and the bureaucratic norms of their schools. She found that, in addition to (or as a concomitant of) pressure from above, strong teacher norms of egalitarianism in the teacher culture inhibited anyone from sticking their neck out too far, exercising leadership without formal invitation or sanction.

What Forms of Leadership Would You Like to Exercise?

The idea of "sticking your neck out" speaks loudly to the nature of the organization and the embedded conventions of "leadership." As Broadhead and colleagues have argued, since the class teacher is the ultimate gatekeeper in relation to change, "perhaps the time has come to enable them to be at the forefront of change, rather than what seems evident at the present time, at the end of a long chain of responsibility passing" (1999, p. 25).

This sentiment is echoed in UNESCO's Addis Abba *Education for All* 2010 conference, pointing to the critical role that teachers play collectively, pro-active in their school decision-making, exercising leadership in addressing marginalization of families and underachieving students. Recognizing that the problem is deeply rooted in communities and the ways in which policy responds to those communities allows teachers to engage with social policy without the associated guilt that the problem lies with them.

This is what Sergiovanni (2001) has described as increasing the "leadership density" of the school. High density means that a larger number of people are involved in the work of others, are trusted with information, are involved in decision making, are exposed to new ideas, and participate in knowledge creation and transfer. In such a situation, a larger number of members of the organization have a stake in the success of the school and the enhancement of individual and collective experience. Bettering human experiences, writes Richard Rorty (1989) means enabling more and more people to be included in what he calls our "we intentions."

Students and teachers are most likely to thrive and grow in schools where leadership is widely exercised rather than resting at the apex of the pyramid; in environments where leadership is emergent, shared, and spontaneous; in work places where leadership is not always an individual activity but rather is embedded in collective action and in networks. In learning and growing schools configurations or patterns of leadership are manifested "in varying combinations and degrees at times individual, at times in couplings and partners, triads, quartets, networks, formal and informal teams and other groupings of temporary, semi-enduring or enduring status" (Waterhouse, Gronn, & MacBeath, 2008).

Do You Ever Break the Rules?

It would be surprising if, as a member of an organization such as a school, you never broke or bent the rules, or allowed/encouraged others to do so. But if you have not, or claim not to have, perhaps you are not leadership material after all. A substantive body of research points to rule breaking as one of the hallmarks of creative, influential leaders. The tighter and more rule-bound the organization, the more conducive it is to rule breaking; the military, for example, offers a test case in which creative rule breaking is a precondition of both survival and promotion. In his book *The Psychology of Military Incompetence*, Norman Dixon offers fifteen incompetence leadership criteria, including "a lack of creativity, improvisation, inventiveness and open-mindedness" and a "tendency to look for, and blame, others" (1994, p. 67).

It is said that Winston Churchill was a young man in a hurry who knew how and when to break the rules. Clearly effective rule breaking is selective and discriminatory. As David Kelley asks, what might be considered valid by way of rules compelling our adherence? Rules that are arbitrary, or issued chiefly as a means of asserting authority, invite rule-breaking by those independent enough to bridle at subjection to another's will. Objectivity requires principles, not rules and an expression of will divorced from reason is arbitrary, with no valid claim on our compliance. It is just another form of subjectivism" (Kelley, 2014).

Are You Ever Subversive?

Leadership is a subversive activity. This is not essentially about breaking the rules but concerned with challenging inert ideas, asking hard, uncomfortable, and uninvited questions, refusing to accept the status quo. As good teaching is subversive of lazy intellectual habits, so good leadership does not settle for easy answers or bow to "the way we do things round here."

When Neil Postman and Charles Weingartner wrote their book *Teaching as a Subversive Activity* (1971), it was not a rebel's charter but a treatise on the place of teaching as intellectual subversion. It was an argument for the place of critical dialogue and a quest for meaning. Good teachers have always practised subversion, particularly when ill-informed policies threaten to stifle creative endeavour and principled dissatisfaction. Socrates had thought of it a few millennia before and in doing so proved just how powerful, and dangerous, thinking for yourself could be.

Subversive leadership aims at creating and recreating cultures in which people — teachers, students, support staff, volunteers, and parents — ask questions. This may be framed as research, teacher-led enquiry, action-learning enquiry, or the very essence of classroom dialogue — "meaning flowing through it" (Bohm, 1983).

In Giroux's terminology, successful leadership means rising above the "grand narrative" and taking hold of practice, although rarely individually and generally in a context where there is collegial resilience and confidence in the direction of travel (1992, p. 45)

What Have You Learned/What Are You Learning?

Is it possible to lead without learning? Are there teachers, principals, young people who have stopped learning? Is it possible to "unlearn"? While it seems, on a conceptual level, impossible to stop learning, there may well be resistance to being challenged or to long-established beliefs being disturbed. However, as an educator charged with helping others to understand and in seeking understanding oneself, the following counsel from David Bridges reminds us that teaching and learning is always about engaging with other, and others', understandings:

> "Understanding" needs always to be replaced by "understandings." Members of the same community will, notwithstanding this identity, have different understandings of the community's experience. Not only that, but any one individual will, at different times and places and for different purposes construct different understandings of the same experience or social situation. Any attempt to understand the other, therefore, has to be interpreted in terms of a collection of understandings engaging with another collection of understandings. (2007, p. 1)

It is with understandings that we start and finish, revisiting, re-appraising, and reframing what we know, what we think we know, and recognizing that at times, "it just ain't so."

References

Bohm, D. (1983). *Wholeness and the implicate order*. New York: Ark Paperbacks.

Bridges, D. (2007). *Education and the possibility of outsider understanding*. Cambridge, UK: Von Hugel Institute, St. Edmund's College.

Dixon, N. (1994). *On the psychology of military incompetence*. London: Pimlico.

Giroux, H. (1992). *Border crossings*. London: Routledge.

Gladwell, M. (2000). *The Talent Myth,: are smart people over rated? The New Yorker, July 22. Retrieved from: Http://www.gladwell.com/2002/2002 07 22 a talent htm*

Kelley, D. (n.d.). *A short course in rule breaking*. Retrieved from http://www.atlassociety.org/tni/short-course-rule-breaking-0 (last accesses 20/9/2014).

Michaels, E., Handfield-Jones, H., & Axelrod, B. (2001). *The war for talent: How to battle for great people*. Boston, MA: Harvard Business.

Postman, N., & Weingartner, G. (1971). *Teaching as a subversive activity*. Harmondsworth: Penguin Books.

Rorty, R. (1989). *Contingency, irony, and solidarity*. New York: Cambridge University Press.

Senge, P. (1990). *The fifth discipline: The art and practices of the learning organization*. New York: Doubleday.

Sergiovanni, T. (2001), *Leadership: What's in it for schools?* London: Routledge Falmer.

Waterhouse, J., Gronn, P., & MacBeath, J. (2008, September) Mapping leadership practice: Focused, distributed or hybrid? *Paper delivered at the British Educational Association*, Edinburgh.

Chapter 4

Why Is the Issue of Indoctrination Important for Educational Leadership?

Charlene Tan and **Hairon Salleh**

Indoctrination is the intention, process, and/or outcome of paralyzing intellectual capacity so that an indoctrinated person is incapable of justifying his or her beliefs and considering alternatives autonomously and rationally (Snook, 1972; Tan, 2008). An indoctrinated person is incapacitated intellectually in at least three ways. First, the person holds to beliefs or values without any good reason or rational justification. Second, an indoctrinated person not only lacks good reasons for holding to certain beliefs, he or she is unable to justify these beliefs. In other words, such a person is incapable of critically inquiring into the worthiness of the beliefs. Third, the inability and unwillingness of the indoctrinated person to consider alternatives reveals a closed-minded or dogmatic style of belief. Indoctrination is reprehensible because an indoctrinated person is no longer capable of thinking independently. It is antithetical to education and to the educational ideals of rationality, autonomy, and open-mindedness.

An indoctrinatory organizational culture is a closed tradition that endorses, prescribes, and permits one uniform monolithic ideology for its members. By insisting that it has the monopoly on truth, it resists learning from other traditions, censors alternative worldviews, and is unwilling to adapt to changing times and places. In the process, it undermines the social conditions for its members to develop independent thinking and become moral agents. It is helpful, however, to distinguish indoctrination from brainwashing; the latter is an extreme form of indoctrination often involving coercive measures whereas the former only requires a deliberate attempt to influence someone or a group of people to incapacitate their intellectual capacity. It is also important to note that indoctrination is not an "all-or-nothing" phenomenon — rather, it comes in varying degrees and forms, and may occur in any content and context, including in the educational domain.

The issue of indoctrination is pertinent to educational leaders because leadership in education is primarily about *influence* (Yukl, 1994; Bush & Glover, 2003). An educational leader exerts influence on one or more followers in such a way that the latter would share the espoused group goals and accomplish a common task in an educational setting. Leadership cannot be defined as merely a set of leadership practices, such as setting direction, communicating, creating the organizational structure, monitoring, and so forth, simply because these actions can take place without the acquisition of influence on the part of followers.

The importance of understanding influence in a leader-follower relationship has been highlighted in the theory of distributed perspective of leadership, whereby influence emerges in and through the interactive relationships between leaders and followers involving multiple groups of people. In such interactive relations, influence is not the sole domain of people in leadership positions. In a school day-to-day context, both school principals and teachers inadvertently find themselves enmeshed in multiple interactive relations, enacting influence over the other — whether from principal to teacher or from teacher to principal. Hence, teachers are also involved in the enactment of influence over their principals through on-going and dynamic processes of rational and autonomous decision making.

Intentional influence by an educational leader may be positive or negative. Negatively, some educational leaders may resort to using their influence to indoctrinate by marginalizing, curtailing, and undermining independent rational thinking, open-mindedness to alternative forms of thinking, and free will to act upon thinking. In school contexts, educational leaders are usually given a substantial degree of power by virtue of their positions and therefore the prerogative to make decisions on many school matters. Unsurprisingly, they also bear the highest degree of accountability. The combination of both power and accountability may lead to these leaders making certain decisions on school matters without considering the thinking, feelings, doubts, questions, and personal agency of teachers. Worse, an educational leader may pre-empt or eliminate teacher resistance by castigating any teacher who offers differing views from those of the leader, demanding acceptance of, and alignment with the leader's views, and undermining the development and expression of independent, rational, and autonomous thinking. Increasing work intensification in school contexts further reinforces the temptation to indoctrinate teachers in this manner, which would lead to the creation of an indoctrinatory organizational culture. Such a culture is characterized, with variations across organizations, by a closed tradition that endorses, prescribes, and permits one uniform monolithic ideology for staff and students, insists that only the organization has the monopoly on truth, resists learning from other sources, censors alternative worldviews, and is unwilling to adapt to changing times and places.

Educational leaders should not resort to indoctrinating their staff for several salient reasons. First, teachers deprived of a healthy exercise of their independent, rational, and autonomous thinking lack a sufficient understanding of and rationale for the espoused direction, vision, and goals given by leaders. This means that teachers are unlikely to internalize and translate the espoused direction and vision in their day-to-day practices. Second, teachers may commit to silent resistance if they feel that the space for voicing rational discourse is minimal or absent, fuelling job dissatisfaction and work frustration. Third, indoctrination is pejorative and objectionable, as it aims to paralyze the intellectual capacity of teachers, de-humanize them, and imperil their growth as teaching professionals.

Rather than using their influence negatively to indoctrinate, educational leaders should positively build up staff and nurture an educative organizational culture. Positive influence requires leaders to provide rational justification for pursuing the espoused goals; followers are encouraged to consider the rationale in pursuing these goals and choose to be a willing part of the team in pursuing these goals. Divergent voices are to be expected, and the leader may not succeed in achieving "buy-in" all the time, but when disagreement happens, contextually appropriate rules of engagement, criteria for critical dialogue, and norms of interaction to facilitate the resolution of such differences should be in place.

The issue of indoctrination is important for educational leaders because a leader who seeks to indoctrinate his or her followers cannot be an effective and moral leader. On the contrary, the ideal educational leader eschews indoctrination by enhancing the intellectual capacities of teachers, thereby improving the teacher performance and student outcomes within an educative organizational culture.

References

Bush, T., & Glover, D. (2003). *School leadership: Concepts and evidence.* Nottingham: National College for School Leadership.

Snook, I. (Ed.) (1972). *Concepts of indoctrination: Philosophical essays.* London: Routledge & Kegan Paul.

Tan, C. (2008). *Teaching without indoctrination: Implications for values education.* Rotterdam: Sense Publishers.

Yukl, G. (1994). *Leadership in organisations*, 3rd ed. Englewood Cliffs, NJ: Prentice-Hall.

Chapter 5

What Is the Relationship between Authority and Educational Leadership?

Nicholas C. Burbules

Educational leadership fundamentally concerns the capacity to inspire collective action toward shared goals within an organization. As Larry Cuban puts it, "By leadership, I mean influencing others' actions in achieving desirable ends. Leaders are people who shape the goals, motivations, and actions of others..." (1988, p. xx). The key words "influence" and "shape" in this definition suggest that an effective leader must be able to motivate others to act. Doing so means having certain kinds of authority — usually authority granted or recognized as legitimate by those other participants. The kind of authority suited to educational leadership, I will argue, depends on the kind of leadership to which one aspires. In this chapter, I will review six of the leading models of educational leadership, and describe the type of authority suited to each. Readers will undoubtedly see advantages and disadvantages to each model — but choosing between them is not my purpose here. Furthermore, these are ideal types: in particular, real-world situations, elements of more than one model of leadership often co-exist.

Authoritarian leadership relies on the status of a position rather than the qualities of the person occupying it. The authoritarian leader tends to rely on coercion and control, expecting conformity with his or her directives because of the power of the office. Authority in this case is impersonal, arising instead out of a position of institutional status; the occupant of the position, by definition, has the authority. To be effective, however, the leader's authority needs to be acknowledged and, in a broad sense, accepted, otherwise there will be resistance and friction within the system. But unlike some of the other models, this kind of authority is not actively granted by the other participants; it is taken for granted as a feature of defined organizational roles.

Charismatic leadership, by contrast, depends entirely on the personal qualities of the leader. The authority granted to the leader is inseparable from the admiration, respect, and trust attaching to that individual in the eyes of others within the organization. Qualities of personality, character, physical appearance, age, and reputation or stature can all play a part in these feelings of affiliation. A different person in the same role or position may not have the same kind or degree of support. Here, authority is based almost entirely on the voluntary willingness of others to follow the leader to whom they are powerfully drawn.

Transactional leadership depends on a series of explicit or implicit *quid pro quos* between the leader and others within the organization. Authority here is entirely conditional, ceded to the leader based on exchanges in which all parties concerned perceive a self-interest in the maintenance of the relationship. These exchanges may be matters of material benefit or of other real or perceived goods. While conditional, this form of authority can be stable so long as the leader has the resources and capacity to fulfill these exchanges. At the same time, loyalty or support conditioned on specific transactions may not transfer to other matters outside the terms of that transaction.

Democratic leadership depends on participatory processes in which the status and position of the leader is endorsed by the other participants, and at least periodically reconfirmed, through some procedure of selection or voting. Authority here grows out of the presumed legitimacy, openness, fairness, and transparency of these procedures and the consensual affirmation they represent. This democratic ethos promotes a more egalitarian spirit within the community, and supports a more direct sense of accountability of the leader to the group.

Transformational leadership depends on the leader's capacity to foster the creation of a shared culture and common set of goals to which a group is committed. Here authority has an essentially moral character. The leader's authority is inseparable from the shared commitment and buy-in participants feel toward that common vision; in other words, the valuative commitment and buy-in reinforce the leader's authority, and vice versa. Over time, these values and goals may become shared and internalized to the extent that the leader's role may become secondary. Indeed, the sense of collective empowerment and shared commitment people feel may be no longer identified with the leader's authority, but in an authority granted to the shared vision, ideas, and values themselves. The leader's role in helping to foster the shared vision, ideas, and values may be extremely subtle, even invisible to many participants.

Distributed leadership advances this decentralizing dynamic even further. Here the purpose of the leader is essentially to make his or her own role and status unnecessary over time; to facilitate processes of collaborative and collective responsibility that in the end belie the need for a specific individual leader at all. Distributed leadership becomes an emergent property of the group as a whole, not the sole province of any individual — even if initially the authority of an individual is the key to guiding and motivating those group processes. Distributed leadership is strongest in recognizing a variety of areas of expertise and wisdom within a community, and, correspondingly, many relations of authority among peers, not just between the group and its leader.

As I noted at the outset, this review is not intended to settle on the proper or "best" form of educational leadership. Thinking about that choice to reflect — not only on the efficacy of a particular leadership model in terms of producing results (which is often the way it is considered) but the dimensions of authority underlying educational leadership — inevitably leads to questions of value and legitimacy. For example, one might judge the trade-off between achieving particular results in the short term, versus forming stable relationships and building institutional capacity in the long term. Or between authority relations that may be relatively powerful, but strongly tied to a particular individual, and so less sustainable if (when) people or personalities change. Or between centralizing versus decentralizing imperatives and how these might give rise to, or reinforce, other structural features of an organization that have consequences of their own.

In the end, as with the process of teaching itself, a key question for educational leadership is whether it works to preserve and reinforce its own importance, or works to become less essential over time.

References

Cuban, L. (1988). *The managerial imperative and the practice of leadership in schools*. Albany, NY: State University of New York Press.

Chapter 6

Why Is the Issue of Accountability Important for Educational Leaders?

Fei Wang

N ever before have we seen such an all-out emphasis on accountability. Never before have we heard the public outcry against
its legitimacy, purpose, and implementation. The word "accountability" seems to bring up more negative emotions than warm fuzzy
feelings in education communities. Its derivatives and artefacts, such as
testing, standards, and assessment remain distasteful and negative for
many. Educational accountability is more about regulation and performance than educational improvement, capacity building, and democracy
in schools (Moller, 2009; Ranson, 2003). However, accountability is an
important dimension of professionalism that can clarify the obligations
and reinforce the relationships of all the stakeholders in the education
system. Moreover, accountability that derives from a strongly held justice
and equity position is critical in dismantling the structural barriers and
challenges within and beyond the school. Exercising leadership — either
moral or subversive — in these situations means moving towards what is
best for students.

Accountability is nothing new for the education community.
Unfortunately, it operates within a hierarchical bureaucracy where
expectations for co-operation are coupled with threatened sanctions for

non-compliance. Over the past decades, concerns about the quality of public education have sparked a variety of educational reforms in countries such as Great Britain, the United States, and Canada. Underlying these reforms is a belief that the existing education system is inadequate to maintain national economic development and augment its competitiveness in a global society. The entrenched neoliberal belief has turned education from a public good into a commodity regulated as a business. It has shifted educational accountability "from a primary concern with optimizing the relation between resource inputs and educational outputs, to a relentless drive to create policies and practices that aim to produce social conditions and forms of subjectivity consonant with the creation and efficient operation of market culture" (Ambrosio, 2013, p. 317).

However, only when expectations become means of control and punishment does accountability become a bad thing, as punishment and control do not teach people accountability. It is time to stop providing all the reasons why something will not work and focus on what can work.

Education is a public undertaking. Stakeholders at all levels of the education system — principals, teachers, parents, school boards, the ministry of education, politicians, and the public — are responsible for contributing to the quality of education. They are (and should be) accountable for their actions and decisions with respect to their responsibilities. This is particularly true for educational leaders who play a pivotal role in educational reform. If doing a great job should be lauded and awarded, then consequences from any decisions and actions should be accountable. Educational leaders must justify their decisions and actions as they have the ability to impact teaching and learning and the quality of education.

Work of educational leaders is about relationships. Such relationships are built through trust. When parents, guardians, and caregivers entrust their sons and daughters to a school or a program, educational leaders have the accountability to ensure that their children are being cared for and provided with a safe environment and quality programs. Educational leaders also have real accountability to the taxpayers to make sure that the money used to operate the system is well spent and well utilized. Such public accountability serves to build trust and stability. When we are held accountable to others, and they to us, we learn who to trust and how trust is built. Trust is a powerful form of social capital that has the potential to make systems more productive and innovative.

Accountability defines a relationship between school leaders and their teachers and staff. When teachers and staff devote their professionalism to a school, educational leaders are accountable to making sure that the working environment is respectful and safe and that teachers and staff have the resources needed to do their jobs. They are also accountable to facilitating the knowledge, skills, and commitment of people working in schools and creating opportunities to discuss the ethics of professional practice and raise issues concerning the public good. The dimension of internal accountability is mutual and reciprocal. As principals are accountable to their teachers and staff, teachers and staff are accountable to maintain good practices, equitable and fair treatment for students, and communication with parents on broader issues in education. Such accountability is established through trust, transparency, and communication. It is paramount to educational leaders, as it constitutes the core of collective leadership. Accountability becomes the key in articulating school vision and goals, optimizing allocation of resources, building school capacity, and enhancing the practice of school improvement.

Accountability also defines political relationships of power and control between different parties. Among these parties are educational leaders pressured to become administrative agents and obedient bureaucrats of school boards, the ministry of education, and other units of government, more so than instructional leaders within schools. This stressor adds to the constant struggle between the right thing to do versus the hard thing to do, between compliance and subversion. However, doing the right thing and doing the hard thing are usually the same. It equally requires leadership with qualities of self-confidence, courage, creativeness, and political savvy. More importantly, the unquestioning following of orders and rules will not lead to accountability. The act of compliance with the rules and regulations is an aspect of accountability that has facilitated some of the worst atrocities in the history of humankind (Jordan & Tuijl, 2006). Accountability means being proactive in examining, questioning, and going beyond expectations that inadvertently work against the wellbeing of students. Being proactive requires educational leaders to employ subversive strategies to question entrenched power structures and to transform counterproductive policies, procedures, and practices. Educational leaders need flexibility and courage to do their jobs within an accountability framework. They also need to learn when to short-circuit or "work" the system and when to ignore or challenge the implicit rules of the game.

Accountability has a moral component. An inner-directed accountability is associated with integrity, passion, and moral responsibility with a strong sense of equity and justice. It justifies *why* they are doing what they are doing. Accountability is not simply about data-driven decision-making, but about recognizing and overcoming the underlying problems that continue to plague public education: "rising poverty and racial segregation in our schools, increasing unemployment, lack of heath care, and the steady defunding of the public sector" (Au, 2011, p. 38). The more complex and prevalent these problems, the greater the accountability required of educational leaders. Unfortunately, ever since the dominant political discourse chose "accountability" as its goal, any commitment to social justice has been driven to the background. Reviving the principles of justice and democracy has become an imperative task for educational leaders who are ultimately accountable for expanding the parameters to encompass moral, social, personal, and professional goals. Educational leaders have a moral accountability to seek solutions to social injustices that remain hostile to the wellbeing of their students. The self-imposed accountability is a starting point from which to advance equity and social justice.

References

Ambrosio, J. (2013). Changing the subject: Neoliberalism and accountability in public education. *Journal of Educational Studies, 49*(4), 316–333. doi :10.1080/00131946.2013.783835

Au, W. (2011). Neither fair nor accurate: Research-based reasons why high-stakes tests should not be used to evaluate teachers. *Rethinking Schools, 25*(2), 34.

Jordan, L., & Tuijl, P. V. (2006). *NGO accountability: Politics, principles, and innovation* London/Sterling, VA: Earthscan.

Moller, J. (2009). School leadership in an age of accountability: Tensions between managerial and professional accountability. *Journal of Educational Change, 10*(1), 37–46.

Ranson, S. (2003). Public accountability in the age of neo-liberal governance. *Journal of Education Policy, 18*(5), 459–480. doi:10.1080/0268093032000124848

How Does Critical Thinking Support Educational Leaders?

Shirley R. Steinberg

I cannot help my knee-jerk reaction when I see the phrase "critical thinking." I envision packaged campaigns costing school districts thousands of dollars, all to create critical-thinking kids. My memory flies back to the late 1980s–1990s, during the dawning age of "critical thinking." I remember political campaigns with candidates claiming that it was time to start teaching critical thinking in the classroom. Walking into an American national teachers' conference book display, I recall looking at the enormous banners, displays, and incentives all calling us to adopt particular programs. Salespeople with hats and buttons and silly toys called out to us, claiming that their product would have an immediate return on our investment in their teaching materials. Critical thinking, in the popular sense, has probably brought in more money to corporate entities than any other curricular topic. And, we, in the second decade of the 21st century, probably teach and graduate the most non-critical kids ever to attend public school.

The following is a trick question: *How does critical thinking support educational leaders?* It implies that critical thinking does indeed support leaders, and that this support is a good thing. In this chapter, I argue that what is generally known as "critical" thinking is instead a neo-liberalized, pseudo-pedagogical scam generated to do three things:

1. Sell critical thinking programs and materials
2. Placate those interested in education into believing that something is being done for our children
3. Lull us into a false sense that those who have taught or been taught via these critical thinking tools and methods *do* indeed think critically

The third item on that list, moreover, is the hegemonic nail in the coffin of North American education.

In 1983, Ronald Reagan's National Commission on Excellence published a document, *A Nation at Risk,* that claimed teachers were not doing their job. In classic Reaganized fear tactics, citizens were told that students were not meeting the minimum requirements, prompting parents to worry that their children would not be successful when leaving school, that gifted children's needs were not being met, and that teachers needed to be watched, measured, and dealt with. The phrase "at risk" no longer meant the ghettoized child in poverty, but the entire nation. Like mushrooms in damp, dark compost, companies popped up, creating measurement strategies, teacher remediation, and full curricula for entire courses, entire school systems. Following the reaction of the American politicians and schools, other English-speaking countries followed quickly in the wake.

The '80s and '90s birthed hundreds of canned, pre-planned, teacher-proof lessons, inquiries into faculties of education, and politically designated "expert" publishing companies claiming expertise to fix the ills of school systems. Throughout the discourse, the notion of critical thinking rose to the top. If our students could learn to think critically, they would be able to lead the world in education. Developmental psychologists claimed that they could create an environment that would allow all students to soar. Robert Sternberg insisted that cognitive styles be acknowledged, yet not confused with abilities. Howard Gardner developed a theory of multiple intelligences, and Robert Slavin created the *Success for All* program, using notions taken from developmental psychology and specifically meant for the urban poor. *All* programs were grounded in the catch-phrase "critical thinking." Developmental psychology was at the forefront of new, packaged programs designed to whip teachers into shape and whip students into critical thinkers.

Unfortunately, there were few critics of the new programs. Millions of dollars and pounds were spent on purchasing full district curricula, and hiring trainers for the programs. Teachers were subject to class evaluations, the arts and physical education disappeared in many public systems, and children's grades became running score sheets calculated and scrutinized by learning analysts. Kozol (2005) summed up this movement best when he denounced the *Success for All* program as a "martial regimen" with an authoritarian and dogmatic underpinning. Kozol, however, was in the minority, and the bulldozer mentality ushered in by Reagan became the norm. The beauty of the new programs was that they sounded so good. Who would not want their child to think critically? In almost every article I surveyed to write this chapter, thinking critically is equated with rationality and clarity. And therein, dear reader, lie multiple issues. Rationality and clarity, of course, are two of the themes woven into *The Bell Curve* (1994), pointing to race as a determining factor in lower school achievement. Kozol attacked these programs as systems of Apartheid created with the expectation that all students would succeed based on one-dimensional implementation.

If *critical thinking* is defined as programized school curricula authored by developmental psychologists, then I do not believe it supports educational leaders. Instead, it turns leaders into corporate pawns who, in the effort to defend the curricular choice, become brash pushers of the public investment. However, if we re-define *critical* as "critically theoretical," and *thinking* as "environmental, cultural, and historical thinking," then my answer is yes, educational leaders would be supported by critical theoretical thinking. Of course, this also calls for educational leaders to become criticalized. In order to create an emancipatory and socially just educational environment, leaders must understand how power works, how capital destroys schooling, and what transformative leadership can be; *and* they must ensure that everyone involved in the educational endeavor understands. With that sentence, there are lifetimes of work to *undo* what has been done *to* education in the past forty years. In the interest of criticalized theoretical thinking, I pose questions to consider in creating a revolution of thought in education:

- What is the relationship of capital and schooling?
- Can schools exist without being driven by capital?
- Can schools continue to be public? Should schools be public?
- Should education be localized?
- Should curricula be designed from one source?
- Can critical be criticalized?
- Can a country accept students becoming critically theoretically educated?
- What is an educational leader? Who is an educational leader?
- How can leadership be transformative?
- Would politicians want educational leaders to become criticalized?
- How can criticalization in education and leadership be measured? Legitimized?
- Would a critical theoreticalized education be subject to becoming indoctrination?
- Who decides what is balanced, critical, socially just?

If we are serious about emancipation, empowerment, shared governance, and a socially just, transformative leadership, we must be able to understand the failures of the past, and not be arrogant about the possibilities for the future. I do believe we must understand past attempts to create a critical thinking, but do it for the right reasons — that we *do* want students to be powerful, decisive, and criticalized. And that, even for radical educational leaders, is a difficult task.

References

Kozol, J. (2005). *The shame of the nation: The restoration of apartheid schooling in America.* New York: Random House.

Chapter 8

Why Should School Leaders Take Equity Seriously in Their Work?

Awad Ibrahim

We-humans are creatures of context. We can think abstractly, but our best understanding is done when we contextualize abstract ideas. So, with your permission, gentle reader (as W.E.B. Du Bois would have called you), I want to *think through* (Derrida, 1996) and contextualize the idea of "equity" and argue that school leaders should take it seriously. First, to contextualize my argument, look at your right hand. Now look at your left hand. If you are sitting beside another person, look at her/him. What have you noticed? That no two hands and no two people are the same? In philosophy, this is called *tautology*; that is, stating the obvious. Equity study is an exercise in tautology. It is an attempt to remind we-humans and school leaders about the obvious: we live in an incredibly multicultural, multilingual, multinational, and hyper-connected world. This, equity study reminds us, is a rich resource to be celebrated and not a challenge to be avoided.

"Equity," Nelson, Palonsky, and McCarthy write, "is a concept directly related to justice, and includes the idea of equal treatment under natural law or rights, without bias or favoritism" (2013, p. 42). As such, the two concepts of equality and equity might rub shoulders, but they can differ significantly. To explain, if two people are never the same, as far as equality is concerned, they would still need to be treated equally. They should be provided with equal opportunities, equal education systems, equal access to jobs, and so on. But in equity studies, to treat everybody equally does not mean treating them the same. Equality in this sense is equality of *condition*, where all *have* the same, or equality of *treatment*, where all are *treated* the same based on a principle such as, "Everyone has the right to be secure against unreasonable search or seizure" (Canadian Charter of Rights and Freedoms [CCRF], Legal Rights, No. 8). As I have previously shown (Ibrahim, 2014), having this right and freedom in the constitution does not guarantee its implementation. In fact, especially with minority populations, we have enough evidence to prove the opposite; so much so that a revision of the Charter is necessary to ensure that these rights and freedoms are not shelved in a dead tradition of the law and the court (Abdi & Schultz, 2008).

This is where we make a strategic and *wide-awake* (Greene, 2005) move from equality to equity and justice. It is a wide-awake move because it does not mean a total decoupling of equality and equity but rather reveals the tension of equality. On the one hand, it sees the necessity of equal access to educational opportunity and jobs but, on the other, recognizes that having individual rights and freedoms enshrined in the law might ironically block people from seeing structural injustices and the need for social change.

Equity, then, is an epistemic framework that attempts to shed light on inequalities and injustices as well as a practice that begins with an extremely difficult but necessary moral question: "Is it possible to distribute things in a truly equal manner?" (Nelson et al., 2013, p. 42). Paulo Freire (2000) refers to this intersection of theory and practice as *praxis*. As a praxis, equity does not just rub shoulders with equality but sees it as a first step in the struggle for justice, rights, and freedoms. Being equal under the law, in other words, is an integral step for justice but does not guarantee fairness. If equality is procedural, it merely ensures that everybody *has* the same or *is treated* the same; as a praxis, equity is a wide-awake internal mechanism that ensures that procedures are fair. In this sense, Nelson et al. argue, "equity provides a concept for judging the procedure of equal treatment. Under equity," they conclude, "exactly equal conditions or results are not required; there is no mandate that good things are distributed to all in an equal manner" (2013, p. 42).

As creatures of context, let us take a concrete example. In 2010, the Ontario Ministry of Education (OME) released a report entitled "Supporting Students in Urban Priority Neighbourhoods" to provide examples of how its Urban Priority High School (UPHS) program has been supporting schools located in regions of Ontario affected by poverty, crime, gang activities, and a lack of community resources. The UPHS initiative offers programs in five key areas: nutrition, student leadership/engagement, lunchtime and after-school programming, staffing, and improving student achievement. The report notes that thirty-four Ontario high schools are recipients of funding for these special programs.

Through the UPHS program, the OME took a wide-awake move from equality to equity. OME operates on the premise that all Ontario schools should have *equal* funding, a minimum base that allows *all* schools to succeed. However, by creating the UPHS program, the OME also recognizes that, given the high concentration of poverty, crime, and gang activities, and the lack of resources, certain communities require extra help dedicated to filling the gaps in the five areas outlined above. The UPHS program is a stellar example of what equity is, how it is implemented, and how it is supposed to work.

Some might argue that programs such as UPHS take away funding that could benefit everyone. Equity is proposed precisely to counter-argue this point. John Rawls (2001) argues that, for justice to deserve its name, it must expect unequal distribution. But this unequal distribution must be justified by some significant social or ethical principle. The whole field of exceptionalities (from mental and physical disability to gifted and talented programs) is premised on a Rawlsian notion of justice and equity, where choices are made based on specific needs and not blanket policies. For example, when we decided to provide special access to public buildings for people who require a wheelchair, this is a principle of equity, which means that equal access for all requires special treatment for some groups. As Nelson et al. note, equity "can include inequality if the basic premise is that of justice" (2013, p. 43). The UPHS program — and all programs constructed to redress previous inequalities, injustices, and discriminations based on gender, race, class, ability, or sexual orientation — are based on addressing equity issues.

James Banks (2014) identifies four ascending levels of school and curriculum reforms related to equity:

1. Contribution level (focusing on heroes, holidays, and culture)
2. Additive level (focusing on themes and perspectives without changing structure)
3. Transformation level (focusing on changing structure and on multiple perspectives and approaches)
4. Social action level (where structure is changed and students, teachers, and school leaders are asked to make decisions on important social issues and take action to help solve them)

In 2012, we conducted ethnographic research in two high schools that have implemented the UPHS program (Ibrahim, Radford, Schmitz, & Toomey, 2012), which showed the exceptionally positive outcome when school leaders make equity the praxis of their school. We saw teachers rallying around justice, advocacy, and commitment to the success of their students. We saw students respectful of their teachers and the physical environment of the school. We saw students who came to school at 7 a.m. to receive extra academic help and did not leave until 8 or 9 p.m. because they were involved in extra-curricular clubs and activities. We saw marginalized groups — especially immigrants, refugees, and First Nations — feel at home. So much so that, in the words of the school principal, the school has turned into a "community hub." In the first level of the school, we met high school students; in the second level, we met their parents receiving instruction in English as a Second Language (ESL). We attended the annual potluck where students and their families gathered to celebrate their togetherness. If you were there, gentle reader, you would have seen almost the whole world (over 65 nationalities), each with their own unique cultural customs, habits, food, dress, dance (performed on stage by students), and you would have heard a rainbow of languages. Above all, we saw an exceptional commitment to First Nations issues; one of the two schools has a First Nations population of 23% and a room designated for First Nations' drum ceremonies.

These two high schools show us that when equity becomes the praxis of the school, and is taken to its highest level thanks to its leadership, then social action finally becomes possible.

References

Abdi, A., & Schultz, L. (2008). *Educating for human rights and global citizenship*. Albany, NY: State University of New York Press.

Banks, J. (2014). *An introduction to multicultural education*, 5th ed. Boston, MA: Pearson.

Derrida, J. (1996). *Monolingualism of the other, or, the prosthesis of origin*. Stanford, CA: Stanford University Press.

Du Bois, W.E.B. (2007). *The souls of black folk*. Originally published in 1903. Oxford: Oxford University Press.

Freire, P. (2000). *Pedagogy of the oppressed*, 30th anniversary ed. New York: The Continuum.

Greene, M. (2005). Teaching in a moment of crisis: The spaces of imagination. *The New Educator, 1*, 77–80.

Ibrahim, A. (2014). *The rhizome of Blackness: A critical ethnography of Hip-Hop culture, language, identity, and the politics of becoming*. New York: Peter Lang.

Ibrahim, A., Radford, L., Schmitz, K., & Toomey, N. (2012). *Urban priority program: Challenges, priorities and hope*. Unpublished report. Ottawa: Ottawa-Carleton District School Board.

Nelson, J., Palonsky, S., & McCarthy, M. (2013). *Critical issues in education: Dialogues and dialectics*. Boston, MA: McGraw-Hill.

Rawls, J. (2001). *Justice as fairness*. Cambridge, MA: Harvard University Press.

What Does Racism Have to Do with School Leadership?

Daniel D. Spikes and Mark A. Gooden

The latest results on the National Assessment for Educational Progress (NAEP) reveal a persistent racial gap in achievement scores. Moreover, high school graduation and dropout rates continue to show wide disparities between races (U.S. Dept. of Education, 2014). Why do these achievement results for many of our students of colour continue to persist despite reform efforts aimed at improving them?

As this essay asserts, a large body of literature has argued that the persistence of racial disparities in schools is attributable, in large part, to institutionalized racism that students of colour, particularly Black and Latino students, face in U.S. schools (Darder, 2012; Gooden, 2012; Howard, 2010; Ladson-Billings, 1998; Milner, 2010; Young & Liable, 2000). However, many of our efforts to reform schools often take a colour-blind approach (Wells, 2014) when what is needed is a more race-conscious approach.

This essay provides a brief overview of the racist practices and beliefs that work to create and perpetuate inequities in schools. Then, we discuss the role of school leaders in helping to ameliorate them. First, however, we provide an overview of the theoretical framework that guides this essay.

Critical Race Theory

Critical race theory (CRT) is an emerging body of scholarship that "challenges the ways in which race and racial power are constructed and represented in American legal culture and, more generally, in American society as a whole" (Crenshaw, Gotanda, Peller, & Thomas, 1995, p. xiii). Moreover, critical race scholars explore the ways in which White privilege and racism work in tandem to control systems and institutions (Bell, 1992a, 1992b; Crenshaw et al., 1995).

A central tenet of CRT is that racism is normal and is woven into the fabric of our society (Delgado & Stefancic, 2001). The nature of seeming "ordinary" often makes White racism difficult to detect, and therefore address (Gooden, 2012). As a result, this allows for concepts like colour-blindness and equality to replace concepts like equity and justice. In addition, White privilege often goes un-interrogated. Thus, critical race theory encourages us to question concepts of neutrality, objectivity, meritocracy, and colour-blindness.

Using critical race theory as our explanatory framework, this essay takes the position that society, and the institutions within them, including schools, are inherently racist. We further argue that White privilege is embedded within our schools. In other words, these spaces were designed by Whites to benefit Whites (Darder, 2012). This places students of colour at a disadvantage. Beliefs in concepts like meritocracy and colour-blindness work together to conceal the systemic challenges that these students face. In the succeeding sections, we describe the racist practices that scholars argue lead to the academic disparities outlined above. Then, we return to how colour-blindness and meritocracy serve to keep these practices in place. Finally, we discuss the role of the school leader.

Inequitable Practices

The literature strongly supports the contention that various inequitable school structures and practices have led to disparate academic outcomes for students of colour (Teranishi, 2002). For example, scholars have argued that the curriculum, both the written and the hidden, serve to create and perpetuate racial gaps (Darder, 2012). Further, other school practices, such as the following, serve as barriers to academic success for these students:

- School tracking (Oakes, 1985)
- Lower teacher expectations (Brown, 2004; McKown & Weinstein, 2008)
- Disparate administration of school discipline (Bryan, Day-Vines, Griffin, & Moore-Thomas, 2012; McFadden, Marsh, Price, & Hwang, 1992; U.S. Department of Education, 2014; Wallace, Goodkind, Wallace, & Bachman, 2008; Wehlage & Rutter, 1986)
- Lack of access to high quality teachers (Darling-Hammond, 2000; Darling-Hammond, 2004; Irvine, 2010; U.S. Dept. of Education, 2014).

The curriculum of K–12 schools in the U.S. often overwhelmingly reflects White middle-class values and norms (Darder, 2012; Young & Liable, 2000). Moreover, school textbooks and other instructional sources often misrepresent or under-represent the contributions of people of colour (Brown & Brown, 2010; MacPhee & Kaufman, 2014; Swartz, 1992). This overvaluing or "privileging" of one culture over all others inherently benefits White students. Further, it also sends a disturbing message that reinforces prevailing racist notions about a person's value (Derman-Sparks & Phillips, 1997). This practice can lead to White students having an over-inflated sense of self-worth, while simultaneously causing students of colour to question their self-worth. Unfortunately, educators are often unaware of and/or refuse to acknowledge this reality. Therefore, to them, this phenomenon remains hidden.

Within an area of research often referred to as the "hidden curriculum," scholars posit that certain values, beliefs, and cultural messages are often transmitted through school structures and practices. This curriculum is often referred to as being "hidden" because many educators are unaware of and/or are unwilling to acknowledge its existence. In addition to the curriculum sending certain messages, other school structures or practices like ability grouping and teacher expectations can convey certain, often hidden, messages as well.

For example, students of colour are more likely to be referred for special education services (Hosp & Reschly, 2004) and are often over-represented in low-track classes (Condron, 2007; Greene, 2014; Futrell & Gomez, 2008; Wyner, Bridgeland & DiLulio, 2007). At the same time, they are often under-represented in higher-track classes and gifted and talented programs. This inequitable practice communicates that a more rigorous curriculum is mainly reserved for students with a certain skin colour.

Related, teachers often hold deficit perspectives regarding the abilities of students of colour (Bomer & Bomer, 2001; Milner, 2010; Valencia, 2010). As such, they often hold low academic expectations for these students. Consequently, they are less likely than Whites to be encouraged to participate in class (Gibbs, 1988) and are not given as much support (Feagin & Barnett, 2004; Young & Liable, 2000). Again, these perspectives and assumptions that teachers carry are often unacknowledged.

Moreover, a recent report released by the U.S. Department of Education's Office of Civil Rights (OCR) chronicles additional barriers that students of colour face in U.S. schools. As the *New York Times* reported, "the Education Department found a pattern of inequality on a number of fronts, with race as the dividing factor." The OCR reveals that Black students are more likely to be taught by inexperienced teachers and are three times more likely to be suspended or expelled than their White peers. This disparate administration of school discipline occurs as early as preschool, where Black students constitute only 16 percent of those enrolled but comprise 48 percent of those suspended or expelled two or more times. Similarly, a study by Wallace, Goodkind, Wallace, and Bachman (2008) revealed that students of colour are often given harsher consequences than White students for the same minor offenses (Wallace et al., 2008).

Each of these structures and practices convey one common theme: most U.S. schools are inherently racist with White privilege embedded throughout. However, most are blind to this actuality. Beliefs in ideals like meritocracy and colour-blindness work together to hide this fact.

Meritocracy

Meritocracy is the hallmark of the "American dream": the belief that success is directly related to hard work, achievement, and ability. Implicit within this belief is the idea that when one does not succeed, it must be due to a lack of these individual behaviours and dispositions (Milner, 2012). However, this belief assumes an equal playing field, which, as Milner relays, is simply not the case:

[E]ducational practices and opportunities are not equal or equitable. There is enormous variation in students' social, economic, historic, political, and educational opportunities, which is in stark contrast to the American dream — one that adopts and supports meritocracy as its creed or philosophy (2012, p. 704).

In this way, Milner suggests that meritocracy is a myth. Darder (2012) also agrees that viewing schools as meritocratic institutions that benefit all who simply work hard is problematic since schools are not value free and are certainly not neutral. Schools benefit White, middle-class students whose values and lived realities directly coincide with the knowledge and skills privileged in these settings (Darder, 2012).

> Educators who buy into the myth of meritocracy can exacerbate achievement disparities between Black and White students (Milner, 2012). By operating under the assumption that student effort and ability alone will lead to student success, educators may ignore structural barriers, racist behaviours, and practices that can negatively impact those students. If left unacknowledged, this colour-blind belief is problematic and can be detrimental to students.

Colour-blindness

Another belief that creates and perpetuates academic disparities between students is colour-blindness. According to Diem and Carpenter, colour-blindness "essentially allows Whites to 'blind' themselves when attempting to make meaning about race" (2012, p. 102). In this way, people claim to not see colour, just people. As a result, there is the belief that discrimination is no longer the central factor determining the life chances of people of colour (Bonilla-Silva, 2010).

While the idea of living in a colour-blind society seems ideal, in fact people do see colour, and people are often treated differently because of the colour of their skin (Bell, 1987). Choosing *not* to see colour then is a privileged position that conveniently allows certain people not to have to acknowledge different lived experiences and allows them to ignore inequities based on race (Banks, 2001; Milner, 2012). Moreover, if we are to believe in one of the basic tenets of critical race theory (CRT) — that racism is pervasive in today's society (Bell, 1987; Delgado & Stefancic, 2001; Derman-Sparks & Phillips, 1997) — then choosing to be colour-blind serves to perpetuate this racism (Banks, 2001; Bonilla-Silva, 2010; Gooden, 2012; Milner, 2012; Parker & Villalpando, 2007).

Further, as Amy Stuart Wells (2014) explains in a recent policy brief for the National Education Policy Center, reform efforts intended to improve academic outcomes for students of colour have largely been ineffective because of their colour-blind nature. Wells argues that, "save for the provision in the federal No Child Left Behind law requiring districts to report test scores by racial/ethnic categories, most recent education policies do not mention race, diversity, or rapid shifts in the public school population" (2014, p. 1). This is problematic because while these policies are seemingly race-neutral on the surface, they have real racial implications for the nation's schools and for the principals who lead them (Wells, 2014).

Discussion

Due to its colour-blind nature, education policy has served to exacerbate disparities rather than improve them (Wells, 2014). Additionally, society's espousal of beliefs like colour-blindness and meritocracy leave inequitable structures and barriers unacknowledged and un-interrogated. Even when schools do acknowledge race or "see colour," it is often in uncritical or distorted ways.

Joyce King (1991) refers to this as dysconscious racism. According to King, "dysconscious racism is a form of racism that tacitly accepts dominant White norms and privileges" (1991, p. 135). It is an uncritical way of thinking of racial inequity. She further states that,

> Unequal critical ways of thinking about racial inequity accept certain culturally sanctioned assumptions, myths, and beliefs that justify the social and economic advantages that White people have as a result of subordinating diverse others (Wellman, 1977 as cited in King, 1991, p. 135).

Therefore, various scholars have expressed that school leadership programs should help to develop this critical consciousness in future leaders, understanding that this development within school leaders is crucial to the success of all students (Brown, 2004; Diem & Carpenter, 2012; Gooden & Dantley, 2012; Young & Liable, 2000). For example, Gooden and Dantley call for preparation programs to "include a prophetic voice, a grounding in critical theoretical traditions, the notion of praxis and a pragmatic edge, and the race language" (2012, p. 244). Brown (2004) calls for preparation programs to develop socially just leaders through transformative learning experiences (Mezirow, 1997). These include providing opportunities for awareness through critical self-reflection, rational discourse, and action as policy praxis.

Further, Diem and Carpenter (2012) similarly advocate for school leadership preparation programs to provide a transformative curriculum. This would include the following steps: 1) refuting colour-blind ideologies, 2) counteracting the misconceptions of human differences, 3) recognizing that student achievement is not always based on merit, 4) engaging in critical self-reflection, and 5) examining the silencing of voices. Finally, Young & Liable go as far as to state that pre-service leaders should not be allowed to get their principal licensure/certification unless they have an "understanding of racism, racial identity issues, racial oppression, and how to work against racism in schools" (2000, p. 21).

Concluding Thoughts

Research suggests that school leaders play a vital role in the educational achievement of all students, regardless of race (Brown, 2004;

Bustamante, Nelson, & Onwuegbuzie, 2009; Theoharis, 2007). Moreover, Howard argues that a "more comprehensive understanding of race and culture can play an important role in helping to close the achievement gap" (2010, p. 1). To improve the educational experiences of students of colour will require school leaders who are culturally proficient (Howard, 2010) and can respond to the unique needs of diverse populations in ways that foster academic growth (Lindsey, Robins, & Terrell, 2003). Therefore, it is important that our school preparation programs provide cultural proficiency/anti-racism training to its pre-service leaders, and it is equally as important that school districts engage their in-service leaders in sustained professional development on these topics.

References

Banks, J. A. (2001). Citizenship education and diversity implications for teacher education. *Journal of Teacher Education*, 52(1), 5–16.

Bell, D. A. (1987). *And we will not be saved: The elusive quest for racial justice.* New York, NY: Basic Books.

Bell, D. A. (1992a). *Faces at the bottom of the well.* New York: Basic Books.

Bell, D. A. (1992b). Racial realism. *Connecticut Law Review, 24*(2), 363–379.

Bomer, R., & Bomer, K. (2001). *For a better world: Reading and writing for social action.* Portsmouth, NH: Heinemann.

Bonilla-Silva, E. (2010). *Racism without racists: Color-blind racism and the persistence of racial inequality in the United States* (3rd ed.). Lanham, MD: Rowman & Littlefield.

Brown, A., & Brown, K. (2010). Strange fruit indeed: Interrogating contemporary textbook representations of racial violence toward African Americans. *Teachers College Record, 112*(1), 31-67.

Brown, K. M. (2004). Leadership for social justice and equity: Weaving a transformative framework and pedagogy. *Educational Administration Quarterly, 40*(1), 77–108.

Bryan, J., Day-Vines, N. L., Griffin, D., Moore-Thomas, C. (2012). The disproportionality dilemma: Patterns of teacher referrals to school counselors for disruptive behavior. *Journal of Counseling and Development, 90*(2), 177.

Bustamante, R. M., Nelson, J. A., & Onwuegbuzie, A. J. (2009). Assessing schoolwide cultural competence: Implications for school leadership preparation. *Educational Administration Quarterly, 45*(5), 793–827.

Condron, D. J. (2007). Stratification and educational sorting: Explaining ascriptive inequalities in early childhood reading group placement. *Social Problems, 54*(1), 139–160.

Crenshaw, K. W., Gotanda, N., Peller, G., & Thomas, K. (Eds.). (1995). *Critical race theory: The key writings that formed the movement.* New York: The New Press.

Darder, A. (2012). *Culture and power in the classroom: Educational foundations for the schooling of bicultural students.* Boulder, CO: Paradigm Publishers.

Darling-Hammond, L. (2000). Teacher quality and student achievement: A review of the policy evidence. *Education Policy Analysis Archives, (8)*1, 1-44.

Darling-Hammond, L. (2004). Inequality and the right to learn: Access to qualified teachers in California's Public Schools. *Teachers College Record, 106*(10), 1936–1966.

Delgado, R., & Stefancic, J. (2001). *Critical race theory: An introduction.* New York: New York University Press.

Derman-Sparks, L., & Phillips, C. B. (1997). *Teaching/learning anti-racism: A developmental approach.* New York: Teachers College Press.

Diem, S., & Carpenter, B. (2012). Social justice and leadership preparation: Developing a transformative curriculum. *Planning and Changing, 43*(1/2), 96–112.

Feagin, J. R., & Barnett, B. M. (2004). Success and failure: How systemic racism trumped the *Brown v Board of Education* decision. *University of Illinois Law Review, 1099,* 1–27.

Futrell, M. H., & Gomez, J. (2008). How tracking creates a poverty of learning. *Reshaping High Schools 65*(8), 74–78.

Gibbs, J. T. (1988). *Young Black males in America: Endangered, embittered, and embattled. Young, Black and Male in America: An Endangered Species.* Dover, MA: Auburn House Publishing Co, 1-36.

Gooden, M. A. (2012). What does racism have to do with leadership? Countering the idea of color-blind leadership: A reflection on race and the growing pressures of the urban principalship [Special Issue]. *Journal of Educational Foundations 26*(1–2), 67–84.

Gooden, M. A., & Dantley, (2012). Centering race in a framework for leadership preparation. *Journal of Research on Leadership Education, 7*(2), 237–253.

Greene, A. D. (2014). Tracking work: Race-ethnic variation in vocational course placement and consequences for academic and career outcomes. *International Journal of Educational Studies, 1*(1), 9–18.

Hosp, J. L., & Reschly, D. J. (2004). Disproportionate representation of minority students in special education: Academic, demographic and economic predictors. *Exceptional Children, 70,* 185–199.

Howard, T. C. (2010). *Why race and culture matter in schools: Closing the achievement gap in America's classrooms.* New York: Teachers College Press.

Irvine, J. J. (2010). Culturally relevant pedagogy. *Education Digest, 75*(8), 57–61.

King, J. (1991). Dysconscious racism: Ideology, identity, and the miseducation of teachers. *The Journal of Negro Education, 60*(2), 133–146.

Ladson-Billings, G. (1998). Just what is critical race theory and what's it doing in a nice field like education? *Qualitative Studies in Education, 11*(1), 7–24.

Lhamon, C.E. & Samuels, J. (2014, January 8). *Dear colleague letter on the non-discriminatory administration of school discipline.* Retrieved February 3, 2015, from the U. S. Department of Education: http://www2.ed.gov/about/offices/list/ocr/letters/colleague-201401-title-vi.html.

Lindsey, R. B., Robins, K. N., & Terrell, R. D. (2003). *Cultural proficiency: A manual for school leaders.* Thousand Oaks, CA: Corwin Press.

MacPhee, D. A., & Kaufman, K. (2014). Exploring bias in elementary history curriculum with preservice and practicing teachers in professional development schools. *The Social Studies, 105*(3), 124–131.

McFadden, A. C., Marsh, G. E., Price, B. J., & Hwang, Y. (1992). A study of race and gender bias in the punishment of school children. *Education and Treatment of Children, 15,* 140–146.

McKown, C., & Weinstein, R. S. (2008). Teacher expectations, classroom context, and the achievement gap. *Journal of School Psychology, 46*(3), 235–261.

Mezirow, J. (1997, Summer). Transformative learning: Theory to practice. In P. Cranton (Ed.), *New directions for adult and continuing education: No. 74. Transformative learning in action: Insights from practice* (pp. 5–12). San Francisco, CA: Jossey-Bass.

Milner IV, H.R. (2010). *Understanding diversity, opportunity gaps, and teaching in today's classrooms: Start where you are, but don't stay there.* Cambridge, MA: Harvard Education Press.

Milner IV, H.R. (2012). Beyond a test score: Explaining opportunity gaps in educational practice. *Journal of Black Studies, 43*(6), 693-718.

Oakes, J. (1985). *Keeping track: How schools structure inequality.* New Haven, CT: Yale University Press.

Parker, L., & Villalpando, O. (2007). A race(ialized) perspective on educational leadership: Critical race theory in educational administration. *Educational Administration Quarterly, 43*(5), 519–524.

Swartz, E. (1992). Emancipatory narratives: Rewriting the master script in the school curriculum. *Journal of Negro Education*, 341–355.

Teranishi, R. T. (2002). Asian Pacific Americans and critical race theory: An examination of school racial climate. *Equity and Excellence in Education, 35*(2), 144–154.

Theoharis, G. T. (2007). Social justice educational leaders and resistance: Toward a theory of social justice leadership. *Educational Administration Quarterly, 43*, 221–258.

U.S. Department of Education, Institute of Education Sciences, National Center for Education Statistics, National Assessment of Educational Progress (NAEP), various years, 1990–2013 Mathematics and Reading Assessments.

Valencia, R. R. (2010). *Dismantling contemporary deficit thinking: Educational thought and practice.* New York: Taylor & Francis.

Wallace, J. M., Jr., Goodkind, S., Wallace, C. M., & Bachman, J. G. (2008). Racial, ethnic, and gender differences in school discipline among U.S. high school students: 1991–2005. *Negro Educational Review, 59*, 47–62.

Wehlage, G. G., & Rutter, R. A. (1986). Dropping out: How much do schools contribute to the problem? *Teachers College Record, 87*, 374–393.

Wellman, D. (1977). *Portraits of White racism.* Cambridge, MA: Cambridge University Press.

Wells, A. S. (2014). Seeing past the 'colorblind' myth: Why education policymakers should address racial and ethnic inequality and support culturally diverse schools. Boulder, CO: National Education Policy Center. Retrieved [August 2014] from http://nepc.colorado.edu/publication/seeing-past-the-colorblind-myth.

Wyner, J. S., Bridgeland, J. M., & DiIulio, J. J. (2007). *Achievement trap: How America is failing millions of high-achieving students from lower-income families.* Lansdowne, VA: Jack Kent Cooke Foundation.

Young, M. D., & Liable, J. (2000). White racism, antiracism, and school leadership preparation. *Journal of School Leadership, 10*(5), 374–415.

Why Should School Principals Think about Social Class?

Pat Thomson

Does Social Class Exist?

Social class can be understood in two ways. First, it can be seen as a sociological metaphor used to describe a social and material reality, the general shared social economic and cultural "space" that we live in (Bourdieu, 1984). Second, it can also be understood as an identity that people claim or have imposed on them.

There is strong evidence for thinking about social class as a metaphor for an actual material reality. The gap between rich and poor has widened significantly over the last century (Piketty, 2014) and twentieth-century "world-leading" nations such as the United States and the United Kingdom are deeply socially and economically divided (Stiglitz, 2012). In 2014, the Great British Class Survey[5] identified seven contemporary class groupings[6] and suggested that about half the population occupied a shared social space where money was tight and everyday life was relatively constrained and stressful. Highly unequal societies, such as Britain and the United States, have serious consequences for those

---

5.   See https://ssl.bbc.co.uk/labuk/experiments/class/

6.   Seven contemporary classes were identified: 1) an elite (6%), 2) the established middle class (25%), 3) a technical middle class (6%), 4) affluent workers (15%), 5) traditional working class (14%), 6) an emergent service sector (19%), and 7) the precariat (15%).

"at the bottom" of the class system: life threatening health conditions (Wilkinson & Pickett, 2010); poor housing (Dorling, 2014); and highly inequitable educational opportunities (OECD, 2009).

Yet there appears to be a reluctance to be identified as "working class." In August 2013, *The Atlantic* carried a story entitled "Why Americans all believe they are middle class" (Shenker-Osorio, 2013). Despite a third of the population earning below the median national income, about half claimed "middle class" as an appropriate social "label." Anat Shenker-Osorio argued that this was because to be seen as "lower class" or "working class" was now a socially stigmatized term strongly associated with suffering and hardship. In everyday life, vernacular derogatory terms such as "trailer trash" and "chav" combine with official policy lexicons — "socially excluded," "marginalized," and "disadvantaged" — to mark those struggling to make ends meet as deficient and feral (Peel, 2003; Tyler, 2013). There seems to be little defence of "working class" as an identity. The UK *Guardian* columnist Polly Toynbee (2011) suggests that people may be generally reluctant to claim to be "working class" because "that's the way politics has led and because, post trade unionism, people no longer know where they stand on the earnings scale." Here, Toynbee points to the ways in which identity and material reality are not divorced from each other but strongly connected, despite the ways in which class-as-metaphor and class-as-identity are commonly separated.

School Principals Thinking about Social Class

The two ways of understanding social class — as a sociological metaphor and as an identity — can orient school principals to their work. Thinking about social class allows school principals to consider *what schools are meant to do*. Through exploring class-as-metaphor, principals come directly to the question of how much schooling, as it is currently practiced, is actually designed to produce and reproduce the social, cultural, and economic realities of social class. A great deal of evidence suggests that, despite the significant increase in mass levels of education, schooling outcomes still largely reflect prevailing social class, race, and gender realities (e.g., Apple, Ball, & Gandin, 2011; Van Galen & Noblit,

2007; Weis & Dolby, 2012). As leaders in their schools, principals must therefore grapple with how, if school is to do otherwise, they might contribute to creating a less divided and more equitable world.

This leads to thinking about *how schools work*. There is a vast literature that analyzes the ways in which policy, school organization, student groupings and promotion practices, language, teaching approaches, curriculum, assessment, and school–community relations generally produce and reproduce existing social classes (e.g., Ball, Maguire, & Macrae, 2000; Connell, Ashenden, Kessler, & Dowsett, 1982; Weis, 2008). A significant body of scholarship and professional knowledge also exists about the ways in which particular identities are privileged in schools while others are stigmatized. Class-as-metaphor and class-as-identity are thus a helpful lens through which to understand not only what happens in schools, but also what needs to change, and how.

Through working with the twin notions of class and considerations of the purposes and practices of schooling, school principals connect with a long and international history of practical intervention and scholarship (e.g., Sahlberg, 2012; Smyth, Angus, Down, & McInerney, 2009; Wrigley, Thomson, & Lingard, 2011). There is much here that is useful in this archive.

However, because every school population is different, and because there is still much to know about how to change schooling to make it more equitable and socially just, school principals are also equipped through their considerations of class, with a frame for action. They are in a position to become active innovators and knowledge producers contributing to the slow process of educational reform. They are in a position to encourage school staff to think about their practices — from the ways in which they talk about and to their students and their families, and the variety of ways in which they locate, value, and use students' home and community knowledge, narratives, and interests, to the ways in which they manage and engage the diverse range of student in their classes. They are also in a position to ensure that every aspect of school administration — from the priorities of timetabling, design of classrooms and school furniture to the ways in which school decisions are made — is directed to support educationally equitable change. Moreover, they are in a position to resist claims that class no longer exists or matters, and that it has nothing to do with the work of school principals. The twin lens of social class as metaphor and as identity make it abundantly clear that the work of school principals is not simply one of management, but is profoundly educational.

References

Apple, M., Ball, S., & Gandin, L. (Eds.). (2011). *The Routledge international handbook of the sociology of education*. New York: Routledge.

Ball, S., Maguire, M., & Macrae, S. (2000). *Choice, pathways and transitions post-16: New youth, new economies in the global city*. London: Falmer.

Bourdieu, P. (1984). *Distinction: A social critique of the judgment of taste* (R. Nice, Trans.). Boston: Harvard University Press.

Connell, R.W., Ashenden, D., Kessler, S., & Dowsett, G. (1982). *Making the difference: Schools, families and social divisions*. Sydney: Allen & Unwin.

Dorling, D. (2014). *All that is solid: The great housing disaster*. London: Penguin.

OECD. (2009). PISA 2009 results: Overcoming social background (Vol. 2). Paris: OECD.

Peel, M. (2003). *The lowest rung: Voices of Australian poverty*. Melbourne: Cambridge University Press.

Piketty, T. (2014). *Capital in the twenty-first century*. Boston, MA: Harvard University Press.

Sahlberg, P. (2012). *Finnish lessons: What can the world learn from educational change in Finland?* London: Routledge.

Shenker-Osorio, A. (2013). Why Americans all believe they are "middle class." *The Atlantic*. http://www.theatlantic.com/politics/archive/2013/2008/why-americans-all-believe-they-are-middle-class/278240/.

Smyth, J., Angus, L., Down, B., & McInerney, P. (2009). *Activist and socially critical school and community renewal*. Rotterdam: Sense.

Stiglitz, J. (2012). *The Price of Inequality*. New York: Norton.

Toynbee, P. (2011, August 29). Money busts the convenient myth that social class is dead, *The Guardian*. http://www.theguardian.com/commentisfree/2011/aug/2029/myth-social-class-dead.

Tyler, I. (2013). *Revolting subjects: Social abjection and resistance in neoliberal Britain*. London: Zed Books.

Van Galen, J.A., & Noblit, G. (Eds.). (2007). *Late to class: Social class and schooling in the new economy.* New York: SUNY.

Weis, L. (Ed.). (2008). *The way class works: Readings on school, family and the economy.* New York: Routledge.

Weis, L., & Dolby, N. (Eds.). (2012). *Social class and education: Global perspectives.* New York: Routledge.

Wilkinson, R., & Pickett, K. (2010). *The spirit level: Why equality is better for everyone.* London: Penguin.

Wrigley, T., Thomson, P., & Lingard, B. (Eds.). (2011). *Changing schools: Alternative approaches to make a world of difference.* London: Routledge.

How Can Educational Leaders Support Sexual and Gender Minority (SGM) Students in Our Schools?

André P. Grace

School administrators are pivotal on-the-ground leaders working in local school contexts across school districts. Teachers see them as driving forces, deeply impacting school culture, school climate, and sociality, expressed as the quality of interrelationships that students have with peers, teachers, school counsellors, and other significant adults. Students see school administrators as persons with power and the capacity and ability to act on their issues and concerns. How their school administrators act deeply influences the degree to which students feel recognized, respected, accommodated, and safe in their schools. Thus, school administrators need to be inclusive educators. As a practicing school administrator, Griffiths positions inclusive educators as advocates for students and leaders who navigate the complexities of "growing inclusion," which he locates as an "uneven process that requires daily dedication" to meet the diverse needs of all students (2013, p. xxi).

From these perspectives, school administrators must find a balance between being transactional and transformational leaders. Fulfilling both dimensions of the leadership role is integral to advancing inclusive schooling as a practical and political project. In this regard, transaction is about developing and engaging policy as a basis for protecting students, teachers, and indeed school administrators themselves. It is also about implementing policy as a practical intervention aimed at school improvement, which is important work that should involve formative evaluation to judge whether the policy is working for the multivariate student population navigating school life. Transaction should be inextricably linked to transformation that is about engaging a politics of visibility and possibility whereby students across differences are seen, heard, and able to thrive and develop to their fullest potential. Inclusive school administrators who are transformational leaders take an integrated approach, positioning teachers, parents and other primary caregivers, *and* students as change agents in the work to make life in schools better *now* for every student. In guiding this work, they engage in ethical leadership, which means that they 1) do no harm; 2) take responsibility for addressing injustice in individual, educational, and civic contexts; 3) scrutinize these contexts to explore limitations and possibilities; and, in the end, 4) act positively and consistently in building schools as socially inclusive spaces where all students experience healthy relationships with peers, teachers, and others in the school community (Starratt, 2004).

Doing this work with sexual and gender minority (SGM) or lesbian, gay, bisexual, trans-spectrum, Two-Spirit Aboriginal, and queer students requires school administrators to challenge heteronormative, genderist traditions that have historically marked the everyday in schools (Grace, 2013). In Canada, it has not been easy work for school administrators to extend truly inclusive education to SGM students. With the public education of children and youth under the control of provinces and territories, there are inconsistencies across ministries of education, teachers' associations, and school districts in addressing SGM issues in schooling (Grace, 2015; Grace & Wells, in press). Addressing non-heteronormative sexual and gender differences is still viewed as a moral and political land mine in many quarters of Canadian education despite protection against discrimination afforded SGM students on the grounds of 1) sexual orientation, as guaranteed by the *Canadian Charter of Rights and Freedoms,* and 2) gender identity, which is increasingly protected in provincial and territorial legislation in keeping with the spirit of the *Charter* as an organic document. Nevertheless, there have been incremental efforts in recent decades to recognize and accommodate sexual and gender minorities in schooling. In this regard, every province and territory has followed its own trajectory of SGM inclusion, with some teachers' associations, ministries of education, and school boards being more progressive than others in policymaking and implementation, resource-and-support creation, and networking across educational and community interest groups (Grace, 2015; Grace & Wells, in press).

If school administrators want to recognize, respect, and accommodate SGM students in their schools, then they need to educate themselves about the efforts of their particular ministry of education, teachers' association, and school district to engage in SGM-inclusive policymaking and its implementation. In my home province of Alberta, for example, pervasive politico-religious conservatism is often viewed as a deterrent to the inclusion of sexual and gender minorities in schooling and other institutional and community contexts comprising Alberta's historically bounded heteronormative sociality. Nevertheless, significant progress has been made in education provincially to recognize and accommodate the multivariate SGM population (Grace, 2015; Grace & Wells, in press). The significant efforts of the Alberta Teachers' Association (ATA) to develop policies, resources, and supports have been a pivotal part of this progress. The ATA's efforts intensified during the decade following the 1998 Supreme Court decision in *Vriend v. Alberta* that granted equality rights to sexual-minority Canadians. Indeed, by 2004 the ATA had become the first teachers' organization in Canada to include both sexual orientation and gender identity as protected grounds of discrimination in its *Code of Professional Conduct* and its *Declaration of Teachers' Rights and Responsibilities*. Currently, school boards in Alberta are under increasing pressure to engage in SGM-inclusive policymaking and implementation to improve life in schools for SGM students. Moving SGM civil rights forward in its schools in November 2011, the Edmonton Public School Board became the first on the Prairies to develop a stand-alone sexual orientation and gender identity policy. Work is ongoing to implement this policy in schools across the district. While the Government of Alberta receives a failing grade in leadership in providing SGM-inclusive education that includes curricular components, in 2008 it became the first Canadian provincial or territorial government to provide resources to address homophobic bullying. Still *Bill 44,* a legislative albatross passed in 2009 that limits what schools can do to advance SGM-inclusive education, remains. The Government of Alberta has yet to find a way out of this encumbering legislation that shakes its finger at inclusive educators, positioning human sexuality among "dangerous" sociopolitical topics to include in the provincial curriculum.

Previously, I have discussed what Canadian school administrators can do to advance the inclusion of SGM students in our nation's schools (Grace, 2007, pp. 33–36). I conclude by quoting the guidelines that I developed in an abridged version here:

- Educate yourself about the realities of sex, sexual, and gender differences, and different constructions of family. As a corollary, learn about heterosexism, sexism, [genderism, and homo/bi/transphobia]....

- Assist your teachers to engage in similar education and learning, and provide them with opportunities for professional development so they can build knowledge of sexual [and gender] minorities and learn about age appropriate ways to address ... [SGM] issues and concerns....

- Build a resource base in your school that will provide material to help mediate conflict with those within and outside the school who resist sexual- [and gender-] minority inclusion. The resource base will also be useful to teachers who want to engage in pedagogical and co-curricular practices inclusive of sexual [and gender] minorities....

- Check with your teacher association and school district to see what educational policies have been developed to assist and support you and your teachers in educational and cultural work to create a school that respects and accommodates sexual [and gender] minorities. If such policies are not in place, then advocate and work to have policies inclusive of sexual [and gender] minorities developed and implemented. Remember, policy enables protection....

- Intervene in your school by supporting students who want to initiate a ... Gay–Straight Alliance Club. Help them find a teacher-facilitator and provide them with advice around safety and security issues.

References

Grace, A.P. (2007). In your care: School administrators and their ethical and professional responsibility toward students across sexual-minority differences. In W. Smale & K. Young (Eds.), *Approaches to educational leadership and practice* (pp. 16–40). Calgary, AB: Detselig Enterprises/ Temeron Books.

Grace, A.P. (2013). Researching sexual minority and gender variant youth and their growth into resilience. In W. Midgley, P.A. Danaher, & M. Baguley (Eds.), *The role of participants in education research: Ethics, epistemologies, and methods* (pp. 15–28). New York, NY: Routledge.

Grace, A.P. (2015). *Growing into resilience: Sexual and gender minority youth in Canada.* Part 2 with K. Wells. Toronto, ON: University of Toronto Press.

Grace, A. P., & Wells, K. (in press). Sexual and gender minorities in Canadian education and society: A national handbook for K–12 educators. Ottawa, ON: Canadian Teachers' Federation.

Griffiths, D. (2013). *Principals of inclusion: Practical strategies to grow inclusion in urban schools.* Burlington, ON: Word & Deed Publishing Incorporated and Edphil Books.

Starratt, R.J. (2004). *Ethical leadership.* San Francisco, CA: Jossey-Bass.

Part II
What Is Education Leadership?

What Is Educational Leadership?

Pierre Wilbert Orelus

B efore endeavoring to define what educational leadership is, it is important to deconstruct the word *leadership*, commonly used in educational and political debates. A person must possess many commendable qualities in order to be identified and selected as a leader. A leader must be visionary, dedicated, disciplined, a good listener, compassionate, knowledgeable, and genuinely caring of others. Leaders are also expected to be inspirational speakers and friendly in the eyes of their followers. These are some of the common characteristics and aspects of leadership.

Situated in the realm of education, leadership entails having inner ability, an appropriate disposition, clear educational goals, and action plans aimed at achieving those goals for transformative social change within the school system and beyond. School leaders in particular need to be deep, creative, imaginative, and innovative thinkers endowed with the innermost ability to assess and analyze problems affecting student learning and achievement and teaching practices. This does not happen in a vacuum. It requires dialogue and for leaders to listen carefully to what students, teachers, families, and administrators have to say about educational and socio-economic issues, and any other issues affecting their academic, professional, and personal lives.

What Is Educational Leadership?

John Roberts

A good educational leader will be dedicated to bridging the gap between the students and their cultural heritage. The leader will create a curriculum that best serves the needs of Aboriginal learners, and will take control of how to educate young people. The leader will work on changing negative attitudes towards education from the parents of Aboriginal learners, and will adopt common core standards provincially for Aboriginal education, making it more culturally appropriate and educationally effective in the community.

Professionally, the educational leader will encourage Aboriginal teachers to take professional development courses, specifically in the areas of mentoring practices, student engagement, Aboriginal content in the curriculum, and ways to inspire success in Aboriginal students. He or she will hire Aboriginal tutors to offer supports to students, both inside and out of the classroom and create links (home–school) between parents and Aboriginal students since the family unit is the centre of Aboriginal society and serves as the primary medium for cultural continuity. Finally, since the majority of teachers have little or no knowledge of Aboriginal languages and terminology, the leader must encourage non-Aboriginal teachers involved in Aboriginal education to become more involved in Aboriginal culture to serve the needs of Aboriginal learners better.

What Is Educational Leadership?

Carolyn M. Shields

E ducational leadership is a moral endeavour. It combines excellent management to ensure that the organization works effectively and efficiently with creative, proactive, and transformative efforts to ensure that it is fulfilling its critical democratic goals in an equitable and socially-just fashion. Educational leadership is grounded in a strong sense of moral purpose, clear goals, and strong personal values. It "must be critically educative; it cannot only look at the conditions in which we live, but it must also decide how to change them" (Foster, 1986, p. 185). Good educational leadership is transformative. It deconstructs knowledge and assumptions within the organization that perpetuate inequities and reconstructs them in ways that are more equitable. It acknowledges that students cannot be forced to fit the system but that the system must adapt to the changing needs and demographics of those within it. It recognizes issues of power and works to overcome the advantages of privilege in order to create a more inclusive and respectful democratic society. Good educational leadership acknowledges our interconnectedness with others throughout the globe and works to help everyone understand his or her place in the global community. In short, "good" educational leadership is both ethical and effective; it fulfils the moral purpose of preparing students to realize the promise of an inclusive, mutually beneficial, deeply democratic society.

References

Foster, W. (1986). *Paradigms and promises.* Buffalo, NY: Prometheus.

What Is Educational Leadership?

William Ayers

Free people are their own leaders, and opening spaces, asking embarrassing questions, confronting orthodoxy, diving into contradictions is everybody's business — and the space from which leadership emerges.

Our democracy includes the descendants of formerly enslaved people as well as recent immigrants; working class people who survive by selling their labour power, sometimes only in the informal economy; folks who have attended inadequate schools, struggled with drugs and homelessness, been in and out of jail or prison. We live in a time when the assault on disadvantaged communities is particularly harsh and at the same time gallingly obfuscated — it is fair to say that these folks have faced and endured institutions that routinely disregard their full humanity.

Access to adequate resources and decent facilities, to relevant curriculum, to opportunities to reflect on and to think critically about the world is unevenly distributed along predictable lines of class and colour. Further, a movement to dismantle public schools under the rubric of "standards and accountability" is firmly in place. Leadership is neither pacification nor accommodation in such circumstances but rather involves staking out a space of refusal. Educational leadership entails active and conscientious listening, drawing out rather than forcing in, and eagerness to learn. Classrooms become spaces where the wisdom in the room — the understandings and experiences, hopes and needs of each — are unleashed and collectively enriched.

Chapter 12

What Is Democratic Leadership?

Philip A. Woods

I f we understand leadership as a process that emerges from the interactions of numerous people — and not simply as the actions of an individual leader — we see organization differently. This insight is encapsulated in the idea of distributed leadership.

If we see leadership as a process that ought to promote social justice and democratic values and elevate human potential, we see the purpose of organization differently. This view is encapsulated in the idea of democratic leadership.

There are good reasons for both perspectives. In this short chapter, I will summarize those reasons and set out what democratic leadership, grounded in a rich conception of democracy, means.

A critic might argue that if we want teachers to produce the educated workforce of tomorrow, we simply need strong, innovative leaders who know what needs to be done and can get others to do it. They might assert that competitive times call for entrepreneurial individuals who can lead the way and create competitive, entrepreneurial students. Schools need this kind of individual leader, they say, just as much as other organizations and businesses. These arguments are, however, completely misleading and ultimately destructive of true education for two reasons.

First, collaboration is key to learning and to innovation (Woods, Roberts, & Woods, forthcoming). Research shows that working and studying collaboratively are conducive to learning. This applies to people who work in all kinds of organizations — business, public sector, voluntary sector, and others — including teachers and students in schools. Lynda Gratton of the London Business School has studied numerous companies and other organizations globally and has found that when "we grow and develop, and we become innovative, energized and stimulated" and work co-operatively, "we are able to create the positive energy that gives us joy and adds value to our companies" (2007, p. xi). Her work directly challenges the idea that commanding and controlling others is the way forward. Where organizations are creative and working well, "rather than be commanded, employees choose to develop important relationships with others, and rather than be controlled, they actively choose to make their time available to [a] collective sense of purpose" (Gratton, 2007, p. 46). In education, R. E. Slavin concludes from his review of research that "co-operative learning offers a proven, practical means of creating exciting social and engaging classroom environments to help students to master traditional skills and knowledge as well as develop the creative and interactive skills needed in today's economy and society" (2010, p. 173).

The value of collaboration has implications for the nature of leadership in schools. To promote learning and creativity, leadership needs to involve everyone from senior leaders to students. A major study on improving schools, for example, found that outstanding leaders create the conditions that lead to a collaborative culture and "the progressive distribution of leadership and growth of confidence and achievement" (Day et al., 2010, pp. 186, 194). Sharing knowledge and improving teaching become embedded processes through teachers engaging in co-leadership in which they pro-actively develop goals and strategies for improvement and working with each other (Frost, 2012).

Second, learning in its fullest sense requires the kind of environment that respects the involvement and growth of the whole person. Learning is not equivalent to measurable achievement through tests and examinations, nor is it reducible to the cognitive and emotional abilities and skills required for employment. True learning includes the nurturing of ethical, aesthetic, and spiritual capabilities; that is, a person's moral compass and those things in life that nourish and uplift the senses and give a feeling of purpose. It includes developing a feel for democratic citizenship and an appreciation of values such as justice, democracy, and the rule of law, tolerance, mutual understanding, and a concern for the welfare of others— all especially important as communities become more diverse. If we take this viewpoint that learning involves developing values and human potential to the fullest, it has implications for the learning that leadership facilitates.

Leadership that fosters this broad and balanced learning creates an environment in which people are treated like, and encouraged to develop into whole human beings with a developed sense of values and rounded capabilities. This kind of leadership is participative. It raises aspirations beyond the measurable attainments that form the basis for national and international indicators of educational success. Values develop as the person is formed through experience, not through being told what their values should be (Joas, 2000). The environment that students experience is key. Frost and Roberts analyzed the results of years of work sustained at the University of Cambridge in developing schools as democratic communities of learning and leadership. They conclude that creating such participative school environments enhances "deep learning" — that is, learning that enhances self-awareness, critical thinking, autonomy, and the process of becoming a person in the sense of "developing the virtues, values and capacity for reason that enable us to live the "good life" and to take our places in the public sphere" (Frost & Roberts, 2011, p. 68). School leadership extends to students through processes such as student consultation, students as researchers, and participative pedagogy.

These reasons commend democratic leadership grounded in what I term holistic democracy (P.A. Woods, 2011; P.A. Woods & G.J. Woods, 2012, 2013). This is leadership that integrates the participation and growth of whole people. In my work, I describe holistic democracy in terms of four dimensions, each integral to democratic leadership:

Two dimensions are about enhancing participation:

> *Power sharing*, which enables people to have a say in what affects them and creates an environment in which involvement is inclusive, responsibility for decision making is shared and all have opportunities for taking and co-leading initiatives and innovation

> *Transforming dialogue*, which encourages dialogue, freedom to share views, and mutual understanding that helps to overcome differences of interests and viewpoints

The other two dimensions concern the development of meaning and learning:

> *Holistic meaning*, which is about learning collaboratively and developing full human capabilities and potential

> *Holistic well-being*, which is about creating a school environment that provides for both individuality and a sense of belonging so that people feel empowered and confident as members of an organization with high self-esteem, the capacity for independent thinking, and feelings of connectedness with deeper purposes and with the natural world

In line with the distributed character of leadership, democratic leadership is a property of the school as an organization, not the possession of a single leader or a small leadership elite. But as Greenfield and Ribbins recognize, an entity called "organization" does not transform social reality; rather, the "transforming mechanism lies within individuals" (1993, p. 17). In the ideal, where all the dimensions of holistic democracy are active, everyone to some degree engages in democratic leadership — and does so collaboratively. The "transforming mechanism" lies in individuals and their everyday interactions and relationships.

To be realistic, we have to recognize nevertheless that some individuals are more powerful than others. In particular, senior leaders can mobilize resources — both symbolic and material — that most others cannot. Hence, they have a key role to play in shaping the leadership culture of a school.

If we want the best and broadest education, we must make opportunities for initiative and for nurturing a culture that spreads leadership in democratic ways, which means being practical. The ideals of democratic leadership are above all a guide to practice. The challenge for school leaders is to move towards these ideals and to increase the "degree of democracy" in light of their own school's circumstances and context (P.A. Woods & G.J. Woods, 2012; G.J. Woods & P.A. Woods, 2013).

Much that is enshrined in holistic democracy may be implicit to school leaders' aspirations for leadership and education. Both making them explicit and reflecting on their implications for leadership practice are critical, however. Without this, the danger is that aspirations for social justice and for nurturing democratic citizenship are lost in the priorities demanded by the pressures for measurable accountability that all schools face.

References

Day, C., Sammons, P., Hopkins, D., Harris, A., Leithwood, K., Gu, Q., Brown, E., Ahtaridou, E., & Kington, A. (2009). *The impact of school leadership on pupil outcomes: Final report* (Research Report DCSF-RR108). London: Department for Children, Schools and Families.

Frost, D. (2012). From professional development to system change: Teacher leadership and innovation. *Professional Development in Education, 38*(2), 205–227.

Frost, D., & Roberts, A. (2011). Student leadership, participation and democracy. *Leading and Managing, 17*(2), 64–84.

Gratton, L. (2007). *Hot Spots.* Harlow: Pearson Education.

Greenfield, T., & Ribbins, P. (1993). *Greenfield on educational administration.* London: Routledge.

Joas, H. (2000). *The genesis of values.* Cambridge, UK: Polity Press.

Slavin, R.E. (2010). Co-operative learning: What makes group-work work? In H. Dumont, D. Istance, and F. Benavides (Eds.), *The Nature of Learning* (pp. 161-178) Paris: OECD.

Woods, G.J., & Woods, P.A. (2013). Degrees of democracy framework: A review of its use and impact. A report prepared for the School of Education, University of Hertfordshire, UK. Available from http://researchprofiles.herts.ac.uk/portal/en/publications/degrees-of-democracy-framework(ef118220-d05b-4b72-81df-37e8ededf050).html

Woods, P.A. (2011). *Transforming education policy: Shaping a democratic future*. Bristol, UK: Policy Press.

Woods, P.A., & Woods, G.J. (2012). Degrees of school democracy: A holistic framework. *Journal of School Leadership, 22*(4), 707–732.

Woods, P.A., & Woods, G.J. (2013). Deepening distributed leadership: A democratic perspective on power, purpose and the concept of the self. Vodenje v vzgoji in izobraževanju (Leadership in Education), *2*, 17–40. English version available at https://herts.academia.edu/PhilipWoods

Woods, P.A., Roberts, A., & Woods, G.J. (forthcoming). Newness against the grain: Democratic emergence in organizational and professional practice. In S. Weber (Ed.), *Organization and the new: Discourses, agents, ecologies of innovation*. Rotterdam: Sense Publishers.

Chapter 13

What Is Ethical Educational Leadership?

Joan Poliner Shapiro

E thical educational leadership can be defined in numerous ways. In this brief chapter, I have chosen to focus on values, virtues, and decision making. These concepts work well together. I strongly believe that educational leaders cannot make wise decisions without possessing an intelligent and worthwhile set of values and virtues. I also believe that leaders need to think rationally, empathetically, and broadly before making an important ethical decision that may affect students, staff, parents, and other constituencies.

Values and Virtues

Over time, educational ethicists have turned to diverse values that they believe are essential for leaders in education to possess. For example, Branson (2009; 2010; Branson & Gross, 2014) highlights wisdom and moral integrity; Haiyan and Walker (2014) focuses on empathy; Begley (2006) stresses self-knowledge and sensitivity; Gross (2014) turns to exemplars who exhibit a wide range of salient qualities; and Bredeson (2005) encompasses values in describing ethical architects as school leaders. Some of these writers emphasize the need to teach values to future educational leaders through moral literacy (Tuana, 2007). While Starratt

(2004) does not turn to values, he does advocate the importance of specific virtues: responsibility, authenticity, and presence.

Another way educational ethical values are gleaned is through the various codes designed by professional organizations. These include the National Policy Board for Educational Administration, ISLLC Standards (NPBEA, 2008); the AASA Statement of Ethics for Educational Leaders (AASA, 2007); and the UCEA Code of Ethics for the Preparation of Educational Leaders (UCEA, 2011). The latter was developed in a participatory process over six years by a number of educational leadership faculty members. Many other local, national, and international organizations have designed their own codes, focusing frequently on important values that educational leaders should possess.

Ethical Decision Making

In the literature, not only are values and virtues emphasized, but the actual process of ethical decision making is also highlighted. There are a few ways to approach educational ethical decision making. Strike, for example, focuses on evidence-driven decision making, where decisions should be "supported by evidence" and "implemented morally" (2007, pp. 111–113).

Starratt (1994) focuses on ethical decision making using three lenses — the ethics of justice, care, and critique. Shapiro and Stefkovich not only utilize the three lenses, but they add a fourth — the ethic of the profession. Starratt's work provided the foundation on which Shapiro and Stefkovich (2001, 2005, 2011) were able to create their Multiple Ethical Paradigms for ethical decision making. When faced with an ethical decision, Shapiro and Stefkovich ask educational leaders to turn to the Multiple Ethical Paradigms of justice, critique, care, and the profession.

Although there is no expectation that educational leaders will turn to the ethic of justice, frequently, in a litigious society, they consider this lens to be the first step in the decision-making process. The ethic of justice (e.g., Beauchamp & Childress, 1984; Sergiovanni, 2009; Strike, 2007; Yodof, Kirp, & Levin, 1992) is concerned with the legal system, fairness, and freedom. It takes into account questions such as the following: Is there a law, right, or policy that relates to a particular case? If there is a law, right, or policy, should it be enforced? Is the law enforced in some places and not in others? Why or why not? And if there is no law, right, or policy, should there be one?

The ethic of critique (e.g., Apple, 2003; Freire, 1970; Giroux, 2006; Portelli, 2007; Reitzug & O'Hair, 2002; S. Shapiro, 1999; H.S. Shapiro & Purpel, 2005), inherent in critical theory and critical pedagogy, is aimed at awakening educational leaders to inequities in society and, in particular, to injustices in education at all levels. It asks leaders to deal with the difficult questions regarding social class, race, gender, and other areas of difference, such as the following: Who makes the laws, rules, and policies? Who benefits from them? Who has the power? Who is silenced?

The ethic of care (e.g., Beck, 1994; Ginsberg, Shapiro, & Brown, 2004; Marshall & Gerstl-Pepin, 2005; Marshall & Oliva, 2006; Noddings, 2003) directs educators to contemplate the consequences of their decisions and actions. It asks them to consider questions such as the following: Who will benefit from what I decide? Who will be hurt by my actions? What are the long-term effects of a decision I make today? And if someone helps me now, what should I do in the future about giving back to this individual or to society in general?

Finally, the ethic of the profession (e.g., Beckner, 2004; Begley & Johansson, 2003; Greenfield, 2004; Murphy, 2005; Normore, 2004; Strike, Haller, & Soltis, 2005) expects educational leaders to formulate and examine their own professional as well as personal codes of ethics in light of standards set forth by Educational Leadership, and then place students at the centre of the ethical decision-making process. It also asks them to take into account the wishes of the community. It goes beyond the ethics of justice, critique, and care to ask the following questions: What would the profession ask me to do? What do various communities expect me to accomplish? What about clashes of codes — does this exist, and is there a problem? And what should the professional educator take into account to consider the best interests of the students, who may be diverse in their composition and their needs (Stefkovich, 2006, 2013; Frick, Faircloth, & Little, 2013)?

There is another ethic currently included under the Ethic of the Profession in the Shapiro and Stefkovich model, but it is considered a separate ethic by Furman (2004; Furman-Brown, 2002). She expands on what she characterizes as the "ethic of the community" and defines it as a process. Furman asks leaders to move away from heroic (solo) decision making and to reach conclusions with the participation of the community or communities.

Although not an ethic, Turbulence Theory (Gross, 1998, 2004, 2006, 2014; Shapiro & Gross, 2008, 2013) adds another dimension to ethical educational decision making. Before making an ethical decision, Gross asks educational leaders to become aware of the organization's stability or vulnerability. In so doing, they can determine if their staff and/or students need a decision that will bring calm to the school/district or a decision that will create some change to overcome complacency. Accordingly, Gross uses the four levels of turbulence employed by pilots: light, moderate, severe, and extreme. He asks educational leaders to create their own turbulence gauge as they weigh their decisions.

Conclusion

In answering the question regarding ethical educational leadership, this essay has looked briefly at values, virtues, and ethical decision making, taking into account some of the literature in this burgeoning field. It is clear that ethical decision making in education is a challenging area. It asks leaders not only to exemplify worthwhile and wise values and virtues, but it also asks them to make decisions that follow their beliefs and consistently place students at the centre of the decision-making process. In an era of accountability, where budgets too often end up at the centre of this decision-making process, this field asks educational leaders to take into account more than money and instead value the needs of their students and staff.

References

AASA (American Association of School Administrators). (2007). *Statement of ethics for school administrators.* Arlington, VA: American Association of School Administrators.

Apple, M.W. (2003). *The state and the politics of knowledge.* New York: Routledge Falmer.

Beauchamp, T.L., & Childress, J.F. (1984). Morality, ethics and ethical theories. In P. Sola (Ed.), *Ethics, education, and administrative decisions: A book of readings* (pp. 39–67). New York: Peter Lang.

Beck, L.G. (1994). *Reclaiming educational administration as a caring profession.* New York: Teachers' College Press.

Beckner, W. (2004). *Ethics for educational leaders.* Boston: Pearson Education.

Begley, P.T. (2006). Self-knowledge, capacity and sensitivity: Prerequisites to authentic leadership by school principles. *Journal of Educational Administration, 44*(6), 570–589.

Begley, P.T., & Johansson, O. (Eds.). (2003). *The ethical dimensions of school leadership.* Boston: Kluwer Academic Publishers.

Branson, C. (2009). *Leadership for age of wisdom.* Dordrecht, Netherlands: Springer Education.

Branson, C. (2010, March). Ethical decision making: Is personal moral integrity the missing link? *Journal of Authentic Leadership in Education, 1*(1), 1–8.

Branson, C., & Gross, S.J. (Eds.). (2014). *Handbook of ethical educational leadership.* New York: Routledge.

Bredeson, P.V. (Fall 2005). Building capacity in schools: Some ethical considerations for authentic leadership and learning. *Values and Ethics in Educational Administration, 4*(1), 1–7.

Freire, P. (1970). *Pedagogy of the Oppressed*, trans. M.B. Ramos. New York: Continuum.

Frick, W.C., Faircloth, S.C., & Little, K.S. (2013, March). Responding to the collective and individual 'Best Interests of Students': Revisiting the tension between administrative practice and ethical imperatives in special education leadership. *Educational Administration Quarterly, 49*(2), 207–242.

Furman, G.C. (2004). The ethic of community. *Journal of Educational Administration, 42*, 215–235.

Furman-Brown, G. (Ed.). (2002). *School as community: From promise to practice.* New York: SUNY Press.

Ginsberg, A.E., Shapiro, J.P., & Brown, S.P. (2004). *Gender in urban education: Strategies for student achievement.* Portsmouth, NH: Heinemann.

Giroux, H.A. (2006). *America on the edge: Henry Giroux on politics, education and culture.* New York: Palgrave Macmillan.

Greenfield, W.D. (2004). Moral leadership in schools. *Journal of Educational Administration, 42*(2), 174–196.

Gross, S.J. (1998). *Staying centered: Curriculum leadership in a turbulent era.* Alexandria, VA: Association for Supervision and Curriculum Development.

Gross, S.J. (2004). *Promises kept: Sustaining school and district leadership in turbulent times.* Alexandria, VA: Association of Supervision and Curriculum Development.

Gross, S.J. (2006). *Leadership mentoring: Maintaining school improvement in turbulent times.* Lanham, MA: Rowman & Littlefield.

Gross, S.J. (2014). Profiles in democratic ethical leadership: Educating for moral literacy through the power of exemplars. 10th Annual Moral Literacy Colloquium. Pennsylvania State University, University Park, PA. April 25–26, 2014.

Haiyan, Q., & Walker, A. (2014). Leading with empathy. In C. Branson & S. J. Gross (Eds.), *Handbook of ethical educational leadership* (pp. xx–xx). New York: Routledge.

Marshall, C., & Gerstl-Pepin, C. (2005). *Re-framing educational politics for social justice.* Boston: Allyn & Bacon.

Marshall, C., & Oliva, M. (2006). *Leadership for social justice: Making revolutions in education.* Boston: Allyn & Bacon.

Murphy, J. (2005). Unpacking the foundations of ISLLC standards and addressing concerns in the academic community. *Educational Administration Quarterly, 41*(1), 154–191.

NPBEA (National Policy Board for Educational Administration). (2008). Educational leadership policy standards: ISLLC 2008, pp. 1–5. Washington, DC: Council of Chief State School Officers. Retrieved 3 January 2010. http://www.ccsso.org/content/pdfs/elps_isllc2008 pdf

Noddings, N. (2003). Caring: A feminine approach to ethics and moral education, 2nd ed. Berkeley, CA: University of California Press.

Normore, A.H. (2004). Ethics and values in leadership preparation programs: Finding the North Star in the dust storm. *Values and Ethics in Educational Administration, 2*(2), 1–8.

Portelli, J.P. (Ed.). (2007, Spring–Summer). Critical democracy and educational leadership issues: Philosophical responses to the neoliberal agenda. *Journal of Thought*, Special Issue, 42(1).

Reitzug, U.C., & O'Hair, M.J. (2002). From conventional school to democratic school community: The dilemmas of teaching and leading. In G. Furman-Brown (Ed.), *School as community: From promise to practice* (pp. 119–141). New York: SUNY Press.

Sergiovanni, T.J. (2009). The principalship: A reflective practice perspective, 6th ed. Boston, MA: Allyn & Bacon.

Shapiro, H.S., & Purpel, D.E. (Eds.). (2005). *Social issues in American education: Democracy and meaning in a globalized world*, 3rd ed. Mahwah, NJ: Lawrence Erlbaum Associates.

Shapiro, J.P., & Gross, S.J. (2008). *Ethical educational leadership in turbulent times: (Re)solving moral dilemmas.* New York: Lawrence Erlbaum Associates/Taylor & Francis.

Shapiro, J.P., & Gross, S.J. (2013). *Ethical educational leadership in turbulent times: (Re)solving moral dilemmas*, 2nd ed. New York: Routledge.

Shapiro, J.P., & Stefkovich, J.A. (2001). *Ethical leadership and decision making in education: Applying theoretical perspectives to complex dilemmas.* Mahwah, NJ: Lawrence Erlbaum Associates.

Shapiro, J.P., & Stefkovich, J.A. (2005). *Ethical leadership and decision making in education: Applying theoretical perspectives to complex dilemmas*, 2nd ed. Mahwah, NJ: Lawrence Erlbaum Associates.

Shapiro, J.P., & Stefkovich, J.A. (2011). *Ethical leadership and decision making in education: Applying theoretical perspectives to complex dilemmas*, 3rd ed. New York: Routledge.

Starratt, R.J. (2004). *Ethical leadership.* San Francisco: Jossey Bass.

Stefkovich, J.A. (2006). *Applying ethical constructs to legal cases: The best interests of the student.* Mahwah, NJ: Lawrence Erlbaum Associates.

Stefkovich, J.A. (2013). *Applying ethical constructs to legal cases: The best interests of the student*, 2nd ed. New York: Routledge.

Strike, K.A. (2007). *Ethical leadership in schools: Creating community in an environment of accountability.* Thousand Oaks, CA: Corwin Press.

Strike, K.A., Haller, E.J., & Soltis, J.F. (2005). *The Ethics of School Administration*, 2nd ed. New York: Teachers College Press.

Tuana, N. (2007). Conceptualizing moral literacy. *Journal of Educational Administration*, 45(4), 364–378.

UCEA (May 2011). *UCEA code of ethics for the preparation of educational leaders.* Charlottesville, VA: University of Virginia.

Yodof, M., Kirp, D., & Levin, B. (1992). *Educational policy and the law*, 3rd ed. St. Paul, MN: West Publishing Company.

Chapter 14

What Is Anti-Racist Educational Leadership?

George J. Sefa Dei

A nti-racism is about race, racism, and the intersections of class, gender, sexual, and [dis]abled oppressions. To engage anti-racist practice is to promote social change by addressing the social oppressions on human lives. This is a collective responsibility; we must share visions of educational leadership if we all care about human dignity. Leadership is about taking responsibility and acting to promote change. In the field of education, the responsibility of leadership is to ensure a fair, just, and equitable educational system, one that is able to promote education for all learners.

Clearly, educational leadership is also an important topic for anti-racism. Effective leadership in schools holds the possibility of anti-racist transformative change. School leadership is about power and authority and, in particular, how power can be used to address questions of justice and equity in today's classrooms. A discussion of leadership brings to the fore the key question of the particular bodies who occupy positions of power and authority in our institutions and whether there is adequate representation of the diverse make-up of communities. This is critical because of the powerful links between identity, knowledge, and social change. The identity, subject position, and social location of the educational leader are significant given the connection of practice, experience, and knowledge; therefore, how schools and school boards select their leaders, what qualities they look for, and the accompanying expectations, roles, and responsibilities of school leadership are all central to anti-racist practice. Weak and ineffective leadership not only serves to maintain the status quo but can also be harmful when we fail to acknowledge the ways that leadership has historically served to cement the power and privilege of particular groups in society.

The question of leadership has received much attention in academic literature. In the field of education, there is general agreement that "leadership matters." A strong leader with vision, able to set agendas with well-defined goals, and able to build collaborative, accountable relationships, it is argued, can successfully ensure school/academic results and community achievements (see Fullan, 2001; Hargreaves & Fink, 2006; Leithwood, Jantzi, & Steinbach, 1999; Leithwood, Louis, Anderson, & Wahlstrom, 2004). The problem is that dominant conceptions of leadership are mired in liberal and neo-liberal agendas that appropriate ideas of quality, competency, standards, accountability, and transparency without any critical engagement of the equity, social justice, and diverse local cultural knowings side of leadership (Logan, 2013; Portelli & Campbell-Stephens, 2009; Ontario Ministry of Education, 2009; Solomon, 2002).

The particular meanings we bring to our concepts are important. The problem with the conventional understanding of leadership is that it is grounded in individual persons. For anti-racist practice, it is important to see leadership as not being about a romantic or charismatic persona. In other words, leadership is not an individual responsibility but a shared one; those who lead are only as good as the people who are led. Anti-racist leadership calls for the heroics of collectivities and communities working together to improve social conditions and resisting domination and oppression, ensuring that we design futures and agenda collectively. Critical anti-racist leadership is also informed by Indigenous knowings. Indigenous leadership — as contrasted with Eurocentric conceptions of leadership — acknowledges that marginalized and colonized communities have long upheld their own conceptions of leadership. Indigenous leadership does not imply any absolute interiority and individuality but rather upholds the agency and power of Indigene/colonized/racialized bodies to name, accord, and affirm leadership in cultural contexts. The

Indigenous conception of leadership is spiritually informed and spiritually based. It is about developing ethical and social responsibility towards all humans [and non-humans] sharing the Earth. It is leadership nurtured by the Land and the teachings of Mother Earth. It is leadership that lives and breathes the sacredness of all activity. It is leadership possessed by all; people choose "leaders" and those chosen are responsible to the communities they represent. Indigenous leadership is about the ethics of caring for everyone, including the non-human. Indigenous leadership is about respecting the sanctity of life and developing interpersonal relations that affirm the bonds between the individual, the group, and the community. Such leadership works with consensus decision making and upholds the integrity of the group.

In order to promote effective educational leadership for anti-racism we must realize that one workshop on "anti-racist leadership" does not cut it!

Leadership in the Canadian context also includes a little discussed additional dimension: how we come to work with our involvements, responsibilities, and implications in settler colonialisms. A leader must first learn to be a critical learner about history and complicity and what these mean for understanding the present and the future. It is a fact that even when school leaders/administrators note or acknowledge the entrapments of White privileges (e.g., Whiteness) and the production of racism towards racialized/colonized and Indigenous peoples, there is still a refusal to link the question of race with colonialism, Aboriginality/Indigeneity, Whiteness, and the ties to colonial lands and settler-hoods (see Pearson, 2014). There are specific instructional, pedagogic, and communicative implications for educational administrators on settled Aboriginal lands. Effective leadership must reframe/re-theorize social justice, anti-racism, and equity education and, more importantly, how we pursue anti-racism work in schools where Aboriginal/Indigenous, anti-racist/anti-colonial knowledge production is professed. The colonial/colonizing knowledge base of the academy (schools, colleges, and universities) continues to be a major challenge of contemporary education; for example, how to decolonize minds and subvert colonial thinking and the colonial hierarchies of schooling/academies. Anti-racist educational leadership will require creating intellectual spaces for sustained critique of the current depoliticized inclusionary approaches, the interrogations of institutional practices and procedures, and the mind-sets of young learners.

Most progressive educational leaders buy into dominant narratives about "social justice for all." Subverting liberal understandings of social justice and complicating social justice (centring race, difference, and power) by legitimizing multiple models of justice that recognize the severity of issues for particular bodies in our institutions (Aboriginal, African-Canadians, etc) is urgent. While "leadership accountability for shaping institutional culture" is key to transformative change in schools (see Pearson, 2014, p. 102), and may be cursorily acknowledged, the issue goes deeper. "Bodies matter" in anti-racist work (e.g., physical representation of faculty, students, and [senior] administrative staff). It is a question of knowledge and power and a need for a "structural hegemonic rupturing" of our educational institutions in order to bring Aboriginal/Indigenous and racialized bodies and their knowledges into positions of leadership. These bodies are equally equipped with leadership skills and attributes, collectively gained from long association with their communities and struggles over oppression, domination, and injustice.

It is through the long histories of struggle that collective leadership is sustained to promote equity and social justice. Anti-racist leadership is birthed in community struggle, and the lessons of history would guide both present and future struggles for better communities and better worlds. In offering education to contemporary learners, the importance of counter-visioning leadership cannot be downplayed. It must be rooted in community and spirituality, it must acknowledge complicities and implications, and it must take responsibility for the promotion of equity and anti-racism. In looking to the future, more accountability and transparency in anti-racist leadership will ensure meaningful educational transformation.

We should also explore more creative ways of developing anti-racist leadership in order to spearhead the total infusion of anti-racism curricular, pedagogic, and instructional approaches in schools for the education of our young learners today. Anti-racist leadership should be pioneering new and innovative ways of co-creation of knowledge with local communities, ensuring educators' responsibility to such knowledge, and promoting the social relevance of anti-racist work for our varied communities. Finally, leadership should explore ways of maintaining ethics and the integrity of anti-racist work, including the ethics and morals that guide the search for new knowledge in order to determine and assess which information is worth searching for.

References

Fullan, M. (2001). *Leadership in a culture of change*. San Francisco, CA: Jossey-Bass.

Hargreaves, A., & Fink, D. (2006). *Sustainable leadership*. San Francisco, CA: Jossey-Bass.

Leithwood, K., Jantzi, D., & Steinbach, R. (1999). Changing leadership for changing times. Buckingham, UK: Open University Press.

Leithwood, K., Louis, K.S., Anderson, S., & Wahlstrom, K. (2004). How leadership influences student learning. New York: Wallace Foundation.

Logan, C. (2013). School leadership. Unpublished PhD Proposal. Ontario Institute for Studies in Education, University of Toronto, Toronto.

Ontario Ministry of Education. (2009). Realizing the promise of diversity: Ontario's equity and inclusive education strategy. Toronto.

Portelli, J.P., & Campbell-Stephens, R. (2009). Leading for equity: The investing in diversity approach. Toronto: Edphil Books.

Pearson, K. (2014). Social justice and equity: Exploring perspectives of senior administrators on whiteness and racism in postsecondary education. Unpublished PhD dissertation, Faculty of Education, Lakehead University, Thunder Bay, Ontario.

Solomon, P.R. (2002). School leaders and anti-racism: Overcoming pedagogical and political obstacles. *Journal of School of Leadership, 12.*

Chapter 15

What Is Advocacy Leadership?

Gary L. Anderson

T he role of the school administrator is changing rapidly. In New York City, under former mayor Michael Bloomberg's administration, principals were modelled after Chief Executive Officers (or "education executives"). The school district essentially disappeared, as did any mechanism for citizen input under mayoral control. Principals instead dealt with networks and "vendors" in a marketplace to contract services (Burch, 2009). They purchased professional development packages that contained different prices for different services. Many aggressively marketed their schools, partnered with the private sector, and engaged in data-driven decision making just like businesses do, except the data is mostly test scores (Shiller, 2011). Although told they were being empowered, most felt more beleaguered (Shipps, 2012). It remains to be seen what of this model survives under Mayor DiBlasio. Whatever ultimately happens in New York City, a powerful and bipartisan policy network is pushing similar market and business-model reforms across the country (Anderson & Montoro Donchik, 2015; Scott, 2011).

Businessmen like Michael Bloomberg believe that all public sector administrators should behave more like businessmen, but this cross-sector borrowing from business has not been carefully examined or empirically studied (Cuban, 2004). Meanwhile, it creates not only dysfunctional policies and a "new professionalism" (Exworthy & Halford, 1999), but also saps the school leadership of its public-service orientation (Denhardt & Denhardt, 2011). Principals are changing their ethos from being advocates for children to being savvy businesspeople maximizing their own school's brand. The very idea of *public* school leadership is at risk.

In an era in which principals are expected to be entrepreneurs of their own schools, what does it mean to be a leader who is an advocate for all children? An example from my own experience as a former principal and from my university experience in preparing teachers to be principals provides a revealing illustration.

Twenty years ago in principal certification programs, we used to tell teachers moving into the principalship that their central task as an instructional leader was to take a teaching staff composed of a continuum of teachers from incompetent to outstanding and help them all improve. If the incompetent ones (usually only one or two) could not improve after working with them over time, then the task was to counsel them out of teaching or use documentation to move them out (Bridges, 1992). We did not scapegoat unions; we taught aspiring principals how to provide due process by helping struggling teachers to improve, while documenting their work in case they didn't.

We taught them how to encourage professional renewal for burned out or "plateaued" teachers, how to target professional development for teachers with specific needs, and how to inspire good teachers to become outstanding. The problem back then was how to carry out both a management and an instructional leadership role given the time constraints (Rallis & Highsmith, 1986). Eventually, we added teacher leader positions, literacy coaches, and critical friends groups to provide additional support for teacher development. Because most teachers saw teaching as a career and stayed in schools longer, there was time to do this kind of capacity building in the school, which also meant building capacity in the system if these teachers moved to another school. All children benefited when teachers improved. This was seen as particularly important in low-income schools where students needed skilled teachers and depended on institutional agents, like teachers, counselors and administrators for access to dominant social and cultural capital (Stanton-Salazar, 2011).

The new entrepreneurial principal, modelled after business CEOs, brings a completely different ethos and internal logic to the public sector

(Ward, 2011). There is now a tendency for principals to recruit low-er-maintenance students and teachers to their schools in order to improve test scores. Charter schools are particularly geared for this kind of entre-preneurialism, but even public school principals in marketized districts are beginning to engage in the same behaviour (Lubienski & Lubienski, 2006). This is why charter schools tend to have far fewer students with special education or English as a second language needs (Baker, 2012). Some principals have figured out that if they recruit good teachers, their job is easier, their test scores improve, and their careers take off. This may seem overly cynical, and I do not think that most principals want to play this market game, but if competition is the game, then they are forced to play it.

But a principal who recruits great teachers to his or her school is not building capacity. Those teachers leave behind a classroom of equally deserving students at their former school. All this does is move resources around the district with the goal of enhancing a particular school's (and by extension, principal's) performance. Closing, "turning around," or "reconstituting" schools does the same thing. It just moves resources around the system on the pretext of getting rid of "bad teachers" (Malen, Croninger, Muncey, & Redmond-Jones, 2002). The yesteryear notion of principals as instructional leaders, helping all teachers improve, increases system capacity. The new entrepreneurial model does not.

At least as an entrepreneurial businessperson, I can argue that my self-interest in building a successful business creates jobs and helps my community. But in public school systems, viewing a school as my "busi-ness" or "start up" usually means that I have to poach good teachers from another school and reject kids who might lower "my" test scores. It is hard to imagine how this model provides advocacy for children.

I am not suggesting here that public schools for poor children were better twenty years ago, but had we continued to focus on an ethos of public service and advocacy for children, I believe we would have made more progress by now than we have by using high-stakes tests and market logics to "incentivize" and punish teachers and principals. We have lost many outstanding teachers and principals because they no longer feel they can use their professional judgment to advocate for what they know is best for children. It is time we had a serious, rigorous discussion about the cross-sector borrowing of ideas. Entrepreneurialism is a wonderful asset for someone starting a business. It is turning out to be disaster for our public educational system.

References

Anderson, G.L., & Montoro Donchik, L. (2015). The privatization of education and policy-making: The American Legislative Exchange Council (ALEC) and network governance in the United States. *Journal of Educational Policy*. Online First. DOI: 10.1177/0895904814528794

Baker, B. (2012). *Review of New York State special education enrollment analysis.* Boulder, CO: National Education Policy Center.

Bridges, E. (1992). *The incompetent teacher: Managerial responses.* New York: Routledge.

Burch, P. (2009). *Hidden markets: The new education privatization.* New York, Routledge.

Cuban, L. (2004). *The blackboard and the bottom line: Why schools can't be businesses.* Cambridge, MA: Harvard University Press.

Denhardt, J., & Denhardt, R. (2011). *The new public service: Serving, not steering.* Armonk, NY: M.E. Sharpe.

Exworthy, M., & Halford, S. (1999). *Professionals and the new managerialism in the public sector.* Buckingham: Open University Press.

Lubienski, C., & Lubienski, S.T. (2006). Charter, private, public schools and academic achievement: New evidence from NAEP mathematics data. New York: National.

Malen, B., Croninger, R., Muncey, D., & Redmond-Jones, D. (2002). Reconstituting schools: "Testing" the "Theory of Action." *Educational Evaluation and Policy Analysis, 24*(2), 113–132.

Rallis, S., & Highsmith, M. (1986). The myth of the great principal: Questions of school management and instructional leadership. *Phi Delta Kappan, 68*(4), 300–304.

Scott, J. (2011). Market-driven education reform and the racial politics of advocacy. *Peabody Journal of Education, 86*, 580–599.

Shiller, J. (2011). Marketing small schools in New York City: A critique of neoliberal school reform. *Educational Studies, 47*(2), 160–173

.Shipps, D. (2012). Empowered or beleaguered? Principals' accountability under New York City's diverse provider regime. *Education Policy Analysis Archives, 20*(1), 1–42.

Stanton-Salazar, R.D. (2011). A social capital framework for the study of institutional agents and their role in the empowerment of low-status students and youth. *Youth and Society, 43*(3), 1066–1109.

Ward, S. (2011). The machinations of managerialism: New public management and the diminishing power of professionals. *Journal of Cultural Economy, 4*(2), 205–215.

Chapter 16

What Is Inclusive Leadership?

James Ryan

Inclusive leadership is a collective process geared to engender a particular outcome — inclusion. In this sense, both the process and the outcome are inclusive. In ideal inclusive leadership situations, all individuals and groups or their representatives participate meaningfully in policy, decision-making, and other influence or power-related processes geared to generate the fair involvement of everyone in what schools and communities have to offer.

Inclusive leadership differs from many of the more traditional approaches to leadership. Many of the latter are exclusive 1) in the relationships organization members have with one another; 2) in the roles individuals and groups assume; and 3) in the ends for which leadership practices are organized. Managerial oriented leadership perspectives, for example, emphasize hierarchical relationships between management and others, embed leadership in single individuals, and promote values of efficiency and effectiveness. In these approaches, those not in management are excluded from policy and decision-making processes; organizations that invest power in single individuals exclude others not in these positions; and the emphasis on efficiency and effectiveness tends to deflect attention away from inclusion. Inclusive leadership, on the other hand, promotes horizontal relationships among organization members, endorses collective enterprises, and works to generate inclusive practices.

Inclusive leadership strives to eliminate unequal power relationships in the leadership process. Hierarchies are not consistent with inclusion. They exclude those not privileged enough to occupy formal positions of authority and those who do not possess personal characteristics that influence others. Some would say, however, that such a goal is unrealistic since hierarchies pervade our organizations and communities. School administrators, for example, are legally invested with power to make decisions about teachers and students; and unequal race, class, gender, and sexual orientation relationships seem to be entrenched in contemporary institutions. But this does not mean that they are right or just or that we should not work toward establishing horizontal, heterogeneous, and equal relationships in schools and communities. Socially just schools and communities can only be attained with leadership practices that display these sorts of relationships.

Inclusive leadership is a collective enterprise. Unlike many contemporary approaches to leadership, it does not assume that leadership resides within single individuals. There are two reasons for this. First, investing power in one individual is not only exclusive, but in extreme cases can be dangerous, as the actions of Pol Pot and Hitler have vividly illustrated. Second, the influence of single individuals on institutions is generally limited. Schools improve not necessarily as the result of individual people doing remarkable things in isolation, but from a variety of many people working together in many different ways and roles, using the multitude of different resources available to them. So in schools, leadership can originate not just with administrators, but also with teachers, parents, students, and other members of the school community. This does not mean that we cannot speak of "leaders"; we can, but when we do so, we must acknowledge that they are just one part of a wider enterprise.

Inclusive leadership is also organized to pursue a particular goal. Unlike many contemporary approaches that focus exclusively on process and ignore ends, or emphasize only effectiveness and efficiency, inclusive leadership strives to achieve inclusion in schools and the wider community. Leadership must get people to recognize exclusive practices and work together to change them. There is little point for the process of leadership to be inclusive if the entire leadership enterprise is not also organized to pursue inclusion in schools and communities. For leadership to be consistent with inclusive ideals, it must be seen and practiced as an inclusive, equitable, collective process organized to promote inclusion.

Practitioners have many ways of putting inclusive leadership into practice. While students, teachers, and parents can be part of an inclusive leadership enterprise, the research on inclusive leadership to date has mostly concentrated on administrators, particularly principals (Ryan, 2006; 2007; 2010a; 2010b; 2012; Ryan & Rottmann, 2009). It illustrates that these administrators adopt particular communication strategies, look critically at their environments, work with their communities, and use their political skills to advocate for inclusion.

Educational administrators who promote inclusive leadership acknowledge the importance of communication to inclusion. They approach inclusive communication strategies in a least two ways: 1) the manner in which they communicate with others, and 2) the ends for which they employ communication. These administrators promote inclusive communication practices, and use these practices to engender inclusion. Many administrators value inclusive two-way interchanges, characteristic of dialogue. Engaging in these dialogues requires establishing relationships with communication partners, understanding others, and listening to people.

Practitioners of inclusive leadership promote critical forms of learning. They acknowledge that they need to help students, teachers, and community members understand one another, recognize exclusive processes like racism, sexism, classism, and homophobia when they occur, and implement inclusive practices. They also know they will have to learn about these same issues from their school communities and help members develop a critical consciousness. This involves consciously pausing, stepping back from daily routines, and inquiring into one's own and others' thoughts and actions. Administrators promote critical consciousness in several ways, including supporting an atmosphere that encourages critique, sponsoring activities specifically designed for such purposes, and asking critical questions.

Inclusive-minded leaders also seek to include incorporate the wider community in school activities. One tactic is to distribute and receive information, employing handbooks, newsletters, and newspapers to inform parents, and surveys and questionnaires to hear from parents. Inclusive-minded administrators also value interacting and establishing relationships with parents. To accomplish this, they interact with parents before and after school, go out into the community to see parents, and encourage teachers to do the same. They employ a number of strategies for bringing parents and community members into contact with the school, including organizing parent nights, barbecues, translation services, drop-in centres, coffee hours, helping with lunch hour supervision, accompanying students on field trips, drawing on parents for their various areas of expertise, and providing ESL services. The best way to get parents involved in the school, however, is to have parental presence as a part of everyday activities.

Given the difficulties of promoting, implementing, and exercising inclusion, practitioners of inclusive leadership may need to advocate for it. Among other things, they may need to persuade reluctant or ignorant others by using various information-circulating techniques, modes of prompting, guided discussions, questioning and provoking, and adopting various arguments to get their points across. Supplying academic articles and student performance data for educators to mull over, and making available stories, videos, and people's experiences may also help to get teachers, parents, and students to buy into inclusion. Leaders also trade and bargain with others, establish links with like-minded others, and, as a last resort, make inclusion non-negotiable, that is, if they are in a position to do this. Although exclusive in some respects, this last practice can, in the right circumstances, generate inclusion in the long run. Towards this end, leaders may do such things as making acts of racism non-negotiable, that is, if they have the power to do so. Leaders will also have to employ their political acumen to understand how power works in their organizations, know how to put these understandings into play, and be prepared to reflect on their actions.

While inclusive leadership may be difficult to achieve in an exclusive world, it is an ideal worth working towards. Schools and communities can be better places for everyone when they are truly inclusive.

References

Ryan, J. (2006). *Inclusive leadership*. San Francisco, CA: Jossey-Bass.

Ryan, J. (2007). Dialogue, identity and inclusion: Administrators as mediators in diverse school contexts. *Journal of School Leadership, 17*(3), 340–369.

Ryan, J. (2010a). Promoting social justice in schools: Principals' political strategies. *International Journal of Leadership in Education, 13*(4), 357–376.

Ryan, J. (2010b). Establishing inclusion in a new school: The role of principal leadership. *Exceptionality Education International, 20*(2), 6–24.

Ryan, J. (2012). *Struggling for inclusion: Leadership in neoliberal times.* Greenwich, CT: Information Age Publishing.

Ryan, J., & Rottmann, C. (2007). Educational leadership and policy approaches to critical social justice. *Journal of Educational Administration and Foundations, 18*(1–2), 9–23.

Chapter 17

What Is Feminist Leadership?

Margaret Grogan

I have thought a lot about leadership — as a feminist who has held formal leadership positions in both post-secondary and secondary education, and has taught leadership to teachers and administrators in several institutions of higher education. In the early 1990s, while studying U.S. women in the superintendency, I was exposed to the power of feminist thinking to help explain why so few women actually held the position. The feminist lens generated interesting insights not only into the ways that gender was enacted in organizational life but also about the traditional discourse of leadership.

Therefore, while I am reluctant to affix yet another label to the word "leadership," I believe leadership can be inspired by feminist thought, particularly in terms of offering alternatives to leadership practices that have not been good for children and their families. I will draw loosely on a spectrum of feminist ideas in this essay. Fundamentally, as Chris Weedon explains, feminism is "directed at changing existing power relations between women and men in society. These power relations structure all areas of life, the family, education and welfare, the worlds of work and politics, culture and leisure. They determine who does what and for whom, what we are and what we might become" (1997, p. 1).

Thus, starting with gender, we learn that others' perceptions of our gender shape our experiences in subtle and not-so-subtle ways, and the playing field is not level. Feminist theories and concepts help us grapple with traditional patriarchal notions of society, where men made decisions on behalf of women and children, men lived their lives in the public sphere, and women undertook domestic duties, including the lion's share of caring for the sick and elderly and raising children. Men's lives have always been seen as informing exemplary work (even for contemporary workers) in the public sphere. By using a feminist historical lens to interrogate women's and men's social and professional roles, we uncovered unequal access to opportunity, power, and self-determination. But, at the same time, we also learned to critique the male-based assumptions underlying social, organizational, and other taken-for-granted practices and beliefs that grew out of an androcentric view of the world. The practice of leadership is a case in point.

In my view, feminist thought contributes the following critical insights to any discussion of leadership: 1) the salience of gender as a social construct; 2) how the intersections of race, gender, and socio-economic status position individuals; 3) the shortcomings in accepted leadership discourse, and the desire to disrupt the status quo. In this essay, I will briefly explore how these understandings require us to reconsider what we teach and espouse in the field of educational leadership if we want to educate all our students. I will confine my comments to the pre-K–12 arena.

The Salience of Gender as a Social Construct

Feminist thought foregrounds the knowledge that women have been positioned historically in many societies as less than men and subordinate to men. Myths of women's inferior intelligence have been thoroughly debunked as well as those surrounding women's capacity to go into armed conflict or to drive heavy machinery. Out of women's lived experiences comes the knowledge that organizational structures, goals, and objectives privilege some members and marginalize others. Despite the fact that women comprise nearly 80 percent of educators, white middle-class men still disproportionally hold positions as principals and superintendents. What becomes clear is that while white middle-class women have made some inroads into leadership positions in the pre-K–12 arena, under-represented minority women and men are far less successful. Thus, access to leadership is shaped by the various intersecting ways gender, race, class, sexuality, ability, and other socially constructed markers position individuals. Feminist thinking heightens our awareness of the extent to which women and marginalized others are even present at the decision making table. Most important, a feminist critique questions why we are still having this conversation when we have so long espoused that gender, race, ethnicity, sexuality, linguistic background, and socio-economic status have no bearing on who leads our schools?

How the Intersections of Race, Gender, and Socio-Economic Status Position Individuals

Feminist thinking draws attention to the social-constructedness of these markers. Again, racist narratives of differences between Black and White intelligence have been exposed and thoroughly refuted. Just as we have understood that perceptions of gender shape beliefs about women's suitability and qualifications for doing work stereotypically associated with men (e.g., leadership), we realize that stereotyping limits options for many individuals depending on local contexts, racism, and homophobia. The white middle-class male principal or superintendent stereotype has particularly adverse effects on white women and women of colour, lesbian/bisexual/transgender women, and gay/bisexual/transgender men. Some white men and men of colour find the traditional aloof, top-down approach constraining as well. And, nobody benefits from the manipulative leadership stereotype that values leadership for the sake of community status and prestige. Moreover, when sexuality, gender, race, linguistic background, and/or ethnicity intersect, individuals seeking leadership roles may be rejected even more vehemently. A critical feminist lens allows us to name these discriminatory practices.

In addition, feminist discourse recognizes that diverse experiences allow leaders to view problem definitions and solutions in ways that the traditional white male middle-class experiences do not. Consequently, a feminist critique not only advocates changing who gets to wield the power in leadership but also promotes the idea of potentially positive changes in perspective and knowledge that emerge from the lived experiences of marginalized individuals. The value of bringing diversity to the practice of organizational leadership lies in the promise of fruitful, productive approaches that challenge the status quo.

A Critique of Accepted Leadership Discourse, and the Desire to Disrupt the Status Quo

Outsiders bring perspectives that differ from insiders' perspectives. Feminist thinking critiques leadership practices that continue to leave out the views of the majority of stakeholders. Community perspectives, involvement in schools, and support for teachers is vital if students are to grow and develop into healthy, compassionate, well-educated citizens. In all our diverse settings, the collective efforts of community members, educators, policy makers, and the students themselves are necessary to interrupt business as usual. Despite years of education reforms, curricular overhaul, and top-down policies, too many of our students are opting out of school, or graduating without the means to access higher education and/or without the skills to find meaningful employment. We must confront the fact that traditional leadership practices have not been successful in transforming last century's schools into engaging learning environments for twenty-first century students. Research indicates that neither girls nor boys all benefit from the way our schools and classrooms are operating (Grogan & Dias, 2015). Feminist approaches advocate using inclusive decision making processes, and rewarding teachers for taking initiatives and leading their own and their colleagues' learning. Traditional control-oriented leadership where principals and superintendents direct the work of others must give way to collective leadership where teachers and leaders share responsibility for taking initiative to change unproductive school practices and policies. Feminist discourse respects teachers as leaders as they take a proactive, action-research-oriented approach to facilitating learning in the classroom.

Leadership inspired by feminist thought, first, casts a critical eye on what is happening to the women and girls in the organization. It includes asking questions such as these: How much formal decision-making power do women hold in this school? What are we doing to equalize or maintain that state of leadership? Do we know which women aspire to leadership? Who is mentoring them? How gendered are our school practices and policies? How do we know whether girls and boys are getting equitable opportunities for learning everything and anything in our school? Are our girls and boys safe from gender-based violence? Are pregnant girls provided a full, inclusive opportunity to graduate?

Second, feminist approaches to leadership flatten the organizational hierarchies so that decision making devolves to those with most expertise in the teaching and learning process. Questions here include the following: Where does the decision making power really lie in this school/district? How can we change that to value the collective? What are we doing to diversify all our committees, task forces, and professional learning communities so that new policies and practices benefit those who have been marginalized in our school? How will we keep from marginalizing others in the future?

Conclusions

Clearly, leadership inspired by feminist critique thrives on interrogating organizational practices and policies for their effects. I believe this lens requires leaders to remain vigilant. My assumptions throughout this essay have been that we are committed to the ideal of educating all students to their fullest potential in our schools. If that is so, we have to keep a critical eye on how we are checking for evidence of students' having reached that goal. Their academic achievement (measured in more nuanced and meaningful ways than at present), social and emotional growth and development, and critical thinking skills to maintain a vibrant democracy must be our priorities. Because organizations differ so greatly in context, this constant vigilance is necessary to ensure that our sometimes lofty rhetoric matches our local realities.

References

Grogan, M. & Dias, S. (2015). Inclusive leadership and gender. Theoharis, G. & Scanlan, M. (Eds.) *Leadership for increasingly diverse schools* (pp. 123-145). New York: Routledge.

Weedon, C. (1997). *Feminist practice and poststructuralist theory*. Cambridge, MA: Blackwell Publishers.

Chapter 18

What Is Culturally Proficient Leadership?

Raymond D. Terrell and Randall B. Lindsey

Students learn what they care about, from people they care about and who, they know, care about them...
— Thirty Years of Stories, 1996

Our purpose in this chapter is to describe culturally proficient leadership as an approach to school leadership centred in a moral purpose that schools and schooling can be successful places for students *because* of their cultural memberships and not in spite of them. Effectively leading in today's schools is both a daunting challenge and a rewarding experience for the administrator, the school, and the community being served. Being a culturally proficient leader in a school that serves diverse communities well provides rich opportunities for educators and communities alike.

Deconstructing the opening epigraph can serve as a personal benchmark on a school leader's journey in developing culturally proficient educational practices for herself and her school. Caring about students in all of their diversity is embodied in a leader's values and behaviours as well as in her school's policies and practices. These values, beliefs, policies, and practices aim to achieve equitable outcomes for all students (Terrell & Lindsey, 2009). Culturally proficient leaders ask the important *why* questions and, as Fullan warned, they *do not get lost in the how to questions*

(2003, p. 61). Culturally proficient leaders pose questions that might explore curiosity and disturb the organization, such as:

- Why do students from this demographic/cultural group lag in achievement and have been doing so for years?
- Why are students from this demographic/cultural group over-represented in special education?
- Why are students from this demographic/cultural group under-represented in honours and International Baccalaureate courses?
- Why are students from this demographic/cultural group suspended and expelled at rates that far exceed their proportion of the school population?

Culturally proficient leaders pose such questions in ways that open themselves and their colleagues to being curious about school-based factors that either facilitate or hinder student access and achievement. Cross, Bazron, Dennis, & Isaacs (1989) in their seminal work on cultural competence and cultural proficiency identified this sense of openness to curiosity as an *inside-out process* of reflection and dialogue that leads to personal and organizational change. These leaders are not naïve; they fully recognize the external realities of community socio-economics, local and national political climates, and the assessment trends that continuously buffet schools. These leaders neither pretend to have all the answers nor shirk their responsibility for keeping focused on what is best for students. Culturally proficient school leaders are guided by a belief that their students deserve high quality education and that they and their colleagues have the capacity to learn how to provide it.

Culturally proficient school leaders know how to work with formal and non-formal leaders in schools across school districts. At the formal level, district- and site-level administrators embrace their primary function of exerting moral leadership at the district and school level. Non-formal leaders are valued and supported at the school and classroom levels. The journey to establishing a culturally proficient school begins with those in formal leadership positions looking closely at internal polices practices, and procedures to ensure that they are aligned to afford all students and community members with equitable access to all areas of the curriculum.

Systemic Leadership and Tools of Cultural Proficiency

Culturally proficient leaders build a systemic culture that takes into account all aspects of the school's educational processes. The leader's continuing focus is on the demographic composition of the students, staff, and community to ensure that diverse voices are represented throughout the formal and informal decision-making processes of the school. The curriculum is designed to provide relevance and rigor for all student populations. Long-range assessment processes are monitored to ensure that all student outcome measures are used in ways that focus on narrowing and closing access and achievement gaps. Similarly, policies and practices are monitored and analyzed to ensure that disproportional representation by race, ethnicity, gender, or social class are mitigated and eliminated over time.

The "Tools of Cultural Proficiency" enable educational leaders to respond effectively in cross-cultural environments by using a powerful set of interrelated tools to guide personal and organizational change (Lindsey, Nuri Robins, & Terrell, 2009). The tools for culturally proficient practices allow school leaders to focus on assets to overcome barriers to student success.

As indicated at the opening of the chapter, Fullan (2003) emphasized the importance of the *why* question. Sinek (2009) describes the relationship among three key leadership questions: *what, how,* and *why.* We view posing these questions as fundamental for developing culturally proficient leadership. Each question has specific importance to reflective and dialogic processes:

- *What?* — identifies the result to be accomplished.
- *How?* — yields the process to attain the desired result.
- *Why?* — reveals your purpose, the cause for which you are working.

When we align Sinek's "golden circle model" with the "tools of cultural proficiency," three phases emerge:

1. **Intention Cycle**: Consideration of Sinek's *why* question fosters deep reflection and dialogue that guides awareness of **barriers** that obstruct access to educational opportunities. Recognition and acknowledgment of barriers provides opportunities to embrace inclusive core values derived from **guiding principles of cultural proficiency.** These guiding principles are grounded in deeply held assumptions and values for diverse cultures. A leader must be intentional in asking *why* questions and choosing to counter the barriers with the core values of cultural proficiency. The work of equity and inclusion requires intention and focus on closing the education gaps for students who have not been served well or need to be served differently.

2. **Assessment Cycle**: The **continuum** provides perspective gained from reflection and dialogue in phase I and provides context for addressing Sinek's *what* question. A range of responses and actions provides language to describe awareness derived from phase I reflection and dialogue. The continuum demonstrates the educator's paradigmatic shift from negative and destructive values, behaviours, and school policies and practices to their positive and constructive values, behaviours, and school policies and practices.

3. **Action Cycle**: The **essential elements of cultural competence** respond to Sinek's *how* question and serve as standards to educators for developing inclusive values and behaviours and for guiding school policies and practices. The new behaviours are based on new beliefs grounded in assumptions derived from accurate and informed meaningful data about cultural groups served by the school.

Figure 1 presents the three cycles representing the interrelatedness of the tools of culturally proficient leadership. The **barriers** inform a **continuum** of destructive behaviour and policies (e.g., cultural destructiveness, incapacity, and blindness), whereas the **guiding principles** as core values inform a **continuum** of constructive behaviour and policies (e.g., cultural pre-competence, competence, and proficiency) and give rise to the **essential elements** that serve as standards for assessing and planning behaviours, strategies, policies and practices.

Figure 1: Cycles of Interrelatedness: Culturally Proficient Leadership

It is important to note that the three cycles are not intended to imply that a person or school must begin at the first cycle and proceed in linear fashion through the other two cycles. Though that may be a logical sequence, many educators have begun their learning at each of the cycles. Educators who are successful and fully embrace cultural proficiency have committed to deep understanding of the three cycles and their interrelationship. Culturally proficient leaders use the tools of cultural proficiency mindfully.

The barriers describe for school leaders individual, institutional, and systemic limitations and roadblocks to change. At this point, leaders consider the various -isms and how they are present in their own values and behaviours, as well as in their school's policies and practices. This self-assessment is often a difficult process for some leaders, as they might feel blamed for systemic -isms. However, once they understand they, like the students and their parents, did not create the conditions that foster inequity, they can see more clearly that they have responsibility to recognize students' capacity to learn and educators' capacity to learn how to educate the students. At that point, leaders must consider how more inclusive core values can be developed. The guiding principles of cultural proficiency provide a template for devising these core values and overcoming the barriers.

The guiding principles are set forth as reflective questions for school leaders' consideration, the responses to which guide their development of core values expressly embracing access and equity for all students. School leaders can also use these questions to guide dialogue in their schools, the responses to which can foster inclusive core values that inform vision and mission statements to guide policy formulation and inclusive practices throughout the school.

- To what extent do you honour culture as a natural and normal part of the community you serve?
- To what extent do you recognize and understand the differential and historical treatment accorded to those least well served in your schools/communities?
- When working with a person whose culture is different from yours, to want extent do you see the person both as an individual and as a member of a group?
- To what extent do you recognize and value the differences within the cultural communities you serve?
- To what extent do you know and respect the unique needs of cultural groups in the communities you serve?
- To what extent do you know how cultural groups in your community define family and the manner in which family serves as the primary system of support for the students (youth) of the community?
- To what extent do you recognize your role in acknowledging, adjusting to, and accepting cross-cultural interactions a necessary social and communications dynamics?
- To what extent do you recognize and understand the bi-cultural reality for cultural groups historically not well served in our schools and societies?
- To what extent do you incorporate cultural knowledge into the policies, practices, and procedures of your organization?

The continuum provides the school leader with language for identifying and overcoming the barriers of non-productive policies, practices, and individual behaviours and replacing them with core values that expressly commit to socially just core values. Culturally proficient school leaders develop skills in directing conversation in ways that empower themselves and their colleagues to focus on their responsibilities and opportunities as educators.

The essential elements provide school leaders with five behavioural standards for measuring, and planning for, growth toward cultural proficiency — assessing cultural knowledge, valuing diversity, managing the dynamics of difference, adapting to diversity, and institutionalizing cultural knowledge.

In Closing

Culturally proficient leadership is essential in today's context of schooling. Culturally proficient school leaders achieve excellence with and for children at risk of school failure by intentionally, emphatically, systematically, vigorously, and effectively ensuring that students can and will develop to their full potential. Leaders must understand and recognize the importance of addressing diversity in all its cultural, linguistic, and human forms as assets for the school community rather than as deficits and problems to be solved.

As a school leader, you can only care for the child when you understand what it is like to be part of that child's culture, what it is like to be unable to speak the language of the classroom, or what it is like to go home to a shelter every night. Culturally proficient school leaders connect with children and youth to get to know and better understand the learner's interests: what they care about, what gives them joy, and what they might wish for if they dared. We invite you to join in the journey toward culturally proficient leadership practices.

References

Cross, T.L., Bazron, B.J., Dennis, K.W., & Isaacs, M.R. (1989). *Toward a culturally competent system of care.* Washington, DC: Georgetown University Child Development Program, Child and Adolescent Service System Program.

Fullan, M. (2003). *The moral imperative of school leadership.* Thousand Oaks, CA: Corwin Press.

Lindsey, R.B., Nuri Robins, K., & Terrell, R.D. (2009). *Cultural proficiency: A manual for school leaders,* 3rd ed. Thousand Oaks, CA: Corwin.

Terrell, R.D., & Lindsey, R.B. (2009). *Culturally proficient leadership: The personal journey begins within.* Thousand Oaks, CA: Corwin Press.

Sinek, S. (2009). *Start with why.* New York: The Penguin Group.

Chapter 19

What Is Social Justice Leadership?

Ira Bogotch

I am very comfortable approaching the topic of social justice as a school leadership question — not as a definitive answer to intractable problems such as discrimination and poverty. I think we can get to those answers, but we have to make some changes in how we see our roles as school leaders.

My studies of social justice within schools and school districts in the US began in 1999. The most obvious conclusion from these works is that the term *social justice* itself is not part of the everyday vocabulary of either teachers as leaders or of school administrators — whether in the US or around the world. School leaders have other, more acceptable terms in place of social justice in everyday practice. Words like "diversity" and "fairness" and phrases like "all children can learn" — a particularly common phrase following the passage in 2001 of the *No Child Left Behind Act* in the US — are widely spoken. But like the phrase "social justice," "diversity" and "fairness" have many different meanings, usually context specific.

The second conclusion can be summed up as follows: school leaders are committed to doing a good job and making a difference, but they tend to define their responsibilities as stopping at the schoolyard gates. That is, governing policies and within-school practices that promote fairness for children, such as free/subsidized lunches, school uniforms to mitigate family disparities in wealth, and subsidizing student fees for school trips are typically considered socially just. As well, pedagogical practices, such as disaggregating data, developing programs for inclusive education, and minimizing both racial and gender discrimination in everything from teaching mathematics to viewing school suspension records would also be included. These efforts speak to the necessity of social justice. But like most school improvement efforts and programs, they do not sufficiently reach the children's home lives or communities in any material way. In other words, these socially just school improvement programs do not extend into the lives of students disadvantaged by schooling (and society) with respect to addressing urgent and intractable conditions of poverty, discrimination, and the lack of opportunities.

Another social justice researcher described the phenomenon of "yes, but," as in "yes, I know what I should do" (with respect to social justice), but "no, I don't always act on these thoughts and beliefs" (Marshall & Ward, 2004). In other words, many of us have the right "socially just" dispositions, but if we can't translate these attitudes and values into socially just programs that make a difference in people's lives, then really, we just have a lot of nice talk, with or without the phrase social justice — and that's not enough to improve schools and communities.

Considering all the good work educators do, my point of view may be considered beyond the scope of a school leader's (or teachers') responsibilities; but for me, this is where the social justice conversation for today needs to begin. The question is how?

My objective is to provoke thoughts and hopefully concrete actions. In so doing, I will try to connect common teaching and learning terms and everyday actions to social justice so that my ideas will not be dismissed out of hand by experienced or aspiring administrators or teacher leaders. To begin, education has five essential elements: processes, ideas, human experiences, shared meanings, and purpose, which can be illustrated like this:

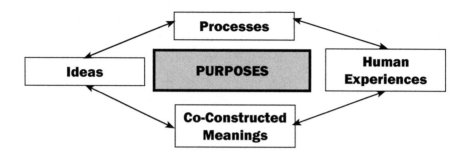

My objective with this figure is to ground the meanings of social justice in education and not write about this topic as if it were some abstract, idealistic concept unrelated to practice. Social justice is doable or it is nothing. It is also necessary. Therefore, putting the figure into simple shapes and words begins with commonly known definitions. For example, at the top of the figure are processes ranging from the straightforward transmission of ideas to the many skillful ways in which teachers and administrators communicate with others: students, colleagues, parents, and community leaders. In classroom lessons, processes invariably have initiating or structuring moves, that is, how curricular topics are introduced, what motivating activities follow, and how to provide ample time for manipulation and practice, whether in-class or as homework. The second essential term, ideas, can be anything from a simple fact — this is an apple — to those that generate thinking about other ideas. The closer the teacher/administrator is able to connect ideas to students' prior knowledge and experiences (scaffolding), the easier it will be for the idea to be learned and subsequently used. A good teacher can break down any complex idea into its constituent parts and begin the lesson with that part most likely associated with students' knowledge and interests.

Human experiences, even when mediated by virtual communications, will always be an essential element in education. We are social beings who relate to others emotionally and cognitively. That is why the old stimulus-response behavioural models were limited in their application at higher levels of learning. Anyone can type in a happy face or LOL, but without the demonstrated care and concern shown by another person, whether standing in front of the room or from afar, the ideas being presented are not as likely to be incorporated into another's thinking and acting. We go through life learning (or not) from experiences; the more human those experiences are, the more we are open to keep on learning.

Consequently, whatever meanings we make of experiences and ideas, the meanings themselves are constructed socially through analyses, syntheses, aesthetic appreciations, and judgments. All of this requires deep discussions about new and old ideas with others. As educators, we know how to take advantage of teachable moments or stimulate the proverbial "aha." Learning may also take place over an extended timeframe, requiring re-teaching using different processes (and mediums) and other ideas as building blocks. Unless meaning is made, lesson or ideas will soon be forgotten once the test is over. We know all this, right?

The above elements are all well-grounded in the literatures on teaching and learning, but what is often omitted or given lip service (rhetorical support) are the purposes of education. Here is where meanings are shaped into a person's core values, not just for the day's lesson, but rather for life. Sadly, schools, particularly US public schools, have lost their meaningful and significant purpose in the eyes of students and the public. The phrase "student achievement" (defined by test scores) has replaced the idea of community working democratically and fairly to promote social justice, making a material difference in people's lives in and out of school. That may not be the sole purpose or even the agreed upon purpose given the diversity of opinion in the US, but it represents a move in the direction of social justice locally and in the world.

What is next? It seems to me that public educators face two challenges today. The first is to insert leadership into educational institutions/practices. The second is to insert education into the minds and hearts of citizens controlled — that is not too strong a word, is it? — socially and ideologically by dominant discourses, such as policies, legal precedents, scientific teachings, technology, religion, and business practices. Where is leadership in terms of vision, questions, and promoting humanity? There is a definite lack of, misuse of, or even the co-optation of leadership in schools and society. There must be a level of calculated risk involved that separates those who strive for social justice from those who play it safe, manage schools, and follow the letter and spirit of their job descriptions and employment contracts. In saying this, I know that I am not being fair to the hardworking and committed teachers and administrators throughout the world doing all they can on behalf of their students. But the truth, for me, is that being a good teacher and even a moral leader is not good enough when it comes to leadership for social justice. We as educators have let the dominant discourses and their specialized expert knowledge drown out our educator voices from social, political, and economic debates. Unfortunately, local and global ideologies deliberately promote anti-educational and anti-humanistic values in order to grab and maintain control/power over students, teachers, parents, and societies. We need educators, educational leaders, willing to take calculated risks and possessing sufficient knowledge of world events happening beyond schools and classrooms. We need educators who are comfortable — through advanced study, beyond what schools call professional development — to articulate what is right for children and their families. In turn, we need an educational system that will protect the rights of those who speak out and, more importantly, build programs and take actions on behalf of others lacking freedom, opportunities, and justice.

The pragmatic question attached to any idea or action including social justice, especially in the US, is whether it makes a material difference. If so, it signifies the truth of such ideas and actions and, therefore, in William James' terms, has a *cash value*. The worth or cash-value of any concept, as James often repeated, was in how the concept helped the individual to cope, how it aided the individual in his or her actual, practical, and concrete experiences (Cotkin, 1985). As such, social justice, like truth, is a bottom-line idea that has social, not just individual, significance in the practical world.

References

Cotkin, G. (Spring 1985). William James and the cash-value metaphor. *Et cetera.http://digitalcommons.calpoly.edu/cgi/viewcontent.cgi?article=1037&context=hist_fac* (retrieved 6 June 2014).

Marshall, C., & Ward, M. (September 2004). "Yes, but...": Education leaders discuss social justice. *Journal of School Leadership, 14*, 531–563.

Chapter 20

What Is Spiritual Leadership?

Njoki Wane

This chapter wrestles with the following questions: what is the role of spirituality in leadership? How do we ensure that spiritual practices are inclusive and not alienating? Is it possible to share a spirituality that does not contravene the faith beliefs of staff and students? Are there any drawbacks to spiritual leadership? How may those in school leadership evoke their spirituality, if at all, in everyday practice for transformative purposes? This chapter aims to make sense of the impact of spirituality in leadership, provide a working definition, call attention to the influence of spirituality on leadership practices, and create greater understanding of the complex nature of spiritual leadership (Houston, Blankenstein, & Cole, 2007; Sergiovanni, 1992; Vaill, 1998; Dantley, 2005).

What Is Spirituality?

There is no universal definition for spirituality since it implies a relationship with what people variously refer to as the life force, god, creator, the higher self or purpose, or the great mystery. What is essential, however, is how you define your own spirituality and spiritual practices. As Director of the Centre of Anti-Racist Studies and of the office of teaching support at the university level, I constantly evoked my spiritual self, contemplating each decision I had to make and its impact on those affected. I also tried to connect with each individual in the office. It was important to "see them" because when I did that, I could gauge their level of inner peace. If it was low, I knew that their productivity would be low; if it was high, then their output for the day would be at its maximum. At the end of each day, I reflected on each action as well as on the wellbeing of each member of staff. After several years of pondering, I came to the heartfelt realization that spirituality is simply that part of me that longs for fulfillment.

The context of spirituality differs from individual to individual and from group to group. For many people, it encompasses a sense of wholeness, healing, and the interconnectedness of all things. For instance, Michael Dantley (2005) argues that spirituality, with components of critical reflection, has been one of the main pillars of the african american experience. "Our spirit," he writes, "enables us to connect with other human beings" (p. 654). Spirituality, therefore, is about meaning making — it is about how people construct knowledge through largely unconscious and symbolic processes manifested through image, symbol, ritual, and music. Spirituality is about the ongoing development of identity or moving towards what many refer to as their greater authentic self. It is simultaneously collective and personal (Wane, 2007, 2011). Derezotes defines spirituality as "a complex, intrapsychic dimension of human development" (1995, p. 1), while Bullis argues that spirituality is "the relationship of the human person to something or someone who transcends themselves" (1996, p. 2). Mazama, writing from an afrocentric perspective, states that spirituality is "cosmic energy that permeates and lives within all that is," which "confers a common sense to everything in the world, and thus ensures the fundamental unity of all that exists (2002, pp. 219–221). In short, spirituality has been defined as "a complex, intrapsychic dimension of human development" (Derezotes, 1995, p. 1), or "the relationship of the human person to something or someone who transcends themselves" (Bullis, 1996, p. 2). Many people include spirituality in a search for meaning that shapes their identities, which enables them to cope with everyday challenges (Watt, 2003). I would say that spirituality is about inner strength, faith, and grounded-ness; it facilitates networking, survival, and collectivity; it connects the personal to larger social systems and meaning-making (Wane, 2007). Moreover, spiritual leaders need to harness these qualities to create a spiritual experience in their schools.

What Is Spiritual Leadership?

In recent years, academics have paid attention to spiritual leadership in education (e.g., Houston, Blankenstein, & Cole, 2008). According to Malone and Fry,

> Spiritual leadership is a causal leadership model for organizational transformation designed to create an intrinsically motivated, learning organization. [It] incorporates vision, hope/faith, and altruistic love, theories of workplace spirituality, and spiritual survival through calling and membership. The purpose of spiritual leadership is to create vision and value congruence across the strategic, empowered team and individual levels and, ultimately, to foster higher levels of organizational commitment and productivity (2003, P. 1).

Vaill (1998) articulates spiritual leadership as leaders reflecting deeply on their experiences and examining the consequences of their decision-making practices; it involves constant dialogue with stakeholders and pays attention to their values and those of their community. According to Bezy (2011), spiritual leaders discipline themselves to get in touch with their inner selves and rid themselves of any distractions and desires that might keep them from achieving their leadership goals. Bezy (2011) says that learning who they are, what motivates them, and what their strengths and weakness are helps leaders to improve their practices.

Houston and Sokolow (2006) advocate the following eight principles of spiritual leadership, arguing that the leaders who employ them are in touch with their spiritual selves and reflect this in their leadership style:

1. Intention
2. Attention
3. Gifts and talents

4. Gratitude
5. Uniqueness of life lessons
6. Connectedness
7. Openness
8. Trust

The principle of *intention* draws people to their leader, while *attention* gathers energy as a leader pays attention to their thoughts, their surroundings, and the issues at hand. This particular principle reduces distraction. Leaders who acknowledge their *gifts and talents* and those of others celebrate the uniqueness of individuals because they "see them" (Degruy, 2005) and are referred to as spiritual leaders. *Gratitude* reminds leaders of their blessings in life, fostering goodness in adversity. Leaders who employ this principle are grateful to be able to help others. In terms of *unique life lessons,* spiritual leaders see their experiences and challenges as part their growth, which can provide a platform for staff growth as well. Leaders who see their schools as having different segments — students, parents, staff, teachers, and community — that contribute to the whole pay attention to the principle of *connectedness.* They see one person's achievement as being integral to overall school goals. *Openness* leads to growth in self and others while *trust* allows spiritual leaders to grow by trusting herself/himself as well as others.

Is there a way of cultivating these eight principles? How can leaders who want to employ spiritual practices make them part of their leadership practice? How do they ensure that spiritual growth is deep-rooted and not superficial? How can they ensure that spirituality is rooted in their thinking, talking, and actions? Such questions allow readers to pause and reflect on their own spiritual leadership practices. There are also some practical ways to cultivate spiritual leadership in a school.

Contemplative knowing is fundamental to the quest for knowledge and wisdom and complements our analytical process. In a school situation, simply acknowledging and appreciating the work of a teacher or rewarding student success will intensify their eagerness to pursue genuine and meaningful inquiry. The leader here would be paying attention to the principles of *attention and intention.* Encouraging teachers to reflect at the beginning or end of the school day to express *gratitude* by reading a short passage from an inspirational book or giving thanks for the many blessings in life can help keep priorities straight. Starting with a motivational quote and asking teachers to reflect on it and share their views can help focus meetings. Different individuals will respond to different modes of the contemplative approach. Contemplative practices in the school encourage the natural human capacity for knowing through silence, sharing, looking inward, pondering deeply, beholding, and observing consciousness (Wane, 2011). These approaches cultivate an inner technology of knowing and learning without the imposition of any religious doctrine. They encourage *openness* and create a community of contemplative and reflective practitioners (teachers) who will begin to see each other in light of the common vision and mission of their school. In the process, the notion of *trust* is cultivated, the contemplative mind is opened through deep thinking and quiet listening to oneself, and meditation creates heightened awareness and concentration. These practices have existed for thousands of years in Buddhism, Hinduism, yoga, Indigenous spiritual practices, and other contemplative religious practices. So why have we ignored them in our roles as educational leaders? When I ran my own community college, I was able to create a oneness of purpose because I encouraged these practices. The teachers began to see themselves as having collective goals as well as individual ones. At the initial stages, these practices made some teachers uneasy, as they were not sure of their source. With time, they became comfortable and joined in. The important thing was to emphasize the notion of spirituality, which can be rooted in a person's culture, religion, or even a favourite hobby. A school led by a spiritual leader will have low rate of teacher turnover, high morale, high student achievement, and few disciplinary issues.

If they originate from an undefinable ritualistic cult, spiritual practices can create alienation. How, then, do we draw the line? How do we create collegiality among the people we supervise while maintaining authority? As spiritual beings created in the image of our creator (who has been given different names), it does not matter whether we are the leader or the worker. The leader, however, is the facilitator of the common vision for the organization. Making spiritual practices part of the everyday routine brings cohesion and focus to important issues.

Contemplation and meditation — taking a few moments to breathe deeply and think of nothing — and ritualizing our lives are the basis of spiritual practices.

Ritualizing our lives means setting aside time for prayer or meditation, meals, reading, exercising, or just sitting quietly doing nothing. In these moments of quietness, we can focus on our breathing. If you have a busy day and no time for a quiet moment, just take a deep breath before conducting a meeting or addressing a gathering. Take a few breaths, close your eyes, and tune in to where you are right in this moment. What are you thinking about? The day ahead? The next meeting? A decision regarding a teacher or student? A decision you have to make in a couple of minutes, weeks, or months? A lesson or emotional hangover from your past? How much are you in your body? How much are you in your head? As you go through these questions, inhale deeply, relax your muscles, make yourself comfortable, and listen to your breathing. As you inhale and exhale, imagine yourself walking through a beautiful, wooded valley towards the sunrise. How do you feel? What thoughts go through your mind? As you breathe deeply, concentrate on the various centres of energy in your body. You will be surprised by how much more you can accomplish after just a few minutes of this simple exercise.

These practices will contribute towards understanding what matters in positions of educational leadership. Your leadership approach will stand out as those working with you realize the influence of spiritual practices. Understanding the complex nature of spirituality requires patience, commitment, and determination. You cannot just pick it from a shelf and return it each day. It must be ritualized to be meaningful and to make an impact on the lives of the people under your leadership.

References

Bullis, R. K. (1996). *Spirituality In Social Work Practice.* Washington, DC: Taylor & Francis.

Bezy, Kevin G. (2011). *An Operational Definition Of Spiritual Leadership.* (Unpublished Doctoral Dissertation). Educational Leadership And Policy Studies, Virginia Polytechnic Institute And State University, Blacksburg, VA.

Dantley, M. (2005). African American Spirituality And Cornel West's Notion Of Prophetic Pragmatism: Restructuring Educational Leadership In American Urban Schools. *Educational Administrative Quarterly, 41*(4), 651–674.

Degruy, J. (2005). *Post Traumatic Slave Syndrome: America's Legacy Of Enduring Injury And Healing.* Portland, OR: Uptone Press.

Derezotes, D. S. (1995). Spirituality And Religiosity: Neglected Factors In Social Work Practice. *Arete, 20*(1), 1–15.

Houston, P. D., Blankenstein, A. B., & Cole, R. W. (Eds.). (2007). *Out-Of-The-Box Leadership* (Vol. 2). Thousand Oaks, CA: Corwin Press.

Houston, P. D., Blankenstein, A. B., & Cole, R. W. (Eds.). (2008). *Spirituality In Educational Leadership* (Vol. 4). Thousand Oaks, CA: Corwin Press.

Houston, P. D., & Sokolow, S. L. (2006). *The Spiritual Dimension Of Leadership: 8 Key Principles To Leading More Effectively.* Thousand Oaks, CA: Corwin Press.

Malone, P. N., & Fry, L. W. (2003). Transforming Schools Through Spiritual Leadership: A Field Experiment. Paper Presented At The Academy Of Management, Seattle ,Washington.

Mazama, M. (2002). *The Afrocentric Paradigm.* Trenton, NJ: Africa World Press.

Sergiovanni, T. J. (1992). *Moral Leadership: Getting To The Heart Of School Improvement.* San Francisco: John Wiley & Sons.

Vaill, P. B. (1998). *Spirited Leading And Learning: Process Wisdom For A New Age.* San Francisco: Jossey-Bass.

Wane, N. N. (2007). Interview With Zulu: Practices Of African Women's Spirituality. In N. Massaquoi & N. Wane (Eds.), *Theorizing Empowerment: Black Canadian Feminist Thought* (Pp. 47–54). Toronto: Innana Publishers.

Wane, N. N. (2011). Spirituality: A Philosophy And A Research Tool. In *Spirituality, Education And Society: An Integrated Approach.* N. N. Wane, E. Manyimo, & E. Ritskes (Eds.). Rotterdam: Sense.

Watt, S. K. (2003). Come To The River: Using Spirituality To Cope, Resist, And Develop Identity. In M. F. Howard-Hamilton (Ed.), *Meeting The Needs Of African American Women: New Directions For Student Services* (Pp. 29–40). San Francisco: Jossey-Bass.

Chapter 21

What Is Rural School Leadership?

Jeanne L. Surface and Paul Theobald

I t may be the prevailing sentiment that kids are kids, schools are schools, and leadership is leadership regardless of where you find them, but there are distinct contextual features that divide schools in the United States according to residential pattern, namely: rural, urban, and suburban. Granted, there are many differences between schools within these large groupings but, overall, they tend to possess more similarities than differences. And to complicate matters, there are sometimes similarities between groups. For example, it is most typical to have schools that struggle with infrastructure issues in rural and urban locales. In fact, those school issues most sensitive to poverty, like attracting and retaining qualified teachers, are likely to be most prevalent in urban and rural America. But in the realm of school leadership, the boundaries of these large school groupings become most pronounced. Leading a rural school is not quite like leading an urban school, which is not at all like leading a suburban school.

In fact, leadership in a rural school is far more than just leading a school. There are never-delineated, but always-understood job duties that go with the rural principalship and superintendancy and they centre on the life of the school's community. Rural school leaders are sought after to assist in creating and maintaining the health of the community at the same time as they are leading the school. There is an expectation of making the school an open environment and sharing space with the elderly, with alumni living close to home, and certainly with families. Participation in school events is a source of common focus. The event might be a football game or helping to clean up the school grounds or paint classrooms. The boundary between a rural community and its school is blurry, at best.

We do not mean to suggest that urban or suburban school leaders are never called upon to assist the communities or neighbourhoods in which they are situated. It is more a matter of degree and, ultimately, influence. Community concerns are a constant in the life of rural school leaders, and their voices wield authority in rural communities in a manner not typically matched in urban or suburban places.

One additional dimension in many ways defines rural school leadership: the extent to which the enterprise is about dealing with decline. Although there are exceptions, leadership in urban and suburban places is much more often about dealing with growth: growth in the number of students, teachers, and buildings; growth in the number of ESL students; growth in the ranks of special education, etc. The typical rural experience is just the opposite.

This means that rural school leaders are intimately familiar with the concept of school consolidation. For more than a century, rural school consolidation was touted as a foolproof path to school improvement (Cubberley, 1914). As if that were not enough, it was also viewed as a way to save tax dollars, making it one of those rare policy initiatives that ostensibly cuts costs and improves the product. While recent research soundly refutes these claims (Berry & West, 2010; Dokoupil, 2010; Duncombe & Yinger, 2005; Howley, Johnson, & Petrie, 2011), such evidence is hardly enough to stop a policy with so much cultural appeal among urban and suburban residents.

This creates a dynamic that often pits rural school leaders against a state legislature dominated by urban and suburban representatives. From a historical perspective, it is not difficult to tell who wins most often. When rural schools close, a "hollowing out" and eventual loss of the community is often the result (Carr & Kefalas, 2009). This is a particularly bitter pill for rural school leaders, as they are well aware that many of the urban and suburban schools applauded for making an impact on the achievement of children living in poverty are those that are purposefully small. We know that small schools have a significant impact on student achievement, especially those living in poverty, which is an overwhelming part of rural demographics (Bickel & Howley, 2000).

More than his or her urban and suburban counterparts, a rural school leader is a "generalist" and must possess talent in multiple areas in order to be successful. School size and barely adequate finances means that rural school leaders are responsible for everything from state and national assessment data, school accreditation, budget, and human resources to athletics, bus routes, and building maintenance. No single leader would ever handle these vast responsibilities in a metropolitan district. Moreover, other than the large numbers involved, school accreditation and state and national assessments entail the same work for leaders and have the same requirements as large districts with personnel specifically hired to do the work.

The tight school-community nexus in rural locales can add positively or negatively to the work-lives of rural school leaders. For example, if (for educational reasons) a teacher who grew up in the community is fired from his position because of poor teaching, the community often becomes involved. If a hometown teacher becomes a verbally abusive coach and must be replaced, she will likely have her followers come to her aid with an attack on school leaders. There is no bureaucracy in place to shield rural school leaders. Further, leadership decisions are often misunderstood by parents and community members and confidentiality concerns sometimes prohibit clear and timely explanations. It is not unusual that such a circumstance can lead to a school board meeting filled with parents and community members angry with the leadership of the school. Because rural school leaders are intimately enmeshed in the community, the job can become very difficult and oftentimes painful and lonely.

On the other hand, rural school leaders have the freedom to carve out curricular and instructional opportunities that most urban and suburban school leaders do not possess. Imagine what it would be like to be in a school of 110 students, K–12, with the freedom to orchestrate a day outdoors working with the Fish and Wildlife Service on a river outside of

Yellowstone National Park. In this real-life example, students examined the rare cutthroat trout native to the region, which have lost about 90 percent of their historical range. The river that the students studied is one of the only pristine places where the species is healthy and genetically pure. The students conducted several studies to determine how they might help the trout expand their range. Through writing and examining policy related to the trout, the students also learned across multiple school subjects, not just science. Obviously, life-changing interdisciplinary lessons like this are beyond the reach of urban and suburban schools. We do not mean to suggest that rural schools are the only type where school leaders can promote the use of place-based curriculum and instruction, but certainly it is far easier, and far more common, in rural schools (Theobald, 1997).

In sum, rural school leadership is often different from that in metropolitan areas and most of that difference stems from the school's tight connection to the community that surrounds it. While this connection can create positive dynamics, while it can add positively to a sense of fulfillment from one's work, it can also go in the opposite direction since there is no buffer between the community and the school administration. No appointment is required by the disgruntled parent for complaints taken up on the street corner, at the post office, or in the local café. Despite this, rural school leaders must often defend the very community that adds so much stress to their work lives, as states continue to promote rural school consolidation whenever their budgets are squeezed. Generalists by necessity, rural school leaders face a large array of issues and work demands and, as a result, must constantly juggle the many issues and items they might work on when they arrive each morning.

References

Bickel, R., & Howley, C. (2000). The influence of scale on school performance. *Education Policy Analysis Archives, 8*(22) p.23.

Berry, C.R., & West, M.R. (2010). Growing pains: The consolidation movement and student outcomes. *The Journal of Law, Economics, and Organization, 26*(1) p.15.

Carr, P.J., & Kefalas, M.J. (2009). *Hollowing out the middle: The rural brain drain and what it means for America*. Boston, MA: Beacon Press.

Cubberley, E.P. (1914). *Rural life and education: A study of the rural-school problem as a phase of the rural-life problem*. Boston, MA: Houghton Mifflin.

Dokoupil, T. (November 1, 2010). Consolidation's failing grade in Indiana. *Newsweek, 156*(18).

Duncombe, W., & Yinger, J. (2005). *Does school district consolidation cut costs?* Syracuse University Center for Policy Research. Syracuse, NY.

Howley, C., Johnson, J., & Petrie, J. (2011). Consolidation of schools and districts: What the research says and what it means. National Education Policy Center, University of Colorado, Boulder, CO.

Theobald, P. (1997). *Teaching the commons: Place, pride, and the renewal of community*. Boulder, CO: Westview.

Chapter 22

What Is Distributed Leadership?[7]

John B. Diamond

As with many concepts in education and the social sciences, the seemingly simple question — what is distributed leadership? — is not easy to answer. The number of answers that one could give continues to grow as multiple definitions have emerged across the worlds of educational research and practice. To date, several books, edited volumes, and journal special issues have been dedicated to distributed leadership and some schools and districts have based their reform efforts on distributed leadership.

In this chapter, I will discuss the distributed perspective as a conceptual framework based on work developed by James Spillane and his colleagues at Northwestern University beginning in the late 1990s. I will then briefly outline some of the numerous ways this construct has been defined and used by other scholars and practitioners.

Theoretical Foundations of Distributed Leadership

The diffusion of the distributed perspective on leadership is quite impressive given that the term only came into use in the last 15 years. While similar ideas may have been around much longer, the contemporary

---

7. This paper borrows concepts and some segments of text from Diamond (2013).

use of the term emerged from research conducted by James Spillane and colleagues (Spillane, Halverson, & Diamond 2001, 2004; Spillane, 2006; Spillane & Diamond, 2007) and Peter Gronn in Australia (Gronn, 2002). In discussing the origins of the concept, I will focus on Spillane and colleagues, whose research has powerfully influenced work on distributed leadership.[8]

The creation of the distributed perspective was an attempt to develop a *conceptual framework* that could be used by researchers to study leadership and by practitioners to reflect on and improve their practice. This perspective critiques, builds upon, and extends prior leadership research. At the risk of oversimplification, we might think of leadership studies as fitting into the following (partially chronological) categories.

1. Studies focused on leadership positions (e.g., principals or CEOs)
2. Studies focused on the people in leadership positions; their unique traits, qualities, characteristics, and behaviours (great man/woman theories of leadership)
3. Studies examining leadership among people not located at the top of the organizational hierarchy (e.g., teacher leader and coalitions of leaders)
4. Examinations of leadership in context (e.g., contingency theory; Fielder, 1973) and leadership as an organizational phenomenon
5. Cognitive perspectives on leadership that emphasized how people understood their roles and acted on those understandings, as well as studies of how leaders' thinking and practice was shaped by the characteristics of educational organizations (institutional theory; Meyer & Rowan, 1978).

This prior work considered multiple elements of leadership practice — the role of individuals, contexts, and cognition — but these core elements were not well integrated. In part to remedy this problem, Spillane and colleagues appropriated concepts from work on distributed cognition and activity theory to argue that leadership was a distributed phenomenon. Work in distributed cognition highlights how thinking and

---

8.   I also focus on this work because I played a role in developing the construct as a postdoctoral researcher and faculty member.

action emerge through social interaction among people in specific contexts using tools and resources that enable and/or constrain thinking and action. In discussing this idea, Spillane et al. (2001, p. 23) discuss work by Hutchins (1995) who "documents how the task of landing a plane can be best understood through investigating a unit of analysis that includes the pilot, the manufactured tools, and the social context." As Hutchins argues, "the successful completion of a flight is produced by a system of two or more pilots interacting with each other and with a suite of technological devices" (Hutchins, 1995, p. 265).

Extending this metaphor of distributed cognition to leadership activity allows us to account simultaneously for individual(s), context, and cognition in an integrated examination of leadership practice. This is a fundamental shift from previous perspectives because the unit of analysis is leadership activity itself — not the people who carry it out, the context in which it happens, or the thinking that goes into leading. Instead, focusing on leadership activity — "activities tied to the core work of the organization that are designed by organizational members to influence ... other organizational members" — allows us to see how each of these constituting elements of leadership activity contribute to its accomplishment (Spillane, 2006, pp. 11–12).

Research using the distributed perspective has focused on two related aspects — the leader-plus aspect and the practice aspect. The leader-plus aspect emphasizes that leadership involves multiple actors who participate in leadership practice. The practice aspect highlights that leadership occurs through "an interactive web of leaders, followers, and aspects of their situation including tools and organizational routines" (Diamond, 2013, p. 85). The leader plus aspect focuses on who leads and under what conditions. It has demonstrated how leadership is stretched across multiple people in organizations and how things like subject matter (mathematics vs. language arts), school size, school student composition, and other factors shape how it is distributed.

The practice aspect emphasizes how leaders work together — co-constructing leadership. For example, previous work has identified at least three ways that leadership is co-constructed:

collaborative distribution in which leaders work together to carry out a leadership routine in the same time and place, collective distribution in which leaders work inter-dependently but separately, and coordinated distribution in which leadership activities are performed in a particular sequence. (Diamond, 2013, p. 85)

While this work was originally developed as a conceptual tool to help researchers and practitioners understand leadership practice better, many uses of distributed leadership have emerged. I turn to some of these definitions below.

Multiple Definitions of Distributed Leadership

As the idea of distributed leadership has become widely used, multiple definitions of the concept have emerged. Table 1 list four such definitions.

Table 1: Four Broad Conceptions of Distributed Leadership

Distributed Leadership as a Conceptual Lens (discussed above)	Distributed leaderships is a conceptual lens that helps researchers and practitioners understand (and perhaps improve) leadership practice
Distributed Leadership as Shared Leadership	Distributed leadership is equivalent to shared or democratic leadership
Distributed Leadership as a Desirable Type of Leadership	Distributed leadership is a desired type of leadership that people engage in within a school or district
Distributed Leadership as Effective Leadership	Distributed leadership is an approach that can improve educational outcomes

Distributed Leadership as Shared Leadership

Some research treats distributed leadership as a form of shared or democratic leadership. This may be the most common way that the concept is used outside of the conceptual model. This is somewhat natural given that the idea of distribution suggests shared activity and the leader-plus aspect focuses on the role of multiple actors in leadership practice. This work has discussed how distributed (shared) leadership is developed, the different types of shared leadership, and the roles of various actors in "shared" leadership structures and practices. While this usage of the concept is common, it is clearly distinct from the conceptual framework developed above.

Distributed Leadership as a Desirable Type of Leadership

Other work, mostly drawing on the conception of distributed leadership as a democratic form, argues that distributed leadership is a desirable form of leadership. This normative conception encourages the adoption of distributed leadership in schools and organizations. From this perspective, school leaders *should* distribute leadership in particular ways. This approach has become popular in scholarly circles as well as in practice, with district leaders "adopting" distributed leadership approaches to organizational change and improvement.

Distributed Leadership as Effective Leadership

A final approach, which builds on the prior two models, attempts to measure the impact of distributed leadership practices on educational outcomes. Some of this work suggests that shared or democratic leadership can lead to positive educational outcomes. Other work acknowledges that the distributed perspective originated as a conceptual framework (not a type of leadership) but should nonetheless move toward examining outcomes. Efforts to measure the impact of what researchers call distributed or shared leadership have yielded very mixed results.

Conclusion

The distributed perspective was originally developed as a conceptual lens that researchers and practitioners could use to understanding leadership practice better. The originators of the construct believed that this perspective would be useful to both research and practitioners because it could frame examinations of leadership that attended to the complexity of practice and integrated the multiple, interactive elements of leadership activity. While uses of the concept have evolved over time, I have tried to highlight the original framing of the concept as a conceptual lens — a lens that has generated substantial new learning for researchers and practitioners.

References

Diamond, J. B. (2013). Distributed leadership: Examining issues of race, power, and inequality. In L. C. Tillman & J. J. Scheurich (Eds.) *Handbook of research on educational leadership for equity and diversity* (pp. 83–104). New York: Routledge.

Fielder, F. E. (1973). The contingency model: A reply to Ashour. *Organizational Behavior and Human Decision Processes, 9*(3), 356–368.

Gronn, P. (2002). Distributed leadership as a unit of analysis. *Leadership Quarterly, 13*(4), 423–451.

Hutchins, E. (1995). How a cockpit remembers its speeds. *Cognitive Science, 19*, 265–288.

Meyer, J. W., & Rowan, B. C. (1978). The structure of educational organizations. In M. Meyer et al. (Eds.), *Environments and organizations: Theoretical and empirical perspectives* (pp. 78–109). San Francisco: Jossey-Bass.

Spillane, J. P. (2006). *Distributed Leadership*. San Francisco: Jossey-Bass.

Spillane, J. P., & Diamond, J. B. (Eds.) (2007). *Distributed leadership in practice*. New York: Teachers College Press.

Spillane, J. P., Halverson, R., & Diamond, J. B. (2001). Investigating school leadership practice: A distributed perspective. *Educational Researcher, 30*(3), 23–28.

Spillane, J. P., Halverson, R., & Diamond, J. B. (2004). Towards a theory of leadership practice: A distributed perspective. *Journal of Curriculum Studies, 36*(1), 3–34.

What Is Urban School Leadership?

Coleen M. Scully-Stewart

U rban school leadership is a term that I have been quite deliberate in avoiding. Although I value and embrace the aims of inclusion, anti-oppression, and substantive parent–community engagement that "urban school leadership" engenders, and I honour much of the work done in teacher training and leadership development under this umbrella, I have reasons for squirming when the term is used. A focus on urban school leadership can create the dangerous notion that leaders in non-urban settings are "off the hook" in thinking deeply about issues of diversity, inclusion, and anti-oppression.

A number of years ago, I set up a conference for intermediate students in a predominantly rural school district to explore the many permutations of communication. To launch the event, I arranged for students to attend a production of Dennis Foon's award-winning play, *Skin*, which focuses on racism "in all its insidious forms," and the effects that it has on the identity formation of several teenagers. I met with opposition on several fronts; one principal in particular strongly opposed plans for the event, arguing that, "Racism is an urban issue. Everyone gets along in this community. Why stir the pot?"

Throughout my career, the phrase "That's an urban issue" has come from principals, teachers, and parents as an argument for avoiding discussion and programming about issues of race, ethnicity, and heteronormativity. Sometimes, as I conducted workshops on equity across the province, this response was overt; at other times, it was the body language and the reticence to engage that sent the same message. The fact is, non-urban settings that appear culturally and racially "homogeneous" are actually laden with issues of race and racism anchored in deep historical roots. For example, there are reasons why First Nations families don't share backyard fences with white neighbours, why the vast acres of farmland that stretch across this continent are not owned by a long lineage of Black or Chinese families, why LGBTQ youth do not openly express their identities in many of the cafes of rural villages and towns, and why same-sex parents avoid parent–teacher interviews about their children's progress. And there are reasons why these topics do not come up in public discourse. They remain hidden — squelched actually — below the veneer of a "harmonious" white heterosexual, non-urban dominant culture. Underlying these normalized practices lie deeply rooted issues of historical and institutional oppression. Focusing our attentions, therefore, on the celebrations, challenges, victories, and tribulations of the diverse "urban" context is essential not only for the betterment of urban communities, but also for the opportunity to create models, raise questions, and keep in the public eye the importance of doing the same in contexts where the need is not always as overtly apparent.

What is it, then, that makes leadership in urban areas both a privilege and a challenge to those focused on making the world a better place? Much depends upon what we mean and whom we refer to when we use the term "urban leadership." In common parlance, the term urban school leaders has come to refer to those faced with the "problems" of "high population density and diversity (racial, ethnic, cultural, and linguistic), poverty, institutional racism, social segmentation and socioeconomic inequalities, unequal distribution of qualified teachers, and problematic funding levels." (Gallager, Goodyear, Brewer, & Rueda, 2012, p. 4). Seldom are they framed as those who can benefit from the advantages of multiple perspectives and the availability of rich cultural resources. In addition, leaders in wealthy urban enclaves, private schools, and seemingly "homogeneous" neighbourhoods are seldom associated with these "urban education" issues, when in fact they need to focus as much on unmasking issues of power and privilege and modelling the importance of activism as do those in schools characterized by diversity and/or poverty. Urban leadership, then, is inclusive, social justice, anti-oppressive leadership that happens to take place in urban settings. It needs to be as visible in enclaves of wealth and privilege and superficially apparent "homogeneity" as it is in pockets of poor and marginalized neighbourhoods. It needs to bleed into contexts that disassociate themselves from the "urban."

Rather than using the term urban leadership as a way to dichotomize the notions of urban and rural, it is more beneficial to consider the inclusive, antiracist, antipoverty, anti-heterosexist emphasis of the former as addressing issues that present themselves in all contexts, but that manifest themselves in different ways. The following paragraphs outline some of the critical elements of "urban" educational leadership while keeping in mind that these elements also apply, perhaps in different ways, to non-urban contexts.

Essentials for Urban School Leadership

If significant change in urban schools is going to hold any traction, we need to abandon the image of a single, heroic agent of change. True, individual principals, teachers, or parents can be a major catalyst for change, but the responsibility for sharing perspectives, unearthing inequities and devising plans to improve the life chances of those who find themselves on the margins needs to be shared until a critical mass of change agents are able to carry momentum forward. Among the many strategies and approaches that would make urban leadership promising in its outcomes, the following are essential: refusal to use a deficit lens, inclusion, critical consciousness, and strategic anti-oppressive action.

Refusal to Use a Deficit Lens

Key to urban leadership is deconstructing and challenging deficit constructions of urban contexts. Unfortunately, the cultural richness and many opportunities woven into urban life are often lost in the negative spin attached to the term "urban education." The magnitude and intensity of diversity in urban settings make the need for addressing issues of equity and institutional oppression more readily apparent. This is a benefit, not a problem. There is much more of an impetus to strategically include diverse voices and to create new spaces that represent these multiple and varied experiences than there is in contexts where the marginalized are sparse and the presence of the dominant culture remains monolithic. This is an opportunity, not a barrier.

Abandoning deficit discourses requires that urban leaders refuse to place the blame for disengagement and poor achievement on the shoulders of marginalized students, their parents, and their communities. It means owning the responsibility for changing the programs and practices that leave many students with no place to see themselves and their experiences represented and understood. It means celebrating the fact that students are able to communicate in more than one language rather than pathologizing the use of first languages other than English. Conversely, urban leaders need to face the deficits in their schools and in the broader educational system. This requires the courage to embrace controversy and expose the realities of school life for those who have little voice rather than seek to portray an image of a harmonious school. This is a difficult task, for the pressure on school leaders to create and maintain positive public images for their schools is immense (Solomon, 2002).

Inclusion

Inclusion requires that we approach leadership as a communal practice. It is a process "in which all members of school communities are involved or represented in equitable ways. The process itself is inclusive in that everyone has a right to contribute. The ends for which it strives are also inclusive. They are geared to work for inclusive, just, and democratic schools and communities" (Ryan, 2003, p. 19).

Urban leaders committed to social justice recognize that it is not enough to welcome all parents into our schools, but proactively solicit and create spaces for their voices to be heard. That requires turning down the volume on the voices that have traditionally felt most comfortable as central figures in decision-making processes. It also means orchestrating multiple times and locations for meetings and events that fit with the life patterns of families in the community.

Substantive parent–community engagement does not mean rallying a diverse group of people merely to promote already established system priorities; it means genuinely seeking their input in helping all participants "see" aspects of the school experience for their students that become normalized with detrimental effects. It means seeking multiple perspectives to improve the school culture, as well as its programs and practices, in ways that not only create more optimistic futures for those in need, but do so in sensitive and humane ways. As Dei (2006) puts it, "Inclusion is not bringing people into what already exists; it is making a new space, a better space for everyone."

Critical Refection

Critical urban leaders begin with — and sustain — a rigorous personal journey to unpack their own experiences, biases, and positioning. This requires engaging the help of those with different life experiences to help them see what they have come to accept as "normal." And then the task is one of modelling the moral courage to "stir the pot" and engage others in unmasking the beliefs and practices that serve to perpetuate the status quo. This collective striving to "see" the effects of content and practices that have become almost doctrinal over time, such as Eurocentric narratives of history, literature that feature only hetero, nuclear families, or school councils comprised only of dominant-culture parents, is crucial for as Chomsky quite optimistically points out,

> There are a vast number of people who are uninformed . . ., but fundamentally decent. . . If they can be brought to raise questions and apply their decent instincts and basic intelligence, many people quickly escape the confines of the doctrinal system and are willing to do something to help others who are really suffering and oppressed. (Cited in Achbar, 1994, p. 195)

As part of this process, urban school leaders might encourage all participants to keep questions such as the following in the forefront of daily school life:

- Am I seeing, understanding, and addressing the ways in which the world treats my students and me as race [culture, gender, class] group members?
- Am I seeing, understanding, and addressing communities and individuals in their full complexity?
- Am I seeing, understanding, and addressing the ways opportunities to learn or thrive are unequally distributed to racial [culture, gender, class] groups?
- What actions offer necessary opportunities to students, families, and communities in such a world? (Adapted from Pollock, 2008, p. xiii)

The responses to these questions would become part of the dialogue in staff meetings and focus groups and would eventually permeate regular formal and informal conversations about school culture, policy, programs, and practices. Discussions of this sort would become a normal part of school culture, so that it would become commonplace to engage students in similar conversations.

Key to urban leadership is a collective effort to unmask and wrestle with aspects of school life and practices that maintain unequal relations of power and privilege. These conversations need to include students as well, for as Torre and Fine found:

> When radically diverse groups of young people come together to discuss their experiences of power and injustice on the basis of their identity-group memberships (i.e., race/ethnicity, class, gender, sexuality, "disability," track level, social clique), then engage and interrogate these differences and debate how to pursue shared social justice goals... When complex identities are acknowledged and valued and power is engaged and interrogated rather than ignored, young people are able to take risks and ask hard questions about racism, oppression, and inequality, all the

while pursuing deeper understandings of complex identities. They build trust and alliances with individuals and
groups across their various lines of difference. (Cited in
Spence, Stewart, & Grewal, 2012, p. 165)

Strategic Anti-Oppression

Urban educational leaders need to develop the political acumen
to navigate complex educational hierarchies and community relations
in pursuing the goals requisite for improving the possibilities for urban
school communities (Ryan, 2010). This requires understanding and
negotiating prevailing power relations, making use of positional power,
and striving to develop new avenues to empower the collective voices and
aims of their diverse school communities.

Urban leaders need the courage to resist the neoliberal urgings
toward standardization, efficiency, and competition. Marginalized students in urban schools may suffer more from the imposition of standardized curriculum and assessment, as there are greater numbers of families
whose life experiences, languages, and cultural and religious practices
are not centrally represented in these artifacts of recent reform. Leaders,
therefore, need to work more strategically and relentlessly to ensure that
culturally responsive and relevant pedagogy permeate both life within
the school and relationships that bridge the school and community.

In the short term, we need to recognize that formally measured student achievement is the "currency of success" in current practice; in the
long term, we need a concerted effort to overhaul these standardized systems that favour some students over others. McKenzie et al. explain the
importance of integrating a focus on student achievement with a commitment to helping students develop in their knowledge and practice of
social justice:

> It is not enough for leaders to focus on student achievement
> only to produce students who can read, write, and compute
> at high academic levels but who do not use their academic
> skills to challenge injustices in society and thus become no

more than uncritical operators in the production economy. Likewise, it is not enough for school leaders to raise student consciousness about inequities and ignore or explain away the gaps in achievement among their students. (Cited in Spence, Stewart, & Grewal, 2012, p. 116)

Conclusion

To call upon individual urban school leaders to be change agents in breaking persistent cycles of oppression is both naïve and unfair. Leadership must be collective and must grow tentacles into the ponderous bureaucracies that block substantive change. If educational leadership broadly is going to hold any legitimacy whatsoever in the eyes of those who are socially, politically, and economically marginalized, then the focus cannot only be on school leaders in diverse and poor urban contexts. This would send a message that the aim of the education system is to manage "hot spots," to keep a lid on justified anger and frustration with inequities, to raise student achievement — in the narrow, measured sense of the term — for political interests rather than to improve the life chances of students and their communities. Those inequities will remain intractable unless educational leadership throughout the system commits to disrupting the assumptions, norms, and practices that continue to favour some groups over others.

Urban school leadership, with its focus on inclusion, antiracism, and culturally relevant and responsive pedagogy, has the potential to catalyze movement more broadly towards a socially just system. If the ideal of a "good" school is one that unmasks inequity and strategically provides students, parents, and educators with the tools to become vigilant and active in promoting just practices, then effective educational leaders in complex, challenging and enriching urban environments stand to provide much needed models for all striving to educate students to become confident, sensitive, contributing global citizens.

References

Achbar, M. (Ed.). (1994). *Manufacturing consent: Noam Chomsky and the media*. Montreal, Quebec: Black Rose Books.

Dei, G. S. N. (2006). Meeting equity fair and square: Keynote address to the leadership conference of the Elementary Teachers' Federation of Ontario, September 28, 2006, Mississauga, Ontario.

Gallagher, K.S., Goodyear, R., Brewer, D.J. & Rueda, R. (Eds.) (2012). Urban education: A model for leadership and policy. New York: Routledge. Pollock, M. (2008). *Everyday antiracism: Getting real about race in school.* New York: The New Press.

Ryan, J. (2010). Promoting social justice in schools: Principals' political strategies. *International Journal of Leadership in Education, 13*(4), 357–376.

Ryan, J. (2003). Leading diverse schools. Dordreht, NL: Kluwer.

Solomon, P. (2002). School leaders and anti-racism: Overcoming pedagogical and political obstacles. *Journal of School Leadership, 12,* 174–197.

Spence, L., Stewart, C., Grewal. P. (2012). *Principal as leader of the equitable school.* Ontario Principals' Council. Thousand Oaks, CA: Corwin Press.

Part III
What Is a Good School?

What Is a Good School?

John Roberts

A good school is there for all students, even those who are not part of the dominant culture. It is more than bricks and wood. When a person says, "I went to a good school," he or she doesn't usually mean the external building, but rather those elements — the leadership and the supports in the school — that contribute to high academic achievement, that minimize the dropout rate, and that offer the tools needed to be successful either in higher education or in the workplace.

Physically, in order to maximize Aboriginal student achievement, the "good" school should have classes of no more than 15 students, have an aide for every teacher in the lower grades, and have classrooms fitted with the latest educational technology. Tribal elders should be enlisted to teach Aboriginal culture and languages, and to offer support to students both inside and outside the classroom.

The legacy of residential schools remains. In order to overcome this stigma, increased funding for Aboriginal education is essential in order to create schools and a school system responsive to the needs of Aboriginal students in order to maximize Aboriginal achievement.

What Is a Good School?

Carolyn M. Shields

A good school provides an exciting, engaging, vibrant, inclusive, and socially-just environment for learning. It promotes the acquisition and interpretation of multiple kinds of information and knowledge. In a good school, all individuals, regardless of their socio-cultural, financial, or religious backgrounds, ability, or sexual orientation are accepted, respected, and included in every learning activity. In a good school, dialogue is encouraged as students and teachers together learn to make sense of, and to critique, the curricular content, others' perspectives, and their own assumptions. Prejudicial comments are challenged, deficit thinking is rejected, and strong, positive, supportive, and encouraging relationships are key.

A good school develops an inclusive sense of community, with the norms not being imposed, but evolving from dialogue among group members. Members recognize that, sometimes, compromise perpetuates the dominance of a powerful group; so, questions about who is marginalized and who is included, who is advantaged and who is disadvantaged by any decision are posed regularly. All policies are based on equitable principles. The academic goal of intellectual growth of all members is balanced with consideration for the social and emotional welfare of the individual and community. In a good school, assumptions are challenged, critique is encouraged, and learning is socially constructed.

What Is a Good School?

William Ayers

S chools for obedience and conformity are characterized by passivity
and fatalism, infused with anti-intellectualism and irrelevance, ob-
sessed with the absorption of facts. They turn on the little technologies of control and normalization — elaborate schemes for surveillance,
knotted systems of rules and discipline, exhaustive programs of sorting
winners from losers. Learning becomes exclusively selfish with no social
motive — every difference becomes a victory for someone and a wound
for someone else.

A good school encourages students to ask fundamental questions,
— Who in the world am I? How did I get here and where am I going?
What is my story, and how is it like or unlike the stories of others? — to
think for themselves, to make judgments based on evidence and argument, to refuse obedience and conformity in favour of initiative, courage,
audacity, imagination, creativity, empathy, and fellow-feeling. Most of all,
a good schools aims to grow free people capable of participating fully in
the world as it is, and, if they choose, transforming all that they inherit. In
a good school questioning, researching, and undertaking active work in
the community is the order of the day. Students learn that helping others
is not a form of charity — an act that impoverishes both recipient and
benefactor — but a type of solidarity.

What Is a Good School?

Pierre Wilbert Orelus

Before attempting to engage this philosophically loaded yet important question, it is worth examining various views informing the social construction and symbolic representation of *a good school*. The definition of *a good school* is contextual and influenced by differing views, ideologies, and interests. Therefore, such a definition needs to be examined through a critical lens to challenge naïve views about the social construction of *good schools* in general.

A school is like a tree; it can and should only be judged by what it produces. A *good school* is commonly judged by its academic outcomes, including higher rates of student academic success. This success has much to do with how the school personnel, particularly teachers, have prepared students to face challenges beyond classroom walls and school fences. This is not coincidental, however. The academic success stories of *good schools* are linked to the financial support they receive from various wealthy donors and the government, and these schools are usually located in relatively safe and affluent neighbourhoods.

How Does Educational Leadership Influence Student Learning?

Jacky Lumby

Influencing student learning is the foundational challenge for educational leadership. It is, however, exceptionally difficult to understand and enact, given that it links two of the most contested concepts in education: learning and leadership.

Learning is an internal process not knowable to others in real time. Rather, we discern learning by retrospective self-reporting by students or by identifying a series of proxies, such as changes in cognition, behaviour, attitudes, or skills. Globally, neoliberal administrations may equate successful learning with test results, but many leaders aim at much broader social, spiritual, and intellectual outcomes (Watkins, 2005). The process of learning is understood in many different ways, spanning behavioural, sociocultural, constructivist, and cognitive theories (Woolfolk Hoy & Hoy, 2013). Whatever the preferred approach, leading learning demands that all who contribute to the leadership of a school create an environment conducive to learning; that is, a process that stimulates and sustains valued change in all learners.

Leadership, too, is a contested concept, enacted by potentially many in a school, including students, if leading is taken to be shaping the emotional and cognitive environment in which shared goals are pursued.

Leading learning is then an indirect process of influencing learners, families, and faculty, the exact nature of which depends on how learning is conceived and on beliefs about the conditions that nurture it. Meta-analyses discern a positive relationship between leadership and learning, although the size and characteristics of its effect remain contested (Robinson, Lloyd, & Rowe, 2008; Swaffield & MacBeath, 2009).

As learning is the primary function of schools, influencing learning can potentially link to every aspect of activity: shaping organizational culture, working with school communities, crafting physical and human resources, and developing curriculum, pedagogy, and assessment processes. A starting point for leaders is to influence underlying beliefs about learning and learners. "Leadership ultimately involves the ability to define the reality of others" (Morgan, 1998, p. 171). Leaders need to ensure that faculty, learners themselves, and the wider community believe in a reality where every student can learn. Though this may seem a statement of the obvious, in many, perhaps most schools, there are children and faculty who do not believe it. Evidence from learners themselves describes the experience of a sizable proportion who feel invisible and unvalued, and who view their peers learning as an outsider watching through a window (Lumby, 2012b). There are children who have accepted any number of deficit labels. There are board members and faculty who, whatever their espoused stance, nevertheless see some children as unlikely to succeed or for whom lesser expectations are appropriate. Establishing the simple belief that all children can learn can be a difficult and draining leadership battle (Garza, 2008).

The primary action to influence learning, then, is insisting — relentlessly and persistently — that every child can learn. A corollary of this stance is the imperative to listen to learners, particularly disaffected learners, as to what they believe will help them learn. There are examples of children of all ages being centrally involved in evaluating and developing learning (Harding, 2001; Prieto, 2001). In some cases, children are trained as researchers and team up with faculty to develop pedagogy (Lumby, 2012a). Leaders here are signalling the value and trust they place in students and reducing the power distance between learners and faculty that some young adults find so counter-productive.

Large-scale studies provide guidance on what learners believe they need. Analysis of data from a national longitudinal study on high school education in the UK distils the following guidance from interviews with disaffected children. The learners' own words are added in italics:

- Clarity of instruction: *"getting it explained properly"*
- Experiential methods: *"activities, not writing"*
- Social learning: *"cos if you are working with other people, if you get stuck on the question, then they can help you out and you are not asking the teacher all the time"*
- Clear direction on improvement: *"they just told us how to improve it and I have"* (Lumby, 2012b, p. 270)

Though such requirements may seem obvious, they are anything but universal. Many learners describe a cycle of incomprehension that triggers aggression or withdrawal. They report being puzzled by the task, spending much time writing, generally being asked to work alone, and receiving minimal constructive feedback; the opposite of what they want (Hamill & Boyd 2002).

Leadership to reverse such patterns is not straightforward. Faculty often become habituated to ways of working that are effective for the most competent or fulfill other requirements, such as maintaining discipline or increasing test scores, rather than supporting learning (Hayes, Johnson, & King, 2009). From Waller (1932) in the US and onward, many scholars have noted a grammar and a deep structure in the community of practice that shapes resistance to transformative change, evident in schools across the world (Pajak, 2012).

In a two-year project in Australian schools, faculty worked with researchers using day diaries, shadowing, and reflection to transform pedagogy. The effort to sustain deep change in pedagogy was innovative and persisted long term, asking that faculty critically interrogate how learning could be achieved. This example demonstrates the degree of leadership, effort, and persistence needed to transform rather than just refresh pedagogy (Hayes et al., 2009).

Inclusive pedagogy is a fundamental challenge for leaders, but there are others. Disadvantage is structurally embedded in relation to race, gender, and other personal attributes. A second foundational challenge for leading learning then is to contest the historic disadvantage experienced by learners perceived as "other" in order to promote social justice. Numerous strategies are suggested in a substantial literature, but the underlying principles are rarely explicitly discussed in schools. A strictly egalitarian approach with the same treatment given to all will not dent existing inequities. Proportional support, with more resources going to those most in need, may provoke cries of unfairness from others (Gorard, 2012). The leader's role is to stimulate and influence debate so that the community can endorse a philosophy and strategies relating to the three dimensions of social justice most widely evident in literature:

1. Redistributing social and physical resources
2. Recognizing, acknowledging, and supporting the culture and experience of marginalized groups
3. Ensuring that learners are empowered to speak for themselves (Brown, 2004; Gewirtz & Cribb, 2002)

Each dimension translates into actions. For example, redistributing resources may include ensuring that those with the least prior attainment receive instruction from the most experienced faculty, and de-tracking to eliminate ghettos of those who have attained less (Theoharis, 2007). Using data to highlight underperformance in order to identify patterns where irrelevant characteristics are associated with lesser attainment is a foundation of initiatives to reduce such discrepancies. The evidence-based focus on key areas of injustice underpins concerted, persistent efforts to rectify matters. As such this strategy appears regularly in narratives of principals who have achieved dramatic, that is swift and significant, improvement in results. But, as one US superintendent who led an apparently remarkable improvement in learning protested, "We did not believe these gains were 'incredible,' to the contrary, we thought it was incredible that bilingual children were performing so poorly!" (Garza, 2008, p. 175). Surprise at sudden or large learning gains generally reflects a deficit viewpoint. Garza's point is that a deficit view of learners constitutes a barrier to learning, not a deficit in the learner.

Above all, leading learning is about the leadership role of creating reality for others; persuading the community that learning is not a competitive sport with losing accepted as inevitable for some. That is the foundational step, but it is just the first. Praxis involves a cycle of entwined reflection and action, driven by clarity of goals and unremitting determination to sustain an environment where all children can learn.

References

Brown, K.M. (2004). Leadership for social justice and equity: Weaving a transformative framework and pedagogy. *Educational Administration Quarterly, 40*(1), 77–108.

Garza, E., Jr. (2008). Autoethnography of a first-time superintendent: Challenges to leadership for social justice. *Journal of Latinos and Education, 7*(2), 163–176.

Gewirtz, S., & Cribb, A. (2002). Plural conceptions of social justice: Implications for policy sociology. *Journal of Education Policy, 17*(5), 499–509.

Gorard, S. (2012). Experiencing fairness at school: An international study. *International Journal of Educational Research, 53*, 127–137.

Hamill, P., & Boyd, B. (2002). Equality, fairness and rights: The young person's voice. *British Journal of Special Education, 29*(3), 111–117.

Harding, C. (2001). Students as researchers is as important as the National Curriculum. *Forum, 43*(2) 56–57.

Hayes, D., Johnston, K., & King, A. (2009). Creating enabling classroom practices in high poverty contexts: The disruptive possibilities of looking in classrooms. *Pedagogy, Culture & Society, 17*(3), 251–264.

Lumby, J. (2012a). Student voice in educational leadership research. In M. Coleman, A. Briggs, & M. Morrison (Eds.), *Researching Educational Leadership* (pp. 236-248). London: Sage.

Lumby, J. (2012b). Disengaged and disaffected young people: Surviving the system. *British Educational Research Journal, 38*(2), 261–279.

Morgan, G. (1998). *Images of organisation.* Thousand Oaks, CA: Sage.

Pajak, E.F. (2012). Willard Waller's sociology of teaching reconsidered: "What does teaching do to teachers?" *American Education Research Journal, 49*(6), 1182–1213.

Prieto, M. (2001). Students as agents of democratic renewal in Chile. *Forum, 43*(2), 87–90.

Robinson, V.M., Lloyd, C.A., & Rowe, K.J. (2008). The impact of leadership on student outcomes: An analysis of the differential effects of leadership types. *Educational Administration Quarterly, 44*(5), **635–674**.

Swaffield, S., & MacBeath, J. (2009). Leadership for learning. In J. MacBeath & N. Dempster (Eds.), *Connecting Leadership and Learning* (pp. 32-52). London: Sage.

Theoharis, G. (2007). Theory of social justice leadership social justice educational leaders and resistance: Toward a theory of social justice leadership. *Educational Administration Quarterly, 43*, 221–258.

Waller, W. (1932). What teaching does to teachers. In W. Waller, *Sociology of Teaching* (pp. 375–440). New York: John Wiley & Sons.

Watkins, C. (2005). Classrooms as learning communities: A review of research. *London Review of Education, 3*(1), 47–64.

Woolfolk Hoy, A., and Hoy, W.K. (2013). *Instructional leadership: A research-based guide to learning in schools,* 4th ed.

Chapter 25

How Has the Increase in Standardized Testing Impacted Educational Leadership?

Wayne Au

B eginning with the 1983 Regan-era report *A Nation at Risk: The Imperative for Education Reform* (National Commission on Excellence in Education, 1983), high-stakes, standardized testing has been ascendant as the guiding metric for education policy in the United States. By 1986, thirty-five states had increased the graduation course-load requirements and instituted reforms revolving around high-stakes tests. By 1994, forty-three states had implemented statewide K–5 assessments, and by 2000, the only US state not to administer a state-mandated test was Iowa. President George W. Bush signed the *No Child Left Behind Act* (*No Child Left Behind Act of 2001*, 2002) into law in 2002, attaching performance goals on high-stakes test scores to various sanctions for public schools, including the loss of federal Title I funding. As of this writing, we currently face the Obama administration's Race to the Top initiative, which demands that, in order to receive special federal funds, states must promote charter schools, adopt the Common Core State Standards (and the tests that come with them), and tie teacher evaluations to test scores, amongst other policies.

The effects of high-stakes testing on students, teachers, classrooms, and even parents are well documented. In many places, and to varying degrees, classroom instruction and curriculum have zeroed in on passing the tests alone, resulting in reductions in non-tested subjects like social studies and science, cuts to the arts and recess, and increases in rote memorization and teacher-centred instruction. Parents have become increasingly disgruntled as well not only about the standardization of curriculum but also about the psychological trauma experienced by their children while taking these tests.

In the midst of the implementation of high-stakes, test-based education policies stand administrators caught in the middle of the political tensions that have arisen. Teachers in most places in the US have unions to advocate for their members and contracts to protect them from malicious attacks. Parents often have Parent–Teacher Associations (PTAs) that serve as a base of influence at the school level, an organization that can provide them with a voice in the education of their children. Administrators, on the other hand, are not as protected and are subject to dismissal without the right to due process. To make things even more complicated for administrators, education reform policies constructed around high-stakes, standardized testing are also notable for being top-down, vertical hierarchies, where, at each level, those at the top use test scores as the central means to hold those below them "accountable" for improvements.

When we take into account all of these factors, administrators are undoubtedly left in an extremely complex and exceedingly difficult position. They are generally obligated to honour the legal rights of teachers and work with them on policy implementation — policies that, like using high-stakes testing for teacher evaluation, might be inaccurate and highly controversial, yet are in vogue in policy circles for ideological reasons. They must also navigate the community politics associated with students and their parents, representing a diverse range of interests and stances on policy, implementation, and the general politics of education. Additionally they exist within, and must negotiate with their own district bureaucracies and hierarchies, institutions that themselves represent a mix of interests, agendas, management styles, and politics. Finally, they are required to survive in a broader policy climate with extremely high stakes where the public, politicians, pundits, and mainstream media are generally critical of public education, placing educators under a high level of scrutiny and potential attack by all stakeholders.

The current policy context that relies on top-down, corporate-style education reforms built on an architecture of high-stakes testing thus places administrators in a highly volatile position where they are held responsible for managing diverse and contradictory expectations and implementing contentious policy, all the while trying to keep their jobs.

The precarious position for administrators inherently raises some difficult questions, choices, and decisions for them within high-stakes test-based policy regimes. For instance, what should administrators do if they do not agree with the testing policy? What if they do not like what the tests are doing to student learning and classroom practices? What are the limits of their power to act or not act within the vertical hierarchies that define most educational bureaucracies? Equally difficult questions arise even if administrators support test-based systems of accountability. For instance, how do they implement policy that many community members — parents, students, and teachers — resist with increasing regularity? How do administrators implement new test-related policies — like using test scores for teacher evaluation or the implementation of new testing regimes like the Common Core testing in the US — where they lack the technical expertise to understand either the problems presented by the policy or the assessment the policy is based upon?

The choices and decisions extending from the above questions are equally difficult for administrators working in the policy context, particularly because any misstep could lead to their nearly immediate dismissal. Administrators generally take one of four broad stances when it comes to high-stakes testing. The first stance is the "true believer" who sees the tests as valid measures of learning and teaching and is committed to test-based systems of accountability to improve learning and to punish failure. True believers tend to back district and state initiatives whole-heartedly with little tolerance for questions or problems raised by those below them in the hierarchal chain. The second administrative type is the "bureaucratic survivalist" who may or may not believe in testing policies per se, but is largely driven by a self-interest in keeping his or her job and surviving within the institutional hierarchies. Bureaucratic survivalists generally do not show initiative of their own, eschew conflict with supervisors, and thus have difficulty either defending or insulating those below them in the institutional structure. The third stance is that of the "pragmatic navigator" who may or may not agree with test-based policies, is genuinely sympathetic to the concerns and questions raised by teachers, students, and parents. This administrator still finds ways to defend and insulate teachers and students from the worst effects of such policies, but is generally compelled to follow test-based policies.

The fourth type is the "public resister" who chooses to protest, speak out against, or resist policies associated with high-stakes, standardized testing, usually on ethical, political, and educational grounds. In July 2012, for instance, Robert Scott, the former Texas state superintendent of schools issued a statement calling high-stakes testing the "end-all, be-all" of education, a "perversion" that is not just "a cottage industry but a military-industrial complex." Another Texas public school administrator, John Kuhn, has become an outspoken critic of high-stakes testing as well. He wrote a letter to his legislators, published in the *Washington Post* (Kuhn, 2012), which became kind of a manifesto of resistance, urging politicians to fund public education, not standardized testing. Kuhn went on to become a speaker at national rallies and publish two books, *Test-and-Punish* (Kuhn, 2013) and *Fear and Learning in America* (Kuhn, 2014). As another example, a group of principals in New York co-authored "An Open Letter to Parents of Children throughout New York State Regarding Grade 3–8 Testing." This letter outlined many critical issues with the new state test, including ambiguous questions, test length, the "visceral" reaction by students, cost of the tests, and its contribution to widening the achievement gap, amongst others. The letter has since been signed by over 1,500 principals in the state of New York, provoking widespread attention in the media and increased public awareness of the problems with high-stakes testing. Yet another example is Thomas Scarice, superintendent of Madison Public Schools in Connecticut. Scarice has been very vocal in expressing his discontent with test-based reforms by writing public letters to his state legislature and publishing them in the *Washington Post*.

The main issue for administrators in high-stakes, standardized testing is their response to the impact of the tests on education generally and their schools and districts specifically. Above all, and as the instances of resistance highlight, administrators are in positions of power, and they have status within our communities. When they speak up, it resonates with teachers, parents, and students across the country. As such, administrators can and should support public education and educational quality for all students. To do so, however, requires that administrators thoroughly explore what high-stakes testing is doing to our schools and our system of education and then weigh that evidence against their personal commitment, bureaucracy, and policy mandate.

References

Kuhn, J. (2012, March 31). A statement of our just grievances. Retrieved from http://www.washingtonpost.com/blogs/answer-sheet/post/a-statement-of-our-just-grievances/2012/03/30/gIQAXTqGmS_blog.html

Kuhn, J. (2013). *Test and punish: How the Texas education model gave America accountability without equity*. Pacific Grove, CA: Park Place Publications.

Kuhn, J. (2014). *Fear and learning in America: Bad data, good teachers, and the attack on public education*. New York: Teachers College Press.

National Commission on Excellence in Education. (1983). *A nation at risk: The imperative for educational reform* (p. 65). Washington D.C.: United States Department of Education.

No Child Left Behind Act of 2001, Pub. L. No. 107-110 (2002). Retrieved from http://www.ed.gov/policy/elsec/leg/esea02/index.html

Chapter 26

What Is the Importance of Critical Self-Reflection for Educational Leaders?

Victoria Handford

For years, school leaders in Canada were granted a form of Weberian "traditional authority," as seen in phrases like "in loco-parentis." Teachers and school leaders were to act "as if" they were the parent of the child (Davies & Guppy, 2014). The ideal parent was whatever the ruling classes said it was. This worldview formed the basis of policies and routines. Difference was suppressed and attempts to extinguish difference were frequently successful. We knew what it was to be ethical — functionally, it was whatever the ruling classes said it was. The slow but steady movement towards creating a body of recognized, effective, and "implementable" practice, a "professionalizing" of the profession, coincided with the significant effects of the 1983 arrival of the *Canadian Charter of Rights and Freedoms*. Along with a plethora of additional important societal changes in the last 40 years, including an increase in immigration and a rise in the educated middle class, this professionalization resulted in what Weber would call a more "legal-rational" organizational and authoritative structure.

Now, central authority has increased. Senior district administrations focus on influencing the power holders at the provincial and state level while maintaining influence with the trustees. Teachers and other school district employees are unionized and marching to the drums of their union leaders, as they try to exert influence on those with influence. In short, the organizational demands on those who once supported school leaders, the large and influential professionalization requirements, the legalistic concerns about responsibility and governance more than overwhelm even the most capable among us. The school leader is left alone, the sole (soul?) voice trying to balance these demands at the school level, addressing the immediate needs of students, parents and staff, on a daily basis in their schools. There is limited or no time for interaction with others that might inform, support, enlighten, or challenge the multitude of daily decisions made by the practicing school leader. Cut loose, it is either sink or swim, and others watch in curious but distracted fleeting seconds to see which will occur.

Socrates served as teacher and role model for Plato. He was a central character in *The Republic*, and perhaps the most significant character in the writings of Western educational values. Socrates said "the unexamined life is not worth living." He challenged the people of Athens to have the courage to engage in critical self-reflection, and then use their voices for frank, unapologetic speech. This did not work out well for him (he died drinking hemlock rather than give up his beliefs). Parrhesia, or what might be called "free speech," was a feature of Dialectic, whereas rhetoric, the tool for persuasion and manipulation, was a feature of Sophistry. Plato's *Dialogues* position one against the other, ultimately pleading with Athens (and therefore civilization since 5000 BC) to engage in honest, self-reflective, and self-critical dialogue. Descartes tells us that whatever can be doubted must be; that it is essential to truth to examine the veracity of everything. Foucault, in his series of lectures at Berkeley in 1983 states, "parrhesia is a verbal activity in which a speaker expresses his personal relationship to truth, and risks his life because he recognizes truth-telling as a duty to improve or help other people (as well as himself)."

Upholding organizational and professional truths, codes of ethics and expectations, requires us to consider the situated reality of each view and each situation in relation to established expectations. In order to view events through multiple lenses, we must first be sure we understand the challenges, strengths, and applicability of our own situated lens. We must embrace our own fallibility. With everyone and everything "for sale," what is honest interaction, how do we best educate our children? Each of our voices, whether used in speaking with ourselves or with others, is as unique as our fingerprints. It is just ours. That voice has to be strong, and balanced with the recognition of our own imperfections. It must be informed, nuanced, and wise, for there is a plethora of hemlock out there.

Critical self-reflection helps us to see our own reflection accurately, thus enhancing our ability to see the humanity of all we serve. In the words of Thomas Greenfield, the long-term goal is to "engage in a continuing process of discovery aimed at gaining an understanding of ourselves and others" (Greenfield & Ribbons, 2005). A "critical friend," or the alternative voice, can be uncomfortable. We tend to shy away from this, or limit the stories by telling only of our "successes," however much this singular view increases our blindness. Many reasons for limiting the ability of a colleague/friend/associate to nuance our thinking are readily available.

Nobel Laureate Daniel Kahneman spent his career researching the "fast, intuitive" versus the "slower, more systematic," making a case for engaging the slower systems as important, we as humans do not see things as they are on first glance (Kahneman, 2011). In the words of the Talmud, "We see things not as they are. We see them as we are." This is the human condition. Critical self-reflection asks that we slow things down and take a closer look at the entire situation. Having borne witness to our own self-critical truths, we are ready to engage in the task of understanding a thicker story. Somehow, we have to step out of Plato's proverbial "cave," turn, and in turning, see that what we thought were the facts are mere shadows of issues frequently disguising the essential work we face. If we see the essential work, if we recognize the magnitude of the issues and our paucity of solutions to issues, do we speak this truth? Do we sip on the hemlock? "Plato's allegory of the cave is not simply to move outside of the cave and into the realm of the ideas, where one is blinded by the sun; it is, rather, to return back into the cave after one has grasped the ideas, and to try to explain them to those who can see only shadows" (De Boever, 2010).

Critical self-reflection is more than a phrase for a page. It opens the cave, revealing the cage. It is essential leadership work.

References

Davies, S., & Guppy, N. (2014). The schooled society: An introduction to the sociology of education. Toronto: Oxford University Press.

De Boever, A. (2010). The allegory of the cage: Foucault, Agamben, and the Enlightenment. *Foucault Studies, 10,* 7–22.

Foucault, M. (1983). Lectures at Berkeley: Truth and subjectivity. SocioPhilosophy, www.youtube.com/watch?v=V0URrVbpjW0

Greenfield, T., & Ribbons, P. (2005). Greenfield on educational administration: Towards a humane craft. London: Routledge.

Kahneman, D. (2011). *Thinking, fast and slow.* Toronto: Doubleday Canada.

Chapter 27

How Should Student Voice Impact Educational Leaders?

Lawrence Angus

I n this chapter, I use the term "student voice" in a way that implies more than just allowing students to speak. "Student voice" has long been associated with educational reform in the interests of disadvantaged and minority students. The idea of giving "voice" recognizes that students have generally not had sufficient power to influence learning environments. A somewhat different concept of "student voice," however, has recently become popularized in some educational leadership literature: a particularly thin voice linked to innocuous notions of student "feedback" rather than to authentic engagement in educational reform. I am therefore referring to "authentic" student voice in arguing that it is important to regard students, particularly those less advantaged, as knowing participants who should have a say in what and how they learn. The onus should be on all educational leaders to recognize, respect, and engage with the diversity of students and the knowledge and cultures that they bring to educational contexts.

I emphasize these points because an excessive concern with accountability and standards has steadily displaced what had been emerging in the 1960s and 1970s as an ethos of equity and social responsibility in schools that required educators to know their students, understand where they were coming from, and "meet" them by negotiating curriculum and pedagogy to make learning more relevant to their everyday lives and experiences. This professional attitude has been displaced by a much more impersonal ethos of competition and performativity that allows little place for understanding and accommodating the social, cultural, and experiential worlds of young people. The hardening of the educational policy regime and of educational attitudes in virtually all Western countries (especially English-speaking ones) has meant that, instead of schools accommodating the diversity of students, both the competitive market arrangements and the heavy accountability regimes of mandatory standardized testing, under which schools now operate, force schools to comply with impersonal and remote standards. Students and teachers are expected to turn themselves into the kinds of people demanded by ostensibly "high performing" schools that excel in high-stakes tests.

To be sure, some students are highly motivated and culturally disposed to acquire the scores and grades that will ensure their future educational and life chances. For them, the "decision" to be successful at school is, as Ball, Davies, David, and Reay (2002, p. 54) put it, "a non-decision" because it is part of a "normal," unthinking and expected social trajectory. But such is not the case for less-advantaged children. For them, the "decision" to make a real effort to be successful at school has to be an "active" decision that is much more problematic because they and their families lack the social and cultural resources and supports that are generally available to more advantaged families. This makes the reproduction of disadvantage especially likely, which is why it is critically important for school leaders and teachers to do everything they can to engage such students — to understand them and their neighbourhoods, to ensure that they have a personal connection with teachers and a stake in what the school is perceived to offer. Students need to know that, while they are trying to understand and belong to the school, their school leaders and teachers are reaching out to them rather than simply expecting them to adjust to entrenched school and teacher paradigms. Students need to recognize the attempts being made to engage them in relevant and interesting school experiences in which they can recognize their own culture and knowledge. But because of high-stakes pressure to prepare students for externally mandated tests, school leaders and teachers have less time to do the difficult educational work of engaging students in the institutional life of schooling. The result is that the students who most need support are more likely to be disillusioned, ignored, and even denigrated by the school system. Small wonder many of them respond with hostility and rejection of schooling.

Promoting student voice means engaging students and treating them in mature and non-patronizing ways that connect with their lives and cultures. As advocates for less-advantaged students in particular, leaders should be prepared to reject the currently dominant "reform" rhetoric and, instead, encourage teachers and students to develop good, relational educational practices. Such leadership is, of course, always difficult, and it always involves tensions and contradictions. It has to be relational within a participative, flexible, democratic environment in which the shaping of the school as an organization is never just top-down, but is an engaged process involving all organizational players, including students. Democratic, transformative leadership takes place in such environments, which are dynamic rather than static, and in which it is recognized that the school is located within a web of complex social and political contexts.

The heavy education policy overlay of managerialism and competitiveness ignores such complexity. Educative leadership that fosters genuine student voice has largely been displaced by accountability frameworks, competition, and standardization. Under such conditions, leaders are more likely to overlook the moral purpose of education that has been asserted by a generation of leadership scholars such as Bill Foster, Thomas Sergiovanni, and Robert Starratt; namely, to promote in schools as social institutions the core values of social justice, democracy, and equity. Such an approach to leadership, and to education more broadly, is necessary to promote fair, equitable, inclusive, truly democratic participation of all young people in education and society. As Shields starkly points out: "Unless all children experience a sense of belonging in our schools, they are being educated in institutions that exclude and marginalize them, that perpetuate inequity and inequality rather than democracy and social justice" (2004, p. 122).

Current accountability requirements emphasize testing, performativity, and managerialism within a moral vacuum that displaces richer, more humane ways of thinking about education. We know from decades of research that schools do not necessarily work to the advantage of all young people. Leaders must therefore try to understand how education as a social institution systematically acts to disadvantage certain types of people, and that we are therefore obliged, as principled educators, to do something about it. The critically important point is that, if we are serious about the authentic participation of students, we must advocate for education that is inclusive of their lives, knowledge, cultures, social circumstances, and hopes. School leadership in such circumstances means being prepared to buck the rules, challenge the status quo, and put students at the centre.

It is a salutary lesson to realize that the kind of school that is likely to be regarded as a star performer within current, mainstream educational thinking is results-oriented and successful in mandatory testing, but is likely to be, at its core, manipulative of students and essentially totalitarian in the way it produces compliance. It is the duty of school leaders and teachers to do more than merely *invite* student voice. They have a moral responsibility to *invoke* student voice — to insist upon, interrogate, and generate student voice. The important thing is to promote, and to act upon, the belief that students do have voices, opinions, and wisdom that must be respected, engaged with, and incorporated into the life of schools.

References

Ball, S.J., Davies, J., David, M., & Reay, D. (2002). 'Classification' and 'judgement': Social class and the 'cognitive structures' of choice of higher education. *British Journal of Sociology of Education, 23*(1), 51–72.

Shields, C. (2004). Dialogic leadership for social justice: Overcoming pathologies of silence. *Educational Administration Quarterly, 40*(1), 109–132.

Chapter 28

Why Is Inquiry Crucial to Educational Leadership?

Heesoon Bai

This short chapter will discuss the crucial importance of inquiry to educational leadership. At the risk of sounding dogmatic, however, only one leadership paradigm allows the exercise of inquiry: democracy. Democracy, in its pure form, is the only system of governance and social arrangement that has a philosophy not based on the top-down exercise of power. While it may recognize the wisdom of the elder and value cultural institutions of authority and expertise that hold and share knowledge and skills with the public, these elders and institutions do not dictate, let alone oppress fellow citizens. With this clarification made, then, let us examine why democratic leadership needs to be informed by inquiry and what are the obstacles to its realization.

My previous work, "What is Inquiry?" (Bai, 2005) characterizes the world as very complex, and life as full of uncertainty. Navigation through this life and this world is characterized by constant change and coping with unknowing and unknowns. While knowledge and skills may help with navigation, they are neither certain nor exact. Given this contingent nature of life and world, we have two basic approaches or attitudes available. The first way is *control and command*: set up your world so that you can tightly control it and predict what will happen. The second way is *track and follow*: move with the flow of contingency and become increasingly proficient in joining in the play of life. As a form of governance and social arrangement, democracy moves closer to the second way than the first. Leaders committed to creating and maintaining democratic culture and society need to learn the ways of tracking, following, and joining. Important dispositions and abilities for this path are curiosity, sensitivity, and care. This is the Dao of Inquiry.

Inquiry as a *modus vivendi* invites us to be *curious* and engage each other in dialogue, instead of the usual host of dazzling things we tend to do to others: mind-reading ("He must be happy"), assuming ("Since she did not respond, I will assume that she does not like me"), pre-judging ("He's got to be the guilty one"), and predicting ("He is going to fail"). Note how these things that we do, mostly unconsciously, represent a form of control that we exercise on the world: on situations and on people that we encounter. We *decide*, in our mind, what is the case, and we act based on unquestioned assumptions. We have not bothered to find out, through inquiry, what is going on — with people and with situations. But why do we not ask? "Oh, hello, what is going on there? What are you experiencing?" Instead of finding out, through inquiry, we have already decided what might, would, could, and should be the case. In fact, often the idea of asking does not even enter one's mind. We see our own projections and take them as reality.

Children are born full of curiosity, full of wonder and questions. All too frequently, however, children are told, "Curiosity kills the cat," or "It is none of your business," or "You don't need to know that," insidiously teaching them that it is not prudent or safe to be curious and to inquire. Children learn to stay out of trouble and avoid emotional hurt by not showing curiosity. They learn to do what parents, teachers, and others in positions of authority — those who know better — told them to do or to be. We need not attribute any ill motives or bad intentions to these figures of authority. In most cases, they genuinely mean well and want children to be protected, safe, and do well in the world. But the unintended consequence is creating distance and disconnection in all relational dimensions of one's being: in the self–other inter-subjective relationship and in the self-to-self intra-psychic relationship. Increasingly, we learn to say, "I won't ask; I will just figure it out myself. I do not want to ask; what will I do if I don't like or understand the answer? It is better not to ask."

Little do we know that these little conversations we have with ourselves in the service of survival and belonging build up our distrust and disrespect of others, and that we become increasingly disconnected from others. Moreover, in the process, we end up splitting ourselves and practising inner oppression of one part by the other; the original part that was all about natural curiosity is now opposed by a split-off part created by external prohibition. This is how fragmented or alienated consciousness is created.

By the time many of us become leaders in various arenas of public life, our curiosity most likely will not have won us these leadership positions. In fact, we may have gotten to our leadership position on the strength of our clear and clear-cut communication, decisiveness in judgment and action, and sure-handed control and command. Now, I am not insinuating that any of these are inherently problematic. I am all for clear communication, and I think decisiveness in some situations is definitely needed. And there might be times when I as a leader will need to take control and command. But the paucity of inquiry and lack of genuine curiosity will tell me whether genuinely democratic leadership is practiced or not. In my experience, leaders often unconsciously foment the very circumstances that justify the negation of curiosity and inquiry, and justify the very controlling and authoritarian actions that occur.

Democracy, if it is to be practiced authentically rather than procedurally, requires a culture of inquiry wherein people (*demos* in Greek) show genuine interest in each other — what they are thinking, feeling, perceiving — and regularly dialogue, consult, and deliberate together, and frequently collaborate. The source of power (*kratos* in Greek) in democracy (demos+kratos) is the mutual sharing of subjectivities (that is, being inter-subjective), attuning to and resonating with each other through empathy (Bai, 2001). Democracy means navigating the seamless flow of self–other mutuality. For democratic citizens, including leaders, self and other are not disconnected. Hence, conflict is never an end point but only a starting point that brings people together to inquire about and undertake an adventure of creative exploration and novel resolutions. Democratic leadership becomes an art of expanding circles of hospitable awareness to include and accommodate greater diversities while maintaining a sense of cohesiveness and integrity. Uniformity and conformity certainly are not the crops that grow in the garden of democracy. Corresponding to bio-diversity, democracy is a social ecosystem with diversity as a marker of resilience, strength, and long-term viability.

Inquiry is invitational, not demanding. Inquiry begins with "I wonder," not "I need to know." "I wonder" goes hand-in-hand with being relaxed, calm, friendly, and even (or, I should say, *especially*) playful. Inquiry is at home in a state of reverie, respect (etymologically, "to look again"), and even reverence. Inquiry does not take things for granted, does not write anything off, and does not explain away. Inquiry grows best in the beginner's mind. As Suzuki says, "In the beginner's mind there are many possibilities, but in the expert's there are few" (2006, p. 1).

Indeed, inquiry is a challenging practice in a culture driven by the greed for speed, worship of technology, cult of efficiency, assessment, and evaluation mania, and the orgy of production and consumption. Our actions are dominated by fear of failure, anxiety about non-conformity, survival stress, and the dire need to relieve our unbearable stress through distraction and addiction. In such a culture, inquiry seems like a luxury we cannot afford. "Don't ask; just do it" has become the *modus operandi*.

Leaders committed to democracy must work carefully and persistently to bring inquiry back into everything they do, which foremost includes reclaiming their birthright of great curiosity. Let us inquire how we may do that.

References

Bai, H. (2001). Cultivating democratic citizenship: Towards intersubjectivity. In W. Hare & J. P. Portelli (Eds.), *Philosophy of education: Introductory readings*, 3rd ed. (pp. 307–320). Calgary, AB: Detselig Enterprises Ltd.

Bai, H. (2005). What is inquiry? In W. Hare & J. Portelli (Eds.), *Key questions for educators* (pp. 45–47). Halifax, NS: EdPhil Books.

Suzuki, S. (2006). *Zen mind, beginner's mind*. Boston, MA: Shambhala Publications.

Why Is Open-Mindedness Important for Educational Leaders?

Douglas J. Simpson and D. Mike Sacken

When thinking about open-mindedness, one's mind may jump from the concept to a specific person who is largely closed-minded. That person may be bright, articulate, and well educated. Paradoxically, that person may also be inflexible, dogmatic, and stubborn. When prized topics arise, he or she is characteristically a closed-minded decision maker who frequently reaches decisions and then acts without considering pertinent alternatives openly and epistemically. The justification for this solo decision-making may include the beliefs that a) the current situation is too critical to delay a choice, b) the directives of supervisors are too sensitive to deliberate, c) the allotted timeframe does not allow input, and d) the views of existing personnel do not merit attention. Alternatively, a person may be so confident in his or her understanding of leadership complexities and change that any situation is deemed manageable alone. Consequently, the person feels warranted in enacting his or others' agenda without thoughtfully considering the views of staff and partners.

Why, then, would any aspiring or practicing educational leader want to encourage the reflective thinking of others — including colleagues, researchers, and parents — when aims, goals, pedagogies, curricula, and facilities are considered? Reasons will vary, but we want to offer six advantages of open-mindedness that may appeal to existing and aspiring educational leaders: a) personal, b) professional, c) organizational, d) structural, e) ethical, and f) educational. These advantages, of course, are usually interwoven and inseparable.

First, the personal advantages of being open-minded include the probability that a leader will become aware of ways to improve his or her personal understanding and judgments. To start, an open-minded person is more inclined to refine his abilities to understand the multiple dimensions of issues, think through controversies, and act with a comprehensive picture in mind (Baehr, 2015; Hare, 1993). From a strictly personal slant, this means that an open-minded person is unlikely to disadvantage himself by limiting his reflections to past studies and experiences and to existing habits and relationships. He is better prepared to function effectively and efficiently in current roles and responsibilities and to acquire new opportunities for growth and service.

Second, the professional consequences of open-mindedness incorporate the personal benefits while adding others, connecting all benefits to serving others. Professional service transports the leader from a largely self-interested focus to an interest in others, including students, colleagues, parents, and communities. When one commits to serving others, leadership foci evolve into deeper, broader, and stronger connections and learning experiences. Ideally, a commitment to serve others brings a self-refreshing mind and spirit and a professional passion and enthusiasm for the well-being of others. A leader should readily be enthusiastic about learning daily from multiple parties, including students, parents, counsellors, and teachers. To consider the ideas of co-partners in education willingly means analyzing their warrant and value (Hare, 2003). Moreover, open-mindedness can attract a broader spectrum of the school to learning and working with an experience-and-research-informed leader.

Third, the value of an open-minded leader in an organizational setting is immense, just as the disvalue of a closed-minded person is enormous. The downside of closed-minded leadership includes stymieing the enthusiasm, creativity, and commitment of many staff and students. Likewise, closed-minded leadership often results in the turnover of talented professionals. Conversely, gifted and highly skilled professionals thrive in environments that value, nurture, and extend their abilities and imagination. They are more likely to enjoy their interactions with students, guardians, partners, and co-workers when they sense respect and regard for them as well as their ideas and strengths. They reflexively become public relations people for their school, including the qualities of its leaders, staff, and students.

Fourth, an open-minded leader — building on her knowledge of organizations — advantages schools because she is responsive to the human dimensions of education (Dewey, 1933; Hare, 2003). That is, because she understands that the school's structure should be adaptable to the lives of children and the work of teachers, she is not dominated by an interest in efficiency but focuses on the countless and mutating needs of teachers and students. She is aware that the core challenges of schools — human development, social interactions, and personal learning — are largely unstructured, novel, and idiosyncratic. Because there is no single answer to every question of teaching and learning, she carefully evaluates multiple potential prescriptions for teachers and students. Understanding that classrooms and schools are working environments with multiple problem-defining-and-solving opportunities, she attends to the interests of students and teachers as an engaged physician listens to individual patients and their caregivers. Recognizing the layered and fragmented nature of organizational structure in terms of identity and experiences, she appreciates the fact that consensus is fragile, perceptions are distinctive, and staff are eager to help students. As an open-minded person, she avoids tempting and easy solutions as she treats school realities as complex, ambiguous, and amenable to more than one legitimate educative response.

Fifth, open-mindedness is an ethical responsibility that accompanies any inquiry into professional questions, including employment practices, fiscal allocations, curricular selections, educational evaluation, and pedagogical practices (Hare, 2003). The open-minded leader has the advantage of being committed to discovering and being influenced by the facts or data and the arguments that emerge during the process of deciding what should be done and evaluating the consequences of decisions.

Reinforcing this professional ethic is a democratic ethic that makes a broader claim: open-mindedness in inquiry is essential to a healthy democratic school and society, because learning the facts about an issue, law, policy, practice, tradition, and situation is essential to learning how to enact and sustain a fair, just, free, and caring school and society (Dewey, 1933). This means that leaders should be characterized and, fortuitously, protected by an open-mindedness to evidence and argument throughout their careers and lives, as they habitually base their judgments and actions on the best available ethical and scientific data, information, and experience. If they do not, they abandon the democratic values of personal and social inquiry and growth, including a concern for the common good.

Finally, the convergence of these educational benefits — personal, professional, organizational, structural, and ethical — means that an open-minded leader is a co-learner with other open-minded educators and colleagues in the pursuit of educating all children well. The pursuit of knowledge and practice necessary to reaching this goal is an ongoing activity. Naturally, embodying the attitudes and abilities of a well-prepared and open-minded leader does not guarantee complete success in fostering learning and in growing students and staff. In short, open-mindedness is important to educational leaders because it unlocks doors to personal and professional learning and service and, thereby, to staff and student development as inquiring members of school and external communities interested in everyone's wellbeing. Being an open-minded leader is no easy task, for it demands a disciplined pursuit of knowledge and values that are not always welcomed, either personally or institutionally.

References

Baehr, J. (2011). The inquiring mind: On intellectual virtues and virtue epistemology. Oxford: Oxford University Press.

Dewey, J. (1933). How we think: A restatement of the reflective thinking to the educative process. Rev. ed. Boston: Heath.

Hare, W. (1993). Open-mindedness and education. Montreal: McGill-Queen's University Press.

Hare, W. (2003). The ideal of open-mindedness and its place in education. Journal of Thought, 38, 2, 3–10.

How Are Educational Leadership and Deficit Thinking Connected?

Kristin Shawn Huggins

According to Valencia, deficit thinking is conceived as the belief "that the student who fails in school does so because of his/her internal deficits or deficiencies. Such deficits manifest, adherents allege, in limited intellectual abilities, limited shortcomings, lack of motivation to learn, and immoral behavior" (2010, pp. 6–7). Therefore, deficit thinking is the kind of thinking that determines a student is incapable of educational success because of the student's deficiencies. This kind of thinking is based upon the belief that student educational success is solely determined by student factors and not at all by educational institutional factors. Historically, deficit thinking has been seen as most prevalent among students of colour and students from low-income homes, with the blame often attributed to the students and their families (Valencia, 2010). However, blaming students and their families for a lack of student achievement ignores the institutional factors that may be linked to student educational success (e.g., Chambers & Huggins, 2014).

Within educational institutions, educational leadership is potentially connected to deficit thinking through the beliefs of educational leaders. Educational leaders must believe their role is to ensure all students, regardless of differences, have the opportunity to learn and be educationally successful. Even further, all educational leaders must not only utter the belief that "all children can learn" but also enact structures and processes to support that belief. Unfortunately, this is often not what occurs. Educational leaders frequently create, or more often, fail to question already-in-place structures and processes within their institutional settings that provide a "description-explanation-prediction-prescription" cycle for students (Valencia, 1997). Skrla and Scheurich (2001) explain this cycle:

> ... first, educators *describe* deficits, deficiencies, limitations, and shortcomings in children of colour and children from low-income homes; next educators *explain* these deficits by locating them in such factors as limited intelligence or dysfunctional families; then, educators *predict* the perpetuation and accumulation of the deficits; and finally, educators *prescribe* educational interventions designed to remediate the deficits. (p. 236)

Once students are seen as being in this cycle, the cycle self-perpetuates. These students then struggle to leave the cycle, while educators fail to see how they have created the cycle. Indeed, despite increasing numbers of children being identified by some form of at-risk label (e.g., poverty, single-parent homes, home language other than English, minority culture), many schools do not look at issues of disparity or discrepancies in achievement from a critical perspective, opting instead for programs already proven to be ineffective in altering inequities (Sheilds, Bishop, & Mazawi, 2005, pp. 3–4).

Yet, educational leaders are in positions to consider and change the structures and processes by bringing a critical lens to those structures and processes. For example, growing evidence exists of school-level educational leaders (Theoharis, 2009) and district-level educational leaders (Skrla & Scheurich, 2001) who have engaged in processes and practices that have been successful in increasing the achievement of students of colour and students from low-income homes, thus debunking the deficit notions that students with certain differences cannot be academically successful. In fact, strategies have been created for educational leaders to consider the ways in which their processes and practices may be prohibiting students of colour and students from low-income homes from achieving academic success. One of those strategies is to conduct a district-level or school-level equity audit (Skrla, McKenzie, & Scheurich, 2009), which includes seven steps:

Step 1: Create a committee of relevant stakeholders.
Step 2: Present the data to the committee and have everyone graph the data.
Step 3: Discuss the meaning of the data; possibly use experts or a facilitator.
Step 4: Discuss potential solutions, again possibly with outside assistance.
Step 5: Implement solution(s).
Step 6: Monitor and evaluate results.
Step 7: Celebrate if successful; if not successful, return to Step 3 and repeat process. (pp. 26–27)

Conducting an equity audit allows districts to see where disparities in achievement exist and create a process to address those disparities. However, it cannot be stressed enough that through engaging in this process, educational leaders must continuously believe that they have the power to increase educational achievement for all students. This may require returning to Step 3 repeatedly until a solution that creates success can be implemented.

While conducting an equity audit provides a process with which to address disparities, having educators engage in the process is not enough to eliminate deficit thinking. Within any educational setting, some people will struggle to believe that they can create processes and practices to ensure that all students will be provided with the opportunities to learn in order to be academically successful. In contrast, to build equitable schools, educational leaders must believe this. In their quest to help other stakeholders (e.g., teachers) eliminate deficit thinking, certain experiences may facilitate a change in beliefs.

McKenzie and Scheurich (2004) suggest three possible experiences for addressing deficit thinking; neighbourhood walks, oral histories, and three-way conferencing. Neighbourhood walks occur when teachers go from student home to student home, knocking on doors and meeting parents. Through these engagements, teachers are able to connect with parents in their own communities, which can provide a better understanding of students' home lives and their parents' concerns for their child's education. Oral histories involve students interviewing community members. Students can capture these oral histories through video or audio recording, presenting them to others in the school in order to provide a more inclusive picture of the surrounding community. Three-way conferencing occurs when the student, the student's family member, and the student's teacher are all involved in discussing the student's academic progress. Through these conferences, all participants gain a greater understanding of the supports needed at home and school for the student to be academically successful. These strategies provide a broader spectrum of understanding student home culture and academic needs for educators, which helps to eliminate deficit-based assumptions about students.

In contrast to deficit thinking is assets-based thinking. Educational leaders must create the structures and processes that provide for learning by assets-based processes and practices. The foundation for all of this must be the unshakable belief that all children can learn. That is, educational leaders should seek to not only eliminate deficit thinking, but also to create thinking that values the assets or "funds of knowledge" that students from various cultures bring to school with them (Moll, Amanti, Neff, & Gonzalez, 1992). Through engaging more closely with communities of difference, educators can expand their understanding of the cultures of those communities, of the resources students from those communities bring to schooling, and of the ways those resources may be used as leverage in creating opportunities for learning and academic success. Therefore, deficit thinking, while pervasive, should not be the status quo, not only because it is incredibly detrimental but also because it fails to capitalize on student resources (Theoharis, 2007).

References

Chambers, T. T. V., & Huggins, K. S. (2014). The influence of school factors on *racial opportunity cost* for high-achieving students of color. *Journal of School Leadership, 24*(1), 191–225.

McKenzie, K. B., & Scheurich, J. J. (2004). Equity traps: A useful construct for preparing principals to lead schools that are successful with racially diverse students. *Educational Administration Quarterly, 40*(5), 601–632. doi: 10.1177/0013161X04268839

Moll, L. C., Amanti, C., Neff, D., & Gonzalez, N. (1992). Funds of knowledge for teaching: Using a qualitative approach to connect homes and classrooms, *Theory into Practice, 31*(2), 132–141.

Sheilds, C. M., Bishop, R., & Mazawi, A. E. (2005). *Pathologizing practices: The impact of deficit thinking on education.* New York: Peter Lang.

Skrla, L., McKenzie, K. B., & Scheurich, J. J. (2009). *Using equity audits to create equitable and excellent schools.* Thousand Oaks, CA: Corwin Press.

Skrla, L., & Scheurich, J. J. (2001). Displacing deficit thinking in school district leadership. *Education and Urban Society, 33*(3), 235–259. doi: 10.1177/0013124501333002

Theoharis, G. (2007). Navigating rough waters: A synthesis of the countervailing pressures against leading for social justice. *Journal of School Leadership, 17*(1), 4–27.

Theoharis, G. (2009). *The school leaders our children deserve: Seven keys to equity, social justice, and school reform.* New York: Teachers College Press.

Valencia, R. R. (1997). *The evolution of deficit thinking: Educational thought and practice.* Bristol, PA: Falmer Press.

Valencia, R. R. (2010). *Dismantling contemporary deficit thinking: Educational thought and practice.* New York: Taylor & Francis.

Chapter 31

How Do Educational Leadership and Leadership Development Impact Student Achievement?

Scott Lowrey

How do educational leadership and leadership development impact student achievement? The arguments in this chapter represent a synthesis of my experience as an elementary school principal, continuous engagement with *Canada's Outstanding Principals Academy* beginning 2005, and my own doctoral research. The ideas that follow are based on the following beliefs:

1. The leadership that influences publicly funded education is foundational to the health of a democratic society
2. School systems exist for schools, not vice versa
3. The moral imperative of improving student achievement is best done at the school level by dedicated principals working with talented teachers
4. The primary goal of principal leadership is to realize collective community efficacy

Experience, Knowledge, and Understanding

Leading schools is complex work in times of constant change. Studies indicate that educational leadership is essential to student achievement (Waters, Marzano, & McNulty, 2003), and principals are second only to classroom teachers in impact on student achievement (Leithwood & Louis, 2012). Leithwood, Day, Sammons, Harris, & Hopkins (2006) state, "As far as we are aware, there is not a single documented case of a school successfully turning around its pupil achievement trajectories in the absence of talented leadership." Educational leadership matters to student achievement; it must be intentionally fostered, not assumed. Moreover, researchers stress that leadership development must be simultaneously embedded in individual and organizational contexts (e.g., Avolio & Hannah, 2008; Fullan 2010).

Bolman and Deal (2003) emphasize that leadership is always situated in both context and relationships. The complexity of demands faced by principals is, in part, a function of serving many constituencies and stakeholders each having a variety of needs. Moreover, principals must balance values and ethics in diverse community settings. Leadership development must be responsive to complex contexts while meeting the developmental needs of principals.

Stewart (2006) stresses that principals must balance input from several, often competing stakeholders while working in complex leadership contexts. Hallinger (2003) cautions that principal authority is challenged when their role is partially defined by meeting the expectations of those both above them and below them in the hierarchy. Consequently, Riehl (2007) asserts that no single form of leadership will likely be effective in all contexts.

Foundationally, the purpose of educational leadership development is to influence student achievement positively. Recognizing that the influence of educational leadership on student achievement is indirect, leadership development experiences provide principals with the capacity to leverage mediating variables. Although leadership is context specific, principals with a larger inventory of leadership strategies, transfer leadership skills to, and from, different contexts. This repertoire represents a balance between continuous job-embedded learning where educational leaders seek precision while navigating personalized problems of practice, multi-year commitment to, and engagement with leadership development programs.

Educational Leadership Development

Waters et al. (2003) explain that McREL's *Balanced Leadership Framework* was derived from a meta-analysis that identified 21 research-based leadership responsibilities (e.g., situational awareness, intellectual stimulation, and change agent) and associated practices, and a knowledge taxonomy (i.e., experiential, declarative, procedural, and contextual). Each of these leadership responsibilities was significantly correlated with student achievement. The impact of leadership on student achievement can be either positive or negative based on the focus of change (e.g., school and classroom practices) and order of change (i.e., first order change versus second order change). The focus of change would be the mediating variable between principal leadership and student achievement. For example, principals who effectively build staff capacity in the area of effective feedback (mediating variable) have a positive, indirect influence on student achievement.

Leithwood, Louis, Anderson, & Wahlstrom (2004) studied how leadership influenced student learning. This document identified core transformational leadership practices as foundational to successful leadership while recognizing that successful leaders draw from their acquired leadership repertoire and leadership experiences. Since leadership is context specific, broader and deeper repertoires enable leaders to navigate new or non-routine leadership challenges effectively. Educational leaders can influence student learning positively by focusing on mediating variables such as developing a positive school culture, implementing collaborative decision-making models with teachers, and fostering positive parental involvement.

Instructional leadership remains a critical element of leadership development. However, instructional leadership cannot be pursued in isolation. Transformational leadership practices such as *building relationships* and *developing people* must be integrated with instructional leadership behaviours to influence student achievement. One colleague offers the opinion that some less than successful leaders, while perhaps having strong expertise in instructional leadership lacked broader knowledge of leadership theory. Both instructional leadership expertise and a foundational understanding of leadership and change are necessary to influence student achievement. In the absence of solid understanding of leadership theory, less successful education leaders may struggle regardless of expertise in other areas, especially in times of dynamic change.

The Wallace Foundation (2008) concludes that traditional educational leadership development programs are out of touch with current realities, especially given the leadership context of constant change. One remedy the Wallace Foundation offered was to incorporate coaching and mentoring opportunities as one critical element of ongoing, job-embedded leadership development. In terms of career stage and trajectory, the current reality for principals differs even within the same school district. The alignment between current realities and leadership development experiences, be they formal or informal, and leadership contexts, requires flexibility and differentiation. Leadership development approaches can be either mandated by school districts, self-selected by school principals, or a combination of both. Influential leadership development experiences of principals at various career stages and trajectories are unique to each individual.

Systems become impediments to building educational leadership capacity when mandating undifferentiated leadership development initiatives that maintain the status quo. Leadership context, articulated at the district level, often precludes principals from applying, or developing, integrative and critical thinking skills to school-based decisions to understanding student achievement. Maintenance of system status quo is an impediment to improving student achievement; systems exist for schools, not vice versa.

Since schools exist within communities, non-educational leadership wisdom relating to what effective leadership is may enhance educational leadership, and vice versa. One theme that emerged during my doctoral research was that well-designed leadership development programs integrate leadership practices from across sectors. Collective community leadership wisdom can then be applied so that our schools can boost student achievement. Over and above an existing skill set, well-designed leadership development programs integrate leadership practices from across sectors.

Conclusion

Educational leadership and leadership development impact student achievement in the following ways:

1. Principal leadership actions, mediated by something, are driven by commitment to improving student achievement
2. Trust of a community transcends and precedes a principal's instructional leadership
3. Leadership lessons from non-educational contexts are important
4. Purposeful integration of theory and practice must focus on student achievement
5. Leadership development is grounded in context, but context is a layered concept

In other words, educational leadership matters to student achievement; it must be intentionally fostered, not prescribed.

References

Avolio, B.J., & Hannah, S.T. (2008). Developmental readiness: Accelerating leader development. *Consulting Psychology Journal: Practice and Research, 60*(4), 331–347.

Bolman, L.G., & Deal, T.E. (2003). *Reframing organizations: Artistry, choice, and leadership* (3rd ed.). San Francisco, CA: Jossey-Bass.

Fullan, M. (2010). *All systems go: The change imperative for whole system reform.* Thousand Oaks, CA: Corwin Press.

Hallinger, P. (2003). Leading educational change: Reflections on the practice of instructional and transformational leadership. *Cambridge Journal of Education, 33*(3), 229–251.

Leithwood, K., Day, C., Sammons, P., Harris, A., & Hopkins, D. (2006). *Seven strong claims about successful leadership.* London: DfES.

Leithwood, K., & Louis, K.S. (2012). *Linking leadership to student learning.* San Francisco, CA: Jossey-Bass.

Leithwood, K., Louis, K.S., Anderson, S., & Wahlstrom, K. (2004). *How leadership influences pupil learning: A review of research for the Learning from Leadership Project.* New York: The Wallace Foundation.

Riehl, C. (2007). Research on educational leadership: Knowledge we need for the world we live in. In F. English & G. Furman (Eds.), *Research and Educational Leadership: Navigating the New National Research Council Guidelines* (pp. 133–168). Lanham, MD: Rowman & Littlefield.

Stewart, J. (2006). Transformational leadership: An evolving concept examined through the works of Burns, Bass, Avolio, and Leithwood. *Canadian Journal of Educational Administration and Policy, 54*, 1–28.

Wallace Foundation (2008). *Mission of the heart: what does it take to transform a school?* New York, NY: Public Agenda.

Waters, T., Marzano, R.J., & McNulty, B. (2003). *Balanced leadership: What 30 years of research tells us about the effect of leadership on student achievement.* Aurora, CO: Mid-continent Research for Education and Learning (McREL).

Chapter 32

What Should Educational Leadership Programs Look Like?

Darrin Griffiths

...if a school does not stand for something more profound than raising achievement levels, then it probably does not make a memorable difference to teachers, students, or parents. Put on a spiritual plan, a school needs a deeper soul.
(Deal & Peterson 2009, p. 62)

Educational leadership programs either as on-going learning or as a requirement to become an administrator in a school are critically important to school improvement. Before outlining the components I believe should be included, first I focus on the purposes of the education and their connection to leadership.

Our basis of moving forward with any type of action or focus should rest on our views about the purposes of education. My view is that education rests on four central and interrelated tenets:

- Students should be considered as ends-in-themselves
- Students are able to understand and shape their world
- Goals of education should be holistic
- All students should be included in or feel that they belong in school (Griffiths, 2013, p. 7)

I understand the purpose of education to be guided by the principle of seeing students as ends-in-themselves and not as means to an end. The end needs to take into account the personal, social, moral, and intellectual development of the individual. The primary purpose of education should be to prepare students to understand, shape, and challenge the world (Smith et al., 1998; Freire, 2000). In other words, students should gain a better understanding of how the world is and how to modify or change it, making it possible for all students (including those from diverse backgrounds) to be democratically included in the school (p. 19). Such a purpose of education goes beyond the popular belief that schools should focus on reading, writing, numeracy, and subject-specific curriculum. Students need to be partners in creating the curriculum (Portelli & Vibert, 2002).

Numeracy and literacy are vital components of education, but equally important are students' abilities to critically understand and change the world, which Freire refers to as "reading the world" and not just the word (Banks, 2004; Freire, 2000). Bertrand Russell discussed a "humanistic conception of education" that would provide the soil, the encouragement, and the freedom for the student to grow; the student would not be destined for a particular calling or vocation until that "seed" began to grow (quoted in Chomsky, 2003, p. 164).

These views of education extend much further than simply producing workers for the capitalist system: students are not reduced to passive pawns in a game where the result (meaning their life choices) has already been determined. Students are not merely able to analyze the world critically, but have the will and confidence to change it — not passive recipients, but active and thinking agents who believe that they can shape their world. In this sense, all students have opportunities to understand the biases and prejudices (at both individual and systemic levels) that oppress some and support others. Borrowing from Russell, this view also includes all students having opportunities in schools to develop their talents, whatever they may be. The question then becomes, "What sort of educational leadership is necessary to reach these aims?"

Equity and educational leadership are intricately connected such that educational leadership has no meaning or purpose without it being directly aligned with broad and robust conceptions of equity. Educational leadership must address the inequities and injustices found in the greater society; through education, these issues can be identified and resisted. That is, those in school leadership have the obligation to work together with educators, parents, guardians, community participants, and students to address and challenge racism, classism, sexism, homophobia, deficit modes of thinking, and other issues.

Educational leadership then, involves leading toward a more equitable future for all students and involves examination, change, and challenge to whatever system is in place. The status quo is always unacceptable if it is inequitable for any individual or group.

In the last few decades, leadership in education has been dominated by positivist, management-type discourses emphasizing efficiency, control, and standardization, which support the reproduction of white, patriarchal, capitalist culture (Dantley, 2002; 2003). Moreover, traditional leadership theories glorify the charismatic leader who uses his/her positional power and character traits to demand and encourage staff to follow. These theories, however, rely more on management skills and traits than on leadership (Marshall, 2004). Many of these traditional approaches can be characterized as "functionalist" in that the administrator's role is to lead and ensure the efficiency and effectiveness of the organization (Watkins, 1989, p. 9). These traditional leadership beliefs and practices not only ignore issues of equity but further cement practices that place the blame for how students fare in schools strictly on the students, their families, and their communities.

Social justice leadership moves away from these traditional leadership practices and is part of the "equity leadership" family in seeking to address such issues as racism, sexism, homophobia, and classism and how they impact students and their families (Larson & Murtadha, 2002; Shields, 2004; Marshall, 2004; Cambron-McCabe & McCarthy, 2005; Lugg & Shoho, 2006; Ryan 2006. Educational leadership must act explicitly and directly to eliminate all forms of exclusionary practice and ideologies. Moreover, the leadership must be educative so that all participants develop at least a nascent understanding of critical consciousness.

As a white, heterosexual, middle-class male, I had no idea about my privilege or how it provided a "passport" in society. It took until my late twenties, when I was teaching in urban schools, for me to reflect on why notions of meritocracy were simply flawed and ignorant of the socially constructed biases found in schools. I finally began to develop critical consciousness about how the world operates. That teaching experience also ignited a passion for me to learn about critical theory and how it connects to the socially constructed world. I wonder, however, what would have happened had I not had those experiences that contradicted the dominant culture? Likely, I would still be a school leader, but one who believed that if surface-level notions of equity (based solely on student achievement data) were addressed, then I was an equity-minded educational leader.

With that in mind, I can now succinctly answer the question at hand. Educational leadership programs must have at their core the curriculum to move participants towards critically understanding the world; how some individuals and groups are disadvantaged while others are not, including ways to overcome such inequities. Such awareness cannot and should not be left to chance. Developing this critical consciousness must be infused in all leadership preparation programs, system or district mandated learning, and leadership selection processes. Educational leadership without targeted, directed, intentional foci on equitable support for all students is not leadership at all and has no place in education. Of course, much of my day as a practising school administrator is filled with completing managerial tasks, dealing with staffing and budgeting issues, ensuring policies are followed, scheduling, evaluating teaching practice, mediating and resolving conflicts, and interpreting system directives. And all of these aspects must be included in any educational leadership program. However, based on my professional work and experience, I believe that such aspects need to be directed by the robust equity perspective, as detailed in my book *Principals of inclusion*.

References

Banks, J.A. (2004). Teaching for social justice, diversity, and citizenship in a global world. *The Educational Forum, 68*(4), 289–298.

Cambron-McCabe, N., & McCarthy, M. (2005). Educating leaders for social justice. *Educational Policy, 19*(1), 201–222.

Chomsky, N. (2003). *Chomsky on democracy & education.* Edited by C.P. Otero. New York: RoutledgeFalmer.

Dantley, M.E. (2003). Purpose-driven leadership: The spiritual imperative to guiding schools beyond high-stakes testing and minimum proficiency. *Education and Urban Society, 35*(3), 273–291.

Dantley, M.E. (2002). Uprooting and replacing positivism, the melting pot, multiculturalism, and other impotent notions in educational leadership through an African American perspective. *Education and Urban Society, 34*(3), 334–352.

Deal, T., & Peterson, K. (2009). *Shaping school culture: Pitfalls, paradoxes, & promises.* San Francisco, CA: Jossey Bass.

Freire, P. (2000). *Pedagogy of the oppressed.* New York: Continuum.

Griffiths, D. (2013). *Principals of inclusion: Practical strategies to grow inclusion in urban schools.* Burlington, Ontario: Word & Deed Publishing Incorporated and Edphil Books.

Larson, C.L., & Murtadha, K. (2002). Leadership for social justice. In J. Murphy (Ed.), *The educational leadership challenge: Redefining leadership for the 21st century* (pp. 134–161). Chicago: University of Chicago Press.

Lugg, C.A., & Shoho, A.R. (2006). Dare public school administrators build a new social order? Social justice and the possible perilous politics of educational leadership. *Journal of educational administration, 44*(3), 196–208.

Marshall, C. (2004). Social justice challenges to educational administration: Introduction to a special issue. *Educational Administration Quarterly 40*(2), 3–13.

Portelli, J.P., Solomon, R.P. (2001). Introduction. In J.P. Portelli & R.P. Solomon (Eds.), *The erosion of democracy of education: From critique to possibilities* (pp. 15–27). Calgary, AB: Detselig Enterprises Ltd.

Portelli, J.P., & Vibert, A. (2002). A curriculum of life. *Education Canada, 42*(2), 36–39.

Ryan, J. (2006). Inclusive leadership and social justice for schools. *Leadership and Policy in Schools, 5*(1), 3–15.

Shields, C.M. (2004). Dialogic leadership for social justice: Overcoming pathologies of silence. *Educational Administration Quarterly, 40*(1), 109–132.

Smith. (1998). In J.P. Portelli & R.P. Solomon (Eds.), *The erosion of democracy of education: From critique to possibilities* (pp. XX–XX). Calgary, AB: Detselig Enterprises Ltd.

Watkins, P. (1989). Leadership, power and symbols in educational administration. In J. Murphy (Ed.), *Critical perspectives on leadership* (pp. 9–38). New York: RoutledgeFalmer.

Part IV
What Is Student Achievement?

What Is Student Achievement?

Carolyn M. Shields

Although all students must master curricular areas and attain high levels of literacy and numeracy, the measure of academic success is not test scores, but rather the ability to construct a clear, cogent argument, to understand and critique complex material, to manipulate mathematical and scientific concepts in real-life contexts, to solve problems, and to communicate persuasively. Moreover, in a world in which change is constant, students must demonstrate an ability to work within volatile, uncertain, changing, and ambiguous contexts. Being able to understand that reality is rarely black or white, that there are usually legitimate, alternate responses is one mark of an educated person. Acknowledging that privilege and advantage are socially constructed, identifying responsibility for less advantaged global neighbours, and recognizing our duty to protect the world-wide ecology are essential components of achievement. Thus, the measure of student achievement is whether each individual has developed the knowledge and skills to open doors to future opportunities and the fulfilment of dreams, to the benefit both of oneself and of society as a whole. Achievement implies real growth — moving beyond the opportunities with which we have been born to acquire new knowledge and skills, to seek new vistas, and to develop critical yet empathic understanding of perspectives yet unexplored.

What Is Student Achievement?

William Ayers

I f education is a commodity like a refrigerator, and if schools are businesses run by CEOs with teachers as assembly-line workers and students as the raw materials bumping along the factory floor as information is stuffed into their little up-turned heads, it is easy to suppose that "student achievement" can be apprehended from a simple standardized metric applied by relentless state-administered (and privately developed and wildly profitable) tests that sort student winners from losers.

But if learning and living are essentially the same thing, — if one lives, one learns; when one is learning, one is living — if the starting point is the child's inherent desire to make sense and become competent in the social world, then "student achievement" is another matter altogether. Children learn to nurse and then eat, babble and then talk, scoot and then walk — innate, natural, self-directed, authentic, discursive, vital, multi-dimensional, self-fulfilling, and accelerating — and achievement is simply part of life. If collaborative participation in the community — inquiry, maintenance, construction, projects, performances, exhibitions — is the standard, learning is no longer a bitter pill to be forced upon the young in preparation for future life; education is understood to be the dynamic process of living life itself.

What Is Student Achievement?

S*tudent achievement* has been at the centre of educational and political discussions for centuries. However, what seems missing in these discussions is the critical examination of important questions, such as *Student achievement, whose definition? Achieving what?* Often, what students achieve in school does not seem to be appreciated and valued by school personnel, including teachers, particularly if their achievement does not fit the norm; that is, meeting the expectations of the school status quo. Even those labelled "deviant" or "rebellious" achieve at school but this is often overlooked, and is not part of the dominant narrative about student achievement. Therefore, our analysis of student achievement will be limited if we do not consider this factor. Other factors, such as uneven distribution of resources among schools, also need to be accounted for in our analysis.

Why some students achieve in schools — that is, meeting the school benchmark and expectations by obtaining good grades and successfully graduating — while others do not? Privileged students who attend private schools often become successful academically, intellectually, professionally, and economically. By contrast, poor kids who go to underfunded schools with overcrowded classrooms led by underpaid teachers tend to perform poorly academically. This category of students is often denied opportunities that could have helped them fulfill their potential and become as successful as their privileged counterparts. Hence, the definition of *student achievement* needs to be situated in the specific educational, socio-economic, and political context.

What Is Student Achievement?

John Roberts

Aboriginal students must connect to their heritage in order to overcome feelings of isolation and low self-esteem. Outside of the mastering the traditional curriculum for all students, Aboriginal students have the additional responsibility of learning the Four Directions teachings as they relate to Indigenous knowledge and philosophy, understanding the connections between student responsibility and the environment, and appreciating the role that Aboriginal literature, art, music, and dance play in the Aboriginal worldview.

Physical statistics are but one way to assess Aboriginal student achievement. According to Statistics Canada, almost half of Canada's Aboriginal population over age 25 has a post-secondary qualification. This is often seen as "good enough" or "better than before," but it is not nearly good enough, since almost 30 percent of the Aboriginal population has no post-secondary qualification, compared to 12 percent of the non-Aboriginal population. In addition, nearly 40 percent of Aboriginal Canadians have not finished high school (161).

Having said this, the measure of Aboriginal student achievement must take into account factors other than mere comparison with non-Aboriginal education. The Canadian Council on Learning states that Aboriginal learning and achievement is life-long and holistic, is found in many different sources, and is rooted in Aboriginal languages and culture. This may be the true measure of student achievement.

Chapter 33

What Are the Fundamental Tensions in Educational Leadership between Tests and Curiosity?

Lejf Moos

C ontemporary societies are becoming ever more complex and governing them is a challenging endeavour. Therefore it is not surprising that politicians have many and often contradictory demands on institutions and their staff. Transnational agencies like the Organisation for Economic Co-operation and Development (OECD) and the European Commission (EC), for example, agree on the need for standardized data on societal progress, including education, in order to be able to govern societies. At the same time, they point to the need to develop innovation in all sectors of society in order to survive global competition. At first glance, those two demands do not conflict with each other. Nevertheless, in terms of education, they may well do exactly that, because now we need to include a third element in the equation: children. At this stage, children, on the one hand, are subject to frequent standardized testing and, on the other, to demands for innovation and creativity.

Multiple analyses have shown that testing is changing the ways that educational systems, schools, and teachers conceive and practise teaching. Tests may make teachers think and act more narrowly or distort curriculum; issues of content may be vulgarized when the focus is placed on facts and instrumental skills and not on problem-based learning and creativity. Political posturing on the need to get back to basics like reading and writing underscores a tendency to teach to the test since teachers want to support their students in performing well in the national league tables.

When the core emphasis in schooling shifts from the learning processes itself to the outcomes of learning, as measured by tests and the like, there is a risk that teachers will adapt their teaching to the ways the tests are constructed. As most standardized tests evaluate skills and knowledge that can be reproduced on command, there is a tendency for teachers to try to "hand over" the information to students, leaving little room and time for creativity, curiosity, testing ideas in practice, experimenting, and self-reflection. Creativity can be defined as a combination of cognitive-social processes and personal competencies, defined as the ability to think outside the box and conceive new ideas, methods, materials, products, and actions.

But often we see that the basics of learning are forgotten: the urge to explore, reflect on, and manage the outer world; relations to other people and ideas; a student's own place and position within those relations and in this world. Students want to learn if learning serves this urge to satisfy their curiosity and put their knowledge into perspective and into practice.

Curiosity is the most pivotal grounding and source of developing pupil competency and thus, in the long run, of societal development. Teachers and schools can expand this natural curiosity by feeding into the processes, by pointing out new targets to focus on, and by nourishing new reflections and investigations. This demands experimentation, testing new knowledge and perspectives, and building on already known understandings, thus pushing students into new and creative investigations of how "things are" versus how they "could be." By letting them find their own place in the midst of all those things, processes, ideas, and features, they find themselves.

The basis for creativity is a critique of the existing state of affairs — asking "what if?" Education should be based on both practical and experimental educational theory that makes room for mistakes, criticism, reflection, deliberation, and collaboration. Innovation involves the creation of new knowledge or new combinations of old insights. It is the result of interaction between people with diverse talents, interests, insights, and experiences in open communication: generalized trust and participatory democracy contribute to creativity.

Unfortunately, creativity is often endangered by prescriptive accountability systems and technologies that monitor and measure student learning: testing the occurrence of specific, prescribed bits of knowledge, for example, is often seen in multiple-choice tests. Those tests would not be worth worrying about except for the fact that they entail specific ways of teaching and of thinking about learning: teachers tend to teach to the test, forcing students to focus only on knowledge that is easily measured. If the system builds only on a detailed, fixed curriculum, it cannot support creativity and innovation. Instead, we shall doubtless see student curiosity dwindling, experimentation declining, and innovation drying up. Innovation confined to measurable outcomes is not innovation at all.

This may be one of the biggest paradoxes of our time: we build educational systems that outline everything that students need to acquire, but any line that cannot be crossed makes it difficult for students to learn. They may acquire old knowledge, but never develop new, critical insights. An approach that fosters creativity and innovation would be to encourage students to construct their own learning through activities based on curiosity, and supported and encouraged by teachers. The effects, however, would be difficult to measure. Schools, therefore, must develop a different accountability logic: the professional accountability trend. Professional standards and ethics are developed in an on-going interplay between the education and experiences of teachers with cultural and political expectations. In some instances, we see strong teacher influence on that interplay, while in others the political and cultural influence is stronger. Presently, it seems that teachers are losing influence, with policy and management taking over and altering classroom practice.

The most important leadership function in schools can be summed up in this way: *educational leadership is about negotiating directions that make sense to professional educators.* Even though schools are forced politically to focus on outcomes (standards, inspections, and tests), schools themselves must find their own ways to achieve these outcomes. They must interpret demands and signals from the outer world and choose the means to respond in reciprocal interactions between all agents. This may diminish the negative effects of accountability regimes while keeping the focus on students, their motivations, their learning needs, and their curiosity.

Chapter 34

How Can Educational Leadership Support Student Engagement?

John P. Portelli

The relationship between educational leadership and student engagement varies according to how one conceives of both rather elusive concepts and their ensuing practices. While student engagement is deemed self-evidently acceptable, for no one would want to argue for disengagement, the existence of educational leadership is more controversial; some have argued that the idea of a select few whose role is to direct (control) the rest is necessarily very undemocratic. However, if leadership is seen as a function shared by many who can assume different but equally valuable responsibilities, then the charge of being necessarily undemocratic is diminished greatly, especially if the relationships between the members of an organization are based on equity, diversity, inclusivity, and social justice rather than a one-size fits all perspective.

There is a "family of concepts" that can be readily associated with engagement and another usually contrasted with it. For example, while terms such as *connections, connectedness, relations, commitment, promise, closeness, belonging, involvement, inspired, interested, motivated, attachment, integration, concentration and effort, ownership, empowerment, authenticity* and *responsibility* remind us of some aspect of engagement, terms such as *alienation, isolation, separation, detachment, fragmentation,* and *boredom* are associated with a lack of engagement or even disengagement. The terms associated with engagement relate to educational aims; the terms associated with disengagement relate to mis-educative aims. Hence the challenge for educational leadership is to create a context for and possibilities for meaningful engagement to flourish for both students and teachers. Unfortunately, very often, unwittingly and unconsciously, those in positions of leadership promote actions that create disengagement with educative learning and with life itself — a situation at the core of push outs (rather than dropouts), the reproduction of inequities, and the marginalization of those that do not fit with the mainstream way of life.

The logical question that arises is this: How can educational leadership support student and teacher engagement? There are different ways that educational leadership can support the engagement of students and teachers in schools. While these vary depending on the qualities and needs of the particular context, we know several things from research that educational leadership can promote and avoid.

First, it is crucial to understand the changing and contextual nature of engagement; it is not fixed and monolithic. Engagement is not always physically visible. While active physical participation may be an expression of meaningful engagement, we need to avoid the behaviourist fallacy that unless one is physically active then one is not engaged. Many other forms of engagement (e.g., emotional, psychological, moral, spiritual, conceptual) are not always empirically discernible. Second, engagement takes time to develop; it requires patience and perseverance, especially when one is trying to go against the grain for the benefit of students. It involves a certain kind of relationship with peers, texts, educators, and community members that implies some hope, commitment, and possibilities; it is co-constructed and developed over time. Above all, no one quick-fix formula will somehow magically create engagement in all contexts and at all times.

Research on student engagement has resulted in some informative data. For example, meaningful student engagement is enhanced by helping students construct positive self-images, ensuring positive and appropriate constructions of students by educators, teachers exhibiting willingness to communicate humanely and fairly with students and caring about them as persons, and developing democratic communities in schools. Conversely, having low academic expectations of students, adopting a deficit mentality, and turning schools into bureaucratic institutions contribute to student disengagement. When students as learners are conceived of as having nothing to contribute to the learning and teaching process, and when students' life conditions, thoughts, feelings, and experiences are deemed irrelevant to their education, then we would be reproducing a deficit mentality that kills any hope or critical ability, so crucial to a genuine education. Moreover, when we assume that all student needs are identical, that they all learn in the same manner, and that there ought to be one curriculum standardized for all, we would be reproducing the one-size-fits-all mentality, which is ultimately colonial and imperialist by its very nature.

Much of the boredom and lack of engagement on the part of students, and often as well on the part of teachers, arises from the fact that a so-called education lacks life and interest — that is, a truly and genuine connection with "being" as the etymology of the term reminds us: "inter" (among, between) and "est" (to be). From this perspective, it becomes crucial to look at life *as* a form of education: education as life, life in education, an education that honours life.

If we truly believe in the democratic values of openness (neither closed-mindedness, nor empty-mindedness, nor an anything-goes mentality), dialogue, equity (not simply equality of opportunity or sameness), critical thinking, creativity and imagination, community and social justice, then we cannot perpetuate a deficit mentality or a one-size-fits-all mentality. Neither should we be fragmenting the educational experience to achieve the bureaucratic aims of an institution that literally kills engagement and creates boredom.

Indeed, even today, in the second decade of the twenty-first century, we have not fully understood that there must be an intricate connection between education and life. An education that is truly worthy of its name takes life seriously, not only at the elementary and secondary education levels but also in all the stages, including higher education. Life, with its complexities, joys, sorrows, doubts, questions, failures, and possibilities, has to be the centre of learning in all of education. Without life and interest, an education becomes formal, fragmented, disconnected, boring, lifeless, and purely mechanical. The responsibility of educators at all levels is to engage students in life and in the different ways it can be perceived throughout the subjects or disciplines. Focusing on life is not a waste of time; it involves genuine engagement that is promising, future oriented, holistic, and ongoing. Without engaging in life as education and education as life, we shall continue to create push outs — a task neither educative nor democratic.

Chavez and O'Donnell argue that engagement entails that students and educators "do not accept the status quo and begin to unconsciously transform themselves to understand the status quo and place themselves into a location for liberatory action based on a praxis of social justice" (1998, p. 2). This is not easy; it requires courage, honesty, integrity, and stamina. Building on the work of Freire (1998) and hooks (1994), Portelli and Vibert's empirical research has shown that the practice of a curriculum of life is possible and that it takes different forms: "Grounded in the immediate daily worlds of students as well as in the larger social and political contexts of their lives, curriculum of life breaks down the walls between the school and the world. It is an approach that presupposes genuine respect for children's minds and experience — without romanticizing either. It is an approach that is inconsistent with a deficit mentality common in many schools" (2002, p. 38). Genuine student and teacher engagement based on education as life and life as education calls for an educational leadership that is emancipatory, inclusive, and democratic and, at times, even subversive in order to be able to reach moral and ethical aims (Portelli 2013).

References

Chavez, R., & O'Donnell, J. (1998). *Speaking the unpleasant: The politics of (non) engagement in the multicultural education terrain.* Albany, NY: SUNY Press.

Freire, P. (1998). *Pedagogy of freedom: Ethics, democracy, and civic courage.* New York: Rowman & Littlefield.

hooks, b. (1994). *Teaching to transgress.* New York: Routledge.

Portelli, J.P. (2013). Deficit mentality and the need for subversion: Reflections on Milani. In C. Borg, M. Cardona, & S. Caruana (Eds.), *Don Lorenzo Milani and education* Boston: Sense Publishers, pp. 213-219.

Portelli, J.P., & Vibert, A. (2002). A curriculum of life. *Education Canada, 42*(2), 36–39.

Chapter 35

What Does Every Principal of Indigenous Students Need to Know?

Jason Price and Nick Claxton

Whatever the context, all school leaders need to know enough to ask this essential question: How do the least advantaged and most oppressed students in my school benefit from this decision? (Price, 2007). If the answer is not directed, clearly and unequivocally, to the well-being of the least advantaged students, then the leader needs to consult, and better yet collaborate with staff, parents, students, and other stakeholders in order to rethink and redirect the decision. What benefits the well-being of Indigenous students is not always easy to determine, for what school leaders may believe to be beneficial may in fact turn out to be otherwise. School leaders working with Indigenous students need to know to ask for help to define what constitutes a benefit by facilitating the inclusion of a diverse intergenerational group of Indigenous parents and community members in their decision-making process. Many Indigenous communities believe in and practice layered, collective decision making rather than unilateral, top-down models.

Some basic understandings and approaches can also assist school leaders in working with and for Indigenous students and communities. School leaders need to recognize that the history of Indigenous "schooling" in the Canadian context is inextricable from colonization and its seemingly inexorable project of cultural and economic assimilation and co-option (Battiste, 2002; 2013; Price, 2007). This colonizing project is still rooted in the covert curriculum of public K–12 educational materials, pedagogies, and policies. Although a process of decolonizing schools through the negotiation and implementation of enhancement agreements between "Aboriginal" communities and provincial school authorities in Canada is advancing, colonial constructs and practices still disadvantage Indigenous students in schools. A significant gap persists between the ideal of "Aboriginal Enhancement" agreements and the reality of daily practice of individual administrators and their staff. For example, the disproportional representation of Indigenous students in special education contexts, and the over-labelling of Indigenous students with behavioural and social "disorders" and "disabilities," like FAS related conditions, still persist (BC Ministry of Education, 2014; McBride & McKee, 2001). Too often, Indigenous students' resistance to — or historically justified mistrust of schooling and its inherent deficit mentality and epidemiological approach to diagnosing students — is interpreted as intellectual "disability" or evidence of behavioural "abnormality." School leaders must understand such predicaments, as well as recognize that Western norms of knowing, being, and proceeding are not universally applicable to all populations. We cannot simply judge Indigenous students' school behaviour from a privileged, historically normative perspective.

While educational leaders need to be acutely aware of embedded racism towards Indigenous peoples in the school or district curriculum, policies, materials, and pedagogies, there are things that they can do to ameliorate these wrongs. We say *do*, rather than *know*, because of the important findings of anti-racist educator Patrick Solomon, who examined Canadian principals' knowledge of, and action in support of anti-racist practices. Solomon (2002) found that while Canadian school leaders could talk the talk, very few walked their talk. For educators wishing to walk the walk on the right path, the following are some ways of approaching teaching and learning that will help transform schools from colonizing spaces to spaces supportive of the diverse ways of being and knowing of Indigenous students, ways that will help transform educators from sympathizers to allies of Indigenous students and communities.

Educational leaders must recognize the too-often inequitable, violent, disturbing historic and contemporary relationships between the government (federal, provincial, or municipal) and Aboriginal peoples in Canada, and ensure that all staff understand these realities and reflect them in the curriculum, pedagogy and staffing decisions. Educational leaders dedicated to social justice must strive to surround all students with Aboriginal cultures, with an emphasis on host nations, in classrooms and hallways, ceremonies and presentations. Of overarching importance is to encourage, and even require all teachers to include experiential and holistic — "minds on, hands on, hearts on" — learning approaches in their pedagogy (Price, 2007).

It is also essential for educational equity that leaders provide all school staff with opportunities to experience firsthand Indigenous approaches to knowing and being, teaching and learning, and to their historical narratives, led by host nations' representatives and other Indigenous peoples. Indigenous education initiatives can provide alternative perspectives and help to reshape educator's knowledge and beliefs and, in so doing, their actions. Noted Indigenous scholar Lorna Williams' guidance for leaders striving to create respectful and welcoming learning environments for Indigenous learners is straightforward and easily achievable if there is a willingness to learn and adapt (Williams & Tanaka, 2007). Williams stresses the importance of inclusive curricula, using culturally responsive pedagogies and culturally responsive assessment strategies and instruments.

Educational leaders must also acknowledge — publically and repeatedly — the deep and significant contributions of Aboriginal peoples to global knowledge in all disciplines in order to support student academic self-confidence and sense of agency. It is also essential for educational leaders to develop thick, rich relationships with a diverse cross-section of Indigenous community members, including Elders and knowledge keepers, parents and the extended families of their students. Transformative leaders will strengthen these relationships by actively participating in Aboriginal community events, and facilitating visits to local cultural sites by students and educators.

The importance of a generous, open approach to communications cannot be exaggerated when working with Indigenous community members. Educational leaders for equity must not be afraid to ask appropriate and respectful questions of Indigenous students, parents, and community members. Ask the students and parents what stories, practices, or elements of their history they want to see explored in their school. Ask the students what they want to learn, and how they want to learn it, and then take them seriously by reflecting their preferences. Teachers and school administrators must consider their roles as members of learning communities; therefore, they must publically acknowledge and respect the Indigenous students' and Indigenous communities' place in that learning (and teaching) community.

In this short chapter, we have shared what we feel all leaders concerned with improving formal educational outcomes for Indigenous students, parents, and communities need to know and do. We have stressed the importance of educational leaders establishing deep, respectful, reciprocal relationships with Indigenous communities; enhancing staff knowledge of Indigenous cultural knowledge, accomplishments, and historical and contemporary perspectives; and adapting curriculum, pedagogies, and policies to reflect the unique needs and aspirations of Indigenous students and communities.

References

Battiste, M. (2002). *Indigenous knowledge and pedagogy in First Nations education: A literature review with recommendations.* Ottawa: National Working Group on Education.

Battiste, M. (2013). *Decolonizing education: Nourishing the learning spirit.* Saskatoon: Purich Publishing.

BC Ministry of Education (2014). Aboriginal report 2009/10–2013/14: How are we doing? Retrieved from http://www.bced.gov.bc.ca/abed/perf2014.pdf

McBride, S.R., & McKee, W. (2001). Over-representation of Aboriginal students reported with behaviour disorders: A report to the Ministry of Education British Columbia. Retrieved from http://www.bced.gov.bc.ca/abed/abed_over.pdf

Price, J. (2007). Democracy: A critical red ideal. *Journal of Thought*, Spring–Summer, pp. 9–25.

Solomon, Patrick (2002) School Leaders and Antiracism: Overcoming Pedagogical and Political Obstacles. *Journal of School Leadership*, 12(2), 174-197.

Williams, L., & Tanaka, M. (2007). Schalay'nung Sxwey'ga: Emerging cross-cultural pedagogy in the academy. *Educational Insights, 11*(3). Retrieved from http://www.ccfi.educ.ubc.ca/publication/insights/ v11n03/articles/william...

How Can Educational Leaders Promote Mental Health in Schools?

Dana Carsley and **Nancy L. Heath**

Mental health is the number one issue in schools today as identified by our teachers, principals, superintendents, directors of education and trustees.
(Ontario Public School Boards' Association, 2011)

Currently one in five children and adolescents will experience significant mental health difficulties during their school years (CMHA, 2014; NIMH, 2015) and mental health challenges are increasingly becoming a focus in our schools (Koller & Bertel, 2006; McMartin, Kingsbury, Dykxhoorn, & Colman, 2014). When students have mental health problems, they are more likely to experience a number of academic and/or school performance difficulties; compared to youth without mental health issues, children and adolescents with mental health concerns have been found to have lower academic performance, greater behavioural and/or attendance problems, and higher levels of dropout (Koller & Bertel, 2006; McLeod, Uemura, & Rohrman, 2012; Owens, Stevenson, Hadwin, & Norgate, 2012).

In 2012, the National Association of School Psychologists (NASP) published a report documenting the overwhelming evidence of the relationship between mental health and academic achievement (Charvat, 2012), as well as asserting that "Mental health is as important as physical health to children's quality of life and directly impacts their learning and development" (NASP Fact Sheet, 2015). Thus, student mental health difficulties are prevalent and clearly impact school performance. However, mental health in schools is frequently considered the responsibility of school psychologists, counselors, or social workers, and not central to the mandate of schools (Reinke, Stormont, Herman, Puri, & Goel, 2011; Weist & Paternite, 2006). Despite the fact that students' mental health is critical for their learning, many classroom-based educators (i.e., classroom teachers, resource-room teachers, classroom paraprofessionals, technicians, and aides) indicate that they are reluctant to deal with mental health issues in schools due to their insufficient knowledge, role confusion, lack of skills, and the priority of the academic mandate (e.g., Mazzer & Rickwood, 2015; Powers, Wegmann, Blackman, & Swick, 2014; Reinke et al., 2011; Splett & Maras, 2011; Stormont, Reinke, & Herman, 2011). Nevertheless, across Canada and internationally, a movement to include mental health initiatives and supports in the school at all levels is emerging (Centre of Excellence for Mental Health, 2015; National Association of School Psychologists, 2008; Ontario Ministry of Education, 2014).

Schools have a unique opportunity to support students' mental health since the services within the schools are highly accessible, minimize stigma, and are potentially cost effective relative to hospital or community service delivery (Stephan, Weist, Kataoka, Adelsheim, & Mills, 2007; Mazzer & Rickwood, 2013, 2015; Weare & Nind, 2011). Indeed, research demonstrates that promoting mental health in schools is associated with significant positive educational outcomes (Charvat, 2012; Weare & Nind, 2011). With this awareness, how can educational leaders facilitate this inclusion, particularly in light of the resistance of school personnel? Drawing on current evidence, there are four key steps to overcoming resistance to addressing student mental health. Each step focuses on one known source of resistance (i.e., insufficient knowledge, role confusion, lack of skills, and the priority of academics). In addition, appropriate resources for school principals and educators are listed with each step.

Recommendations

Step 1. Insufficient Knowledge: Psychoeducation

The first step is to provide staff with basic information that will enhance their willingness to highlight mental health concerns in the classroom. This basic psychoeducation includes information on the prevalence of mental health issues in the schools, the effects of mental health on academic success and classroom functioning, and the importance of the prevention of mental health difficulties in our day-to-day environments. Resources include fact sheets to share and discuss with school staff to emphasize how mental health needs to be an integral part of the educators' concern for student learning.

Online resource. The ABC's of Children's Mental Health: Information for School Principals. National Association of School Psychologists http://www.nasponline.org/resources/handouts/abcs_handout.pdf

Description. This downloadable fact sheet includes basic information on the prevalence of mental health issues in youth, how to address mental health issues in the schools, and steps to help teachers in supporting the needs of their students.

Step 2. Role Confusion: System Clarification

The second step targets educators' resistance to dealing with mental health problems, which arises from misunderstanding and fear concerning their role and responsibilities. The main concerns of many educators are that 1) they fear they will be expected to serve as a mental health professional, which is beyond their role, and 2) increasing their role with these students may result in less support from school mental health professionals. It is therefore important to clarify the role of the educators, and to incorporate school protocols/procedures for their involvement and collaboration with school mental health professionals. As Figure 1 illustrates, in a continuum of services for mental health in the schools, educators have a leadership role in providing a classroom environment that enhances/promotes mental well-being. With the help of school mental health professionals, educators can incorporate information and strategies for the enhancement of mental health resilience (e.g., student mental health literacy, stress management, mindfulness) into their curriculum. Although mental health professionals will lead in assessment, diagnosis, and intervention to support students with emerging or existing mental health disorders, educators remain essential partners in effective referral, providing information about classroom behaviours for assessment, and, most importantly, helping to implement appropriate interventions and supports in the classroom. It is essential, however, for educators to understand that they will only lead in promotion of well-being and universal/generalized prevention programs within their classroom.

Catch Figure 1

Role of the Teacher

Promote well-being through building mental health resilience

Universal in-class prevention programs to enhance mental health

Providing supports, accommodations, and strategies for students at-risk or with mental health issues

Referral, assessment, and diagnosis of mental health disorders

Interventions and therapy

Role of the Mental Health Professional

Figure 1: Role Clarification. Teachers are concerned that they are responsible for the full-continuum of mental health services for their students. The inverted triangle on the left shows that teachers are responsible for certain mental health needs with consistent support from the mental health professionals (MHPs). The triangle on the right demonstrates the role of the MHPs in supporting the teacher. As suggested by the whole figure, neither group has complete responsibility for the full continuum of services, as each plays a vital role in supporting students' mental health needs.

Resources for system clarification focus on the role of the educational leader in building a clear system and effective protocols for supporting mental health in their schools.

Online resource: Leading Mentally Healthy Schools: A Vision for Student Mental Health and Well-Being. School Mental Health-ASSIST http://sncdsb.on.ca/assets/uploads/MentalHealth/Leading%20 Mentally%20Healthy%20Schools.pdf

Description. Downloadable resource with strategies, tools, and resources to help administrators and school leaders organize the school system in order to promote school mental health and student well-being.

Book resource. The Teacher's Guide to Student Mental Health (2014). William Dikel, MD.

Description. In addition to essential information on mental health and mental health programs in the school, administrators will learn how to clarify roles for principals, teachers, and mental health staff, and how to communicate effectively with school teams.

Step 3. Lack of Skills: Empower Educators

One of the most significant obstacles influencing educators' willingness to engage in supporting students around mental health issues is their assertion that they do not have appropriate skills (Graham, Phelps, Maddison, & Fitzgerald, 2011; Mazzer & Rickwood, 2015; Reinke et al., 2011). Therefore, professional development and resources that develop their capacity to address these issues is paramount. Following role clarification in step 2, educators will likely be more receptive to professional development and resources that focus on the promotion of well-being and the universal prevention programs that build mental health resilience, as well as specific strategies for effective identification for referral and support of students with specific mental health difficulties in the classroom. Resources for empowering educators are organized around the different continuum of services, focusing on the areas where the educator holds a leadership position.

Online resource. Talking About Mental Illness: A Guide for Developing an Awareness Program for Youth. Canadian Mental Health Association, Centre for Addiction and Mental Health http://www.camh.ca/en/education/Documents/www.camh.net/education/Resources_teachers_schools/TAMI/tami_teachersall.pdf

Description. Downloadable guide for an awareness program designed to enhance students' and teachers' knowledge and understanding of mental illness; includes basic information, support, and tools for teachers.

Online resource. The ABCs of Mental Health. The Hincks-Dellcrest Centre http://www.hincksdellcrest.org/Home/Resources-And-Publications/The-ABC-s-of-Mental-Health.aspx

Description. With this resource, the teacher/school professional can indicate the actions or behaviours observed in their students by age, and determine whether these behaviours are developmentally appropriate (green light), somewhat worrisome suggesting referral (yellow light), or a serious problem suggesting urgent referral (red light).

Step 4. Priority of Academics: Changing School Culture

Finally, educators repeatedly indicate that a major barrier to addressing mental health promotion, prevention, or support in the classroom is the lack of time; curricular and other school needs have greater priority (Graham et al., 2011). For this final step, the educational leader plays a pivotal role through their communication to staff of the importance of the inclusion of mental health promotion, prevention, and intervention services throughout the school. Specifically, a review of relevant research has found that school leaders can best enhance mental health within their schools by making it a priority for the student, collaborating with families, and ensuring standard procedures within the schools (e.g., role clarification, community partnerships, referral and communication, monitoring progress; SMH-ASSIST, 2013).

> **Book resource.** Mental Health in Schools: Engaging Learners, Preventing Problems, and Improving Schools (2010). Howard Adelman PhD and Linda Taylor PhD.
>
> *Description.* In addition to information on school mental health programs, this book is designed to assist educators and school leaders in creating and supporting a healthy school environment that meets the academic and mental health needs of students.

Conclusion

Students' learning is inextricably linked to their mental health. As a result, it is critical for schools to support the mental health needs of students. The greatest challenge in meeting this need is to persuade educators that some aspects of mental health issues are best addressed within the school. In this chapter, we have provided the steps and resources to equip school leaders and administrators to overcome these challenges. In order to prepare students to become responsible citizens in society, an exclusive focus on academics is not sufficient; we can no longer disregard mental health concerns and separate them from the mandate of the school. With the support of school leaders and administrators, schools are in the best position to make a difference in enhancing mental health resilience.

References

Adelman, H. S. & Taylor, L. (2010). *Mental health in schools: Engaging learners, preventing problems, and improving schools.* Thousand Oaks, CA: Corwin Press Inc.

CMHA (Canadian Mental Health Association) (2014). *Mental illness in Canada.* Retrieved from http://alberta.cmha.ca/mental_health/statistics/#.VO9zckJNla8

Centre of Excellence for Mental Health (2015). *The Centre of Excellence for Mental Health: Promoting mental health to strengthen school communities.* Retrieved from http://cemh.lbpsb.qc.ca

Charvat, J.L. (2012). Research on the relationship between mental health and academic achievement. Bethesda, MD: National Association of School Psychologists.

Dikel, W. (2014). *The teacher's guide to student mental health.* New York, NY: W. W. Norton & Company.

Graham, A., Phelps, R., Maddison, C., & Fitzgerald, R. (2011). Supporting children's mental health in schools. *Teachers and Teaching, 17*(4), 479–496. doi: 10.1080/13540602.2011.580525

Koller, J.R., & Bertel, J.M. (2006). Responding to today's mental health needs of children, families and schools: Revisiting the preservice training and preparation of school-based personnel. *Education and Treatment of Children, 29*(2), 197–217.

Mazzer, K.R., & Rickwood, D.J. (2013). Community-based roles promoting youth mental health: Comparing the roles of teachers and coaches in promotion, prevention, and early intervention. *International Journal of Mental Health Promotion, 15*(1), 29–42. doi: 10.1080/1462370.2013.781870

Mazzer, K.R., & Rickwood, D.J. (2015). Teachers' role breadth and perceived efficacy in supporting student mental health. *Advances in School Mental Health Promotion, 8*(1), 29–41. doi: 10.1080/1754730X.2014.978119

McLeod, J.D., Uemura, R., & Rohrman, S. (2012). Adolescent mental health, behavior problems, and academic achievement. *Journal of Health and Social Behavior, 53*(4), 482–497. doi: 10.1177/0022146512462888

McMartin, S.E., Kingsbury, M., Dykxhoorn, J., & Colman, I. (2014). Time trends in symptoms of mental illness in children and adolescents in Canada. *Canadian Medical Association Journal, 186*(18). doi: 10.1503/cmaj.140064

NASP Fact Sheet (2015). Removing barriers to learning and improving student outcomes: The importance of school-based mental health services. *The importance of school mental health services* (Position Statement). Bethesda, MD: National Association of School Psychologists.

National Association of School Psychologists (2008). *The importance of school mental health services* (Position Statement). Bethesda, MD: Author.

NIMH (National Institute of Mental Health) (2015). *Prevalence of any disorder among children.* Retrieved from http://www.nimh.nih.gov/health/statistics/prevalence/any-disorder-among-children.shtml

Ontario Ministry of Education (2014). *Supporting minds: An educator's guide to promoting students' mental health and well-being*. Retrieved from http://www.edu.gov.on.ca/eng/document/reports/SupportingMinds.pdf

Ontario Public School Boards' Association (2011). *Let's put our heads together*. Retrieved from http://www.opsba.org/index.php?q=news/let039s_put_our_heads_together

Owens, M., Stevenson, J., Hadwin, J.A., & Norgate, R. (2012). Anxiety and depression in academic performance: An exploration of the mediating factors of worry and working memory. *School Psychology International, 33*(4), 433–449.

Powers, J.D., Wegmann, K., Blackman, K., & Swick, D.C. (2014). Increasing awareness of child mental health issues among elementary school staff. *Families in Society: The Journal of Contemporary Social Services, 95*(1), 43–50. doi: 10.1606/1044-3894.2014.95.6

Reinke, W.M., Stormont, M., Herman, K.C., Puri, R., & Goel, N. (2011). Supporting children's mental health in schools: Teacher perceptions of needs, roles, and barriers. *School Psychology Quarterly, 26*(1), 1–13. doi: 10.1037/a0022714

SMH-ASSIST (2013). *Leading mentally healthy schools: A vision for student mental health and well-being in Ontario schools*. Retrieved from http://sncdsb.on.ca/assets/uploads/MentalHealth/Leading%20Mentally%20Healthy%20Schools.pdf

Splett, J.W., & Maras, M.A. (2011). Closing the gap in school mental health: A community-centered model for school psychology. *Psychology in the Schools, 48*(4), 385–399. doi: 10.1002/pits.20561

Stephan, S.H., Weist, M., Kataoka, S., Adelsheim, S., & Mills, C. (2007). Transformation of children's mental health services: The role of school mental health. *Psychiatric Services, 58*(10), 1330–1338.

Stormont, M., Reinke, W., & Herman, K. (2011). Teachers' characteristics and ratings for evidence-based behavioral interventions. *Behavioral Disorders, 37*(1), 19–29.

Weist, M.D., & Paternite, C.E. (2006). Building an interconnected policy-training-practice-research agenda to advance school mental health. *Education and Treatment of Children, 29*(2), 173–196.

Weare, K., & Nind, M. (2011). Mental health promotion and problem prevention in schools: What does the evidence say? *Health Promotion International, 26*(51), 29–69. doi: 10.1093/heapro/dar075

Why Do Educational Leaders Need to be Concerned About "Dropouts"?

John Smyth

The short answer to why be concerned with so-called "dropouts" is that it is a social justice issue, and as such, impacts all of us, not just the young people most profoundly affected by the act of giving up on school. At its core, acting in ways that make schools hospitable and amenable places for the most marginalized and least attractive students, ought to be the *sine qua non* of educational leadership. In other words, educational leaders ought to be fervent advocates for those made most vulnerable by the way we choose to construct our societies and, by implication, the way we organize and conduct our schools.

In this chapter, I want to rehearse the arguments as to why educational leaders — and here I include policy makers, administrators, site principals, and other leaders — need to act in ways that actively prevent young people from becoming "collateral damage," as Bauman (2011) calls them. In the contemporary context of casting schools as business competitors jockeying to shove one another out of the way in order to secure "market share," students who are an untidy fit are discarded as "consumers."

Schools are arguably *prima facie* middle-class institutions; as a consequence, they need to be realigned and recast in ways that make them inclusive of *all* students, not just those whose lives, backgrounds, families, and cultures happen to fit with the ethos of the school. Given this kind of default position, it takes a particular kind of educational leader, one with the courage to bring into existence the kind of conditions that make school possible for students who have a strong predilection to give up or leave school for a variety of reasons.

The conventional interpretation — in my view, quite disingenuous — is that for students whose backgrounds are different from the prevailing one at the school, it is acceptable to label them as being "at risk" or having a range of "risk factors." This label leads to detachment, disengagement, a feeling of the inevitability of failure, and ultimately the act of early school leaving. Notice that I am holding back from using the term "dropping out," and for good reason; to deploy this term is to pin blame on students for their supposed inability to connect with and sustain a rewarding educational life. Such a view makes obvious where the finger of blame is to be pointed — to inadequacies and deficits on the part of students, their backgrounds, and the lives they bring with them to school. In this reading, it is the student who has "failed" at school; there is no space for the view that it is the school that has "failed" the student.

The alternative is to start from the position that when young people give up on school, it is for good reason. For example, they cannot see that school has anything of value to offer them. They cannot see the relevance of schooling in their present or future lives. The pedagogical approach is hostile, authoritarian, uninspiring, and often punitive. There is no sense that school is a place for them, nor that anyone cares about what kind of futures young people want to create for themselves. Such schools provide no place for students to have a "voice" — everything is predetermined by others, often at a distance, and there is no attempt to understand their lives. Thus construed, schools become demeaning, fearful, low-trust places where the overwhelming agenda is to ride roughshod over young lives by imposing somebody else's agenda. Under these conditions, it is not surprising that an increasing number of students make the active decision to withdraw — as a conscious and courageous act of defiance.

So, what are the implications for educational leaders when young people give up on school? The agenda is nicely captured by the metaphor of the miner's canary, carried to warn them of toxic gases:

> The canary's more fragile respiratory system would cause it to collapse from noxious gases long before humans were affected, thus alerting the miners to danger. The canary's distress signalled that it was time to get out of the mine because the air was becoming too poisonous to breathe. (Guinier & Torres, 2002, p. 11)

In other words, the miner's canary is the warning signal as to the wider existence of symptomatic and systematic dangers in need of attention. The canary metaphor also "captures the association between those who are left out and the social justice deficiencies in the larger community" (pp. 11–12). If the problem were simply "located in the canary," then it could be solved "by outfitting the canary with a tiny gas mask to withstand the toxic atmosphere" (p. 12). In like manner, trying to convert students of difference into middle-class clones that fit the institution of schooling is failing to grasp the more profound point that what is required is "to do something different from what has been done in the past [and] with that understanding" (p. 12). Here are some pointers gleaned from my extensive research in this area over four decades of research.

It is important to read the early warning signals around "dropping out" or disengagement and begin to do something different. Young people are profound witnesses and knowledgeable experts about what works for them educationally, if they are given the chance to speak. Most important is to acknowledge that all young people are educable, and that the challenge for schools and educational leaders is to find the appropriate and relevant starting points. While pursuing forms of learning that are rigorous, rather than dumbed-down, the focus needs to be on celebrating successes rather than punishing failures or apportioning blame to individuals. The backgrounds students bring with them to schools need to be regarded as repositories of strengths and assets for constructing and pursuing more expansive and enriching opportunities. Young people have social and emotional lives and it makes no sense to tell them to park them at the school gate. When relational problems occur, they need to be dealt with in a calm and mature manner that is educative and instructive rather than punitive. Rather than seeing students as "behaviour management" problems requiring discipline, the issue needs to be turned around; perhaps the curriculum is not engaging young people.

In pursuit of these ideas, leaders need to have the courage to speak back to educational regimes that they know are damaging young people, and have the fortitude to speak the alternatives into existence (for more on this see the notion of the *Socially Just School*, Smyth, Down, & McInerney, 2014). As Wathington put it, if in the current stressed presence in schools worldwide, "we choose to pathologize the canaries instead of interpreting their signals of distress as vulnerabilities in our capacity to serve them," then we will knowingly be doing so "at our own peril" (2013, p. 21).

References

Bauman, Z. (2011). *Collateral damage: Social inequalities in a global age*. Cambridge, MA: Polity Press.

Guinier, L., & Torres, G. (2002). *The miners' canary: Enlisting race, resisting power*. Cambridge, MA: Harvard University Press.

Smyth, J., Down, B., & McInerney, P. (2014). *The socially just school: Making space for youth to speak back*. Dordrecht, The Netherlands: Springer.

Wathington, H. (2013). Heeding the canary: How higher education can improve outcomes for all students. In J. DeVitis (Ed.), *Contemporary colleges and universities* (pp. 20–27). New York: Peter Lang Publishing.

Chapter 38

What Factors Are Associated with Educator Leader Burnout?

Kathryn Whitaker

The literature has documented significant role changes in the principalship, not only in the US, but also in other Western countries (Whitaker, 2003a; IPPN, 2002). Role changes for principals in select Western countries include issues such as local management of schools, a tension between leadership and management, increased accountability, altered relationships with parents and the community, federal and state mandates, and school choice.

In the US, federal data-driven education reform acts such as *No Child Left Behind* and *Race to the Top* initiated an era of massive accountability that holds principals and schools responsible for student outcomes, requiring principals to learn a new set of skills for which they were not trained (Dubois, 2012). By 2014, most states had adopted the Common Core Curriculum and its associated assessments, which require a new set of skills for both principals and teachers. Principals are now faced with evaluating teachers in new, prescribed ways.

Concomitant with the literature on the changing role of the principal, a good deal of attention has been devoted to the number of principals who have left or will be leaving the profession. Whitaker (2003b) found that 90 percent of school district superintendents reported a moderate to extreme shortage of qualified principal candidates. Other studies have documented the particular difficulty of filling high school principal positions (Pounder & Merrill, 2001). A recent study at the University of Texas that examined data on Texas public schools found that only half of newly hired principals stay on the job for three years; 70 percent leave before their five-year anniversary (Viadero, 2009).

The retention rates for principals in low-performing schools and those with high concentrations of student poverty are worse. According to a Texas study, 20 percent of newly hired principals at secondary schools with a high proportion of low-income students leave after one year (Viadero, 2009).

Most principals in the US and internationally are competent, hard-working professionals; their frustrations with the role are related to sheer role overload as they find themselves unable to accomplish the many tasks and responsibilities assigned to the principal. Increased demands and pressures related to accountability and instructional leadership from the federal, state, and local levels can overwhelm them. Some principals become frustrated over the overwhelming nature of the job and its impact on their personal lives. In a study of burnout among elementary principals, tasks related to accountability for student achievement and relationships with parents presented the greatest challenges. Other principals reported the difficulty of juggling all the roles of curriculum, professional development, special programs, classroom monitoring, and motivating teachers to improve (Combs, Edmondson, Jackson, 2009). These challenging issues have caused some educational leaders to reach the educator burnout stage, which has been much studied over the past three decades. The term "burnout" conjures up different meanings but typically represents high stress levels and role overload. Burnout negatively affects personal and professional lives and interpersonal relationships.

Several definitions of burnout have emerged over the past three decades:

1. Feelings of low personal accomplishment coupled with strong feelings of emotional exhaustion and depersonalization (Maslach & Leiter, 2005)
2. A state of fatigue or frustration brought about by devotion to a cause, way of life, or relationship that failed to produce the expected rewards (Freudenberger, 1980)

3. A construct used to explain observable decrements in the typical quality and quantity of work performed by a person on the job (Carroll & White, 1982)
4. An extreme form of role-specific alienation (Dworkin, 1987)

Whitaker (1995) found that educator leader burnout was specifically related to several issues:

1. *Increasing demands of the principalship*: Increased accountability pressures, increased paperwork, and time management issues contributed to increased demands.
2. *Lack of role clarity*: Principals expressed frustration over the lack of clarity in new roles related to various education reform issues.
3. *Lack of recognition*: Principals perceived a need for more intrinsic and extrinsic rewards, especially from the district office in the way of support given the new demands of the job.
4. *Decreasing autonomy*: Principals felt that autonomy was slipping away due to more national, state, and local mandates for K–12 education.

According to Brock and Grady (2002), burnout has early warning signs, including the following:

- Feelings of mental and physical exhaustion
- Feeling out of control, overwhelmed
- An increase in negative thinking
- Increased isolation from family, friends, and colleagues
- A sense of declining productivity or lack of accomplishment
- Dreading going to work in the morning

When educational leaders experience burnout, the costs are enormous, both personally and for their organizations. There is a diminished commitment to the organization at a time when commitment and energy levels need to remain high given the high-stakes accountability. Absenteeism and physical illness is likely to be higher for those leaders who experience burnout. Turnover in principals' jobs is also likely to be high with principals choosing to exit their roles early.

If educator leader burnout is a problem, what can educational organizations do to address this issue? Staff development experts and school district administrators share in the responsibility of offering assistance to educational leaders in danger of becoming burned out. Many talented leaders need greater support systems, enhanced professional development, and growth opportunities to renew their energies. I offer several recommendations to consider in designing professional development for educational leaders:

1. Re-examine the roles of principals and other educational leaders. The principalship and other leadership roles are very stressful. In particular, the role of principal has become overwhelming. School districts need to find ways to reduce the role overload for principals, such as hiring more assistant principals and other instructional support personnel.

2. Develop better support systems for principals and educational leaders. Most educators in leadership roles need greater support systems to carry out their roles. They desire opportunities to brainstorm and problem solve with their peers. Establishing mentors for new principals is also helpful.

3. Establish better training for new principals. Many educational leaders have not had the training necessary to carry out new and expanded roles with their increased demands, new technologies, and fluctuating political realities.

4. Enhance growth opportunities for educational leaders. As with most professions, those in leadership positions become tired of the same old grind day in and day out, especially since the workdays are so stressful. They require assistance in developing personal and professional development plans. Even a temporary change in role, such as a job exchange, might reinvigorate principals and other leaders to remain in their positions over the long term.

Educational organizations must explore the phenomenon of burnout seriously. With leaders' roles becoming increasingly complex, burnout will escalate. Attending to one's own personal and professional growth can be the perfect antidote to burnout.

References

Brock, B.L., & Grady, M.L. (2002). *Avoiding burnout: A principal's guide to keeping the fire alive.* Thousand Oaks, CA: Corwin.

Carroll, J.F., & White, W.L. (1982). Theory building: Integrating individual and environmental factors within an ecological framework. In W.S. Paine (Ed.), *Job stress and burnout: Research, theory, and intervention perspectives* (pp. 41–61). Thousand Oaks, CA: Sage.

Combs, J., Edmondson, S., & Jackson, S. (2009). Burnout among elementary school principals. *Journal of Leadership and Practice, 5*(4), 10–13.

Dubois, L. (2012 Summer). Creating professional development to help today's principals excel at leading teachers and schools. *Peabody Reflector,* Vanderbilt University, 17-21

Dworkin, A.G. (1987). *Teacher burnout in the public schools: Structured causes and consequences for children.* Albany, NY: SUNY Press.

Freudenberger, H.J. (1980). *Burnout: The high cost of high achievement.* New York: Anchor Press.

IPPN (Ireland Primary Principals' Network). (2002). Press release for annual conference, Galway. Dublin, Ireland.

Maslach, C., & Leiter, M.P. (2005). Stress and burnout: The critical research. In C.L. Cooper (Ed.), *Handbook of stress and medicine,* 2nd ed. (pp. 153–170). Boca Raton, FL: CRC Press.

Pounder, D.G., & Merrill, R.J. (2001). Job desirability of the high school principalship: A job choice perspective. *Educational Administration Quarterly, 37*(1), 27–57.

Viadero, D. (2009, October 9). Study shows Texas principals don't stay on the job long. *Education Week.* http://www.edweek.org/ew/articles/2009/10/09/09

Whitaker, K.S. (1995). Principal burnout: Implications for professional development. *Journal of Personnel Evaluation in Education, 9,* 287–296.

Whitaker, K.S. (2003a). Principal role changes and influence on principal recruitment and selection: An international perspective. *Journal of Educational Administration, 41*(1), 37–54.

Whitaker, K.S. (2003b). Superintendent perceptions of quantity and quality of principal candidates. *Journal of School Leadership, 13*(2), 159–180.

Chapter 39

How Can Educational Leaders Contend with the Political Aspects of Their Role?

Sue Winton and Katina Pollock

A n educational leader's role is diverse. It involves many overlapping areas including leadership/management, health/wellness, cultural identity/language, and mental health (Pollock & Hauseman, forthcoming). These areas are part of the social processes of education, and like all social processes, they involve politics. "Politics" can be defined many ways, but one way to think of politics is "who gets what, when, and how" (Lasswell, 1965).

The work of leaders involves both formal and informal politics. In terms of formal politics, who gets what, when, and how is largely determined by legislation and regulations of governing bodies. Alternatively, informal politics involve actions and decisions aimed at influencing practices outside of formal government processes. What makes them "political" is that they affect people differently: some individuals and groups benefit while others do not. Furthermore, these processes involve diverse actors with varying amounts of power. School leaders engage in both kinds of politics daily as they participate in, and are affected by, decision-making processes about who gets what, when, and how at the international, national, provincial, community, district, and school levels (Crow & Weindling, 2010; Cuban, 1988). Leaders should follow and participate in debates about policy at these different levels so they understand their work's larger political context. In this chapter, we propose ways school principals can contend with political aspects of their role while recognizing that this is not an exhaustive list.

First, principals must acknowledge that their role *is* a political one. Principals make numerous choices, including how teaching will occur, how resources and opportunities will be distributed, and how decisions are made. Principals' choices can challenge or perpetuate inequities (Anderson, 2009). Even the (impossible) decision to be "apolitical" is political since an unwillingness to engage actively in politics has political consequences.

Second, principals must recognize that their role involves engaging in politics arising outside their schools (e.g., funding decisions, new policy mandates, union activities) and within them. People in schools use power in efforts to get what they want and to protect themselves (Blase, 1991). These micro-political actions (so-called because they occur at the school level) may be conflictive or co-operative (Bjork & Blase, 2009). They may be enacted consciously or unconsciously, individually or with others (Blase & Blase, 2002). How principals act politically affects learning, teaching, relationships, school governance, and democracy in education (Blase & Anderson, 1995; Malen & Ogawa, 1988).

Third, principals can develop knowledge and skills to engage in politics purposefully and effectively. For example, they should know the wide range of micro-political strategies commonly employed in schools. Principals' micro-political actions include using rewards and sanctions; controlling decision-making processes, committee memberships, and meeting agendas; buffering; listening; avoiding; and using data strategically (Blase & Anderson, 1995; Crow & Weindling, 2010). Teachers' micro-political strategies include documenting, managing their reputations, conforming to conservative norms, and participating in extracurricular activities (Blase & Anderson, 1995). Parents and students act politically as well.

Importantly, principals need to cultivate and use political acumen or wisdom. Political acumen is the ability to read one's political environment and determine which political strategies to use, when, and with whom (Ryan, 2010). To learn about their environment, principals may listen to others, interact with a range of individuals, participate in district-wide committees, work in multiple schools districts, and conduct focus groups and surveys of their school communities (Ryan, 2010). Important knowledge to glean about one's environment includes channels of informal communication; key people, groups, and networks and their relative amounts of influence; and the local conventions and priorities.

This knowledge can help principals enact a range of political strategies. While we hope they will be used in the pursuit of social justice, these strategies can be used to pursue any kind of goal. One key political skill is agenda setting, which involves identifying goals and a plan to achieve them (Lashway, 2006). The plan must recognize and address others likely to be affected and other influences. Principals can use knowledge of their environment to determine who and what must be considered. As part of their efforts, principals must develop alliances; this involve determining whose support they need, developing relationships with these individuals, and learning how to mobilize them (Lashway, 2006). Strategies for building relationships include being visible and networking in places where they are likely to meet those with whom they want to work (Ryan, 2014). Principals should work with allies within and outside their schools to problem solve, achieve shared goals, and enhance public schools' legitimacy (Abowitz, 2011; Anderson, 2009).

Knowledge of their environments can also help principals identify individuals and groups who may challenge their goals or resist their efforts and understand their reasons for doing so. Principals can use this knowledge to communicate, educate, and negotiate with these individuals and to identify possible counter arguments (Bolman & Deal, 2008). Indeed, negotiation — a process of back-and-forth communication used to come to an agreement when participants share some but not all interests — is an important political skill for principals (Bolman & Deal, 2008). Fisher, Ury, and Patton (2011) describe an approach wherein principals separate the people with whom they are negotiating from the issue under discussion; focus on interests rather than positions; identify mutually beneficial options; and develop and use objective criteria to make decisions.

Another skill that will help principals manage political aspects of their role is the ability to persuade others. Logical and emotional appeals, as well as emphasizing one's credibility, are some important persuasive strategies (Higginbottom, 2010). Again, principals use their political acumen to determine which persuasive strategies are likely to be effective with different individuals and in various circumstances.

In addition to possessing political acumen and the skills outlined above, principals must understand policy appropriation, which inevitably occurs when a policy created in one site is interpreted and ultimately remade by those who encounter it someplace else (Levinson, Sutton, & Winstead, 2009). Individuals in schools appropriate policies in relation to their local contexts. Principals can act strategically as they engage in this process. One strategy involves identifying policy language with many possible meanings and defining it in ways that support principals' goals (Anderson, 2009). "Democracy" and "equity," for example, can be defined to pursue social justice outcomes. Another strategy is to look for omissions and contradictions in policy texts and exploit them.

Possessing political knowledge and skills is not sufficient; principals must also communicate effectively using the most appropriate means for their audiences: newsletters, podcasts, phone messages, websites, video messages, community bulletin boards, local media, email, text messages, and computer screens in school hallways (Hopkins, 2008).

So far, we have discussed strategies for directly engaging with the politics inherent in principals' work. However, principals must be selective; there may be times when it makes sense politically not to engage. Also important is active *dis*engagement (to the greatest extent possible), even if only for a short time. Healthy disengagement strategies include exercising, spending time with loved ones, taking a holiday, or reading (Pollock, Wang & Hauseman, 2014). Indeed, knowing *when* and *how* to engage can help principals contend with political aspects of their role.

References

Abowitz, K.K. (2011). Achieving public schools. Educational Theory, 61(4), 467–489.

Anderson, G.L. (2009). Advocacy leadership: Toward a post-reform agenda in education. New York: Routledge.

Bjork, L., & Blase, J. (2009). The micropolitics of school district decentralization. Educational Assessment, Evaluation and Accountability, 21(3), 195–208.

Blase, J. (1991). The micropolitical perspective. In J. Blase (Ed.), The politics of life in schools (pp. 1–18). Thousand Oaks, CA: Corwin Press..

Blase, J., & Anderson, G.L. (1995). The micropolitics of educational leadership: From control to empowerment. New York: Teachers College Press.

Blase, J., & Blase, J. (2002). The micropolitics of instructional supervision: A call for research. Educational Administration Quarterly, 38(1), 6–44.

Bolman, L.G., & Deal, T.E. (2008). Reframing organizations: Artistry, choice and leadership (4th ed.). San Francisco, CA: Jossey-Bass.

Crow, G.M., & Weindling, D. (2010). Learning to be political: New English headteachers' roles. Educational Policy, 24(1), 137–158.

Cuban, L. (1988). The managerial imperative and the practice of leadership in schools. Albany, NY: State Univeristy of New York Press.

Fisher, R., Ury, W.L., & Patton, B. (2011). Getting to yes: Negotiating agreement without giving in. Toronto, ON: Penguin.

Higginbottom, K. (2010). What can educational leaders learn from Oprah Winfrey's ability to persuade? Unpublished master's thesis, Western University, London, ON.

Hopkins, G. (2008). Principals share lessons learned about communicating with parents, others. Retrieved 10 June 2013 from http://www.educationworld.com/a_admin/admin/admin511.shtml

Lashway, L. (2006). Political leadership. In S. Smith & P. K. Piele (Eds.), School Leadership (pp.226-281) Thousand Oaks, CA: Corwin Press

Lasswell, H.D. (1965). Politics: Who gets what, when, and how (9th ed.). Cleveland, OH: Meridian Books, The World Publishing Company.

Levinson, B.A.U., Sutton, M., & Winstead, T. (2009). Education policy as a practice of power: Theoretical tools, ethnographic methods, democratic options. Educational Policy, 23(6), 767–795.

Malen, B., & Ogawa, R.T. (1988). Professional-patron influence on site-based governance councils: A confounding case study. *Educational Evaluation and Policy Analysis, 10*(4), 251–270.

Pollock, K., & Hauseman, C. (2015). Principals' work in the Canadian context: What does the research tell us? In H. Arlestig, C. Day, & O. Johansson (Eds.), *Cross Country Histories of School Leadership Research: Focus and Findings* (pp. 202-232).Dordrecht: Springer.

Pollock, K., Wang, F. & Hauseman, D.C. (2014b). *The Changing Nature of Principals' Work. Final Report for the Ontario Principals' Council* (41 pp.). Toronto, ON: Ontario Principals' Council. http://goo.gl/DKdV52

Ryan, J. (2010). Promoting social justice in schools: Principals' political strategies. *International Journal of Leadership in Education: Theory and Practice, 13*(4), 357–376.

Ryan, J. (2014). Promoting inclusive leadership in diverse schools. In I. Bogotch & C.M. Shields (Eds.), *International Handbook of Educational Leadership and Social (In)Justice* (Vol. 29, pp. 359–380). Dordrecht: Springer International Handbooks of Education.

Chapter 40

How Can Educational Leaders Support Parent Engagement in Schools?

Herveen Singh and Jeewan Chanicka

E ducational leaders are power brokers. How they choose to operationalize their executive powers in schools is a direct reflection of their theoretical conceptions of leadership. In this chapter, we argue that there is a direct link between an administrators' theoretical conception of leadership and their actions/leadership activities.

To date the idea of "inclusion" and varying degrees of "diversity and equity" has proliferated in the leadership literature (Dantley, 1990; Dei, 1996; Hallinger, 2003; Portelli, Shields, & LaRocque, 2002; Ryan, 2006; Stewart, 2006; Theoharis, 2007). To argue *for* inclusion without recognizing the complexities of marginalization is simply cliché. Our position is that *exclusion* is systemic. We are cognizant of the responsibilities that leaders have in addressing the incredible barriers that discriminate against diverse students, their families, and communities. We examine the concept of "power engagement" within the lived realities of intersecting oppressions, including eurocentrism, patriarchy, race, gender, sexuality, disability, class, indigeneity, and historical marginalization.

Leading in Diverse Contexts: Reconceptualizing Power and Engagement

Leading in diverse urban contexts requires leaders to know the community that their schools are meant to serve. We argue that it is the leader's responsibility to be connected to local neighbourhoods and to understand their intricacies, such as the histories of the people living there, their experiences, and lived realities. This responsibility is *not* an added duty; rather it is part and parcel of *being an effective educational leader.*

While conducting professional development and training sessions with educational leaders, we often hear administrators complaining that *"while it is important to connect with parents and communities, it can be challenging."* We recognize that there are barriers for all stakeholders (parents, communities, and leaders) seeking to engage with schools, especially given the rapidly changing demographics of most major cities in Canada. The concept of inclusion, therefore, becomes muddled and is either at risk of being seen as a cliché or deemed too cumbersome to engage with substantively. While it may be difficult, however, it is *not* impossible. Supporting parental and community engagement requires an orientation and conception of leadership that prioritizes and values such connections.

Embracing the Position of Power Broker: Reconceptualizing the *Means and Ends* of Power in Supporting Parental and Community Engagement in Schools

In this section we examine bell hooks' (2000) concept of "the power to end domination" and heed her call for a reconceptualization of power to include educational leaders as "power brokers" who embrace the concept of power and substantively support parental and community engagement in schools. Heeding this call for a reconceptualization of power, we argue that educational leadership requires an intentional focus on reconceptualizing the fundamental purposes of "power" to become the *power to end domination.* In parental and community engagement, domination by schools includes having the terms of parental and community engagement dictated by the school, having parameters of engagement determined by the school, and a lack of recognition and follow up on input received from parents and community members.

The current climate of educational leadership rewards those (in the form of hiring, retention, and promotion, as well as social acceptance) who emulate narrow neoliberal conceptions of accountability and performance. Neoliberal conceptions of leadership do not substantively support parental and community engagement; at best, such engagement is tokenistic. Such neoliberal conceptions breed a standardized form of leadership that rewards those who mimic imperialistic norms as measured by mainstream notions of leadership (Singh, 2010). In this way, the standardization of leadership continues to marginalize students, their parents, and communities. In reconceptualizing power, we seek to disrupt such neoliberal conceptions of power by deliberately prioritizing leadership agendas to engage the parents and communities it is meant to serve.

1. Being a Power Broker: Structures Drive Practice and Reflect Attitudes and Values

Principals must recognize that their positions are anchored in power. To simply state, "I am fair" or "I have an open-door policy," is not enough. Ultimately, they have control over most decisions that occur in a school and have the ability to affect the day-to-day lives of families. Deconstructing such power within a school is critical, especially if the intent is for all children to be successful and for all families to engage meaningfully.

A principal must pay attention to the specific structures in place in a school and whether or not they serve some students better than others. Which students are identified, who is sent to the office and how often, which staff members are leaders, who is vocal, who is silent, which parents have access to the school — or are most vocal — and which parents are not are all structures that require attention. Patterns emerging from all of these will suggest where power discrepancies exist, especially when marginalized voices are over-represented.

Hiring policies provide one way to work towards evening out the power structures in a school. Hiring should be diverse for many reasons, including preparing students for the world into which they will graduate. However, in terms of understanding the community in which the school is located, hiring staff who reflect the community will give access and voice to community members who may not feel comfortable approaching the principal. Culturally, some families will not approach a principal out of respect for authority; however, being able to see other staff members who may look like them, or speak a similar language, provides access to sharing concerns or feedback.

Office structure and set up also reflect power dynamics. The following questions should be considered: How are parents spoken to by front office staff? How long do they have to wait? How are the conversations held? Heavy use of educational terminology can also create barriers for families. When a family comes into the principal's office, what do they see? Degrees on the wall? Family pictures? Where do they sit? All of these send messages that convey power.

The principal can also be accessible by being present around the school and outside when families are dropping off students or picking them up by greeting and welcoming them. These simple strategies allow for communication and relationship building on an ongoing basis.

2. Removing Barriers for Parental and Community Engagement

In reconceptualizing power to be "the power to end domination" in educational leadership, an intentional focus on removing barriers for parental and community engagement is necessary. Parental and community engagement is vital to ensuring pertinent and relevant connections to school programming, student learning, and general well-being.

Recognizing that significant challenges and barriers to parental and community engagement exist, we advocate for a conception of leadership that consciously *ends domination* by intentionally creating pathways for parents and communities to engage with schools.

Principals can help to remove the structural power and domination perpetuated by schools by making transparent their structures, processes, and work connected to the school's improvement plan and allowing themselves to be held accountable by their community. A Community Report Card, for example, has the principal reporting back to the community and allows the community to grade the school anonymously based on these goals.

3. Providing Platforms for Parent and Community Leadership in Schools

Often mentioned in a tokenistic way, substantively removed from the examination of marginalization and other barriers to engagement in schools, is the practice of providing platforms for parental and community voices. While parental committees and trustees exist, they do not necessarily represent the needs or voices of parents and community stakeholders. In reconceptualizing power for engagement, major stakeholders should be engaged in a substantive manner, which includes giving them site-based decision-making power that cannot simply be vetoed by governing educational bodies. Further, the need to mandate leaders to capacity build beyond the confines of the educational system and build alliances with formal and informal groups that represent the interests of those they serve within the institution is critical. This often requires leaders to lean into their discomfort zone and make alliances even if they are far from their own lived reality and/or traditional norms of educational leadership.

Families can be engaged in schools in many ways, the most common being the School Council. It is critical to keep in mind, however, that this is often most accessible to middle- and upper-class families who understand how structures work and understand the role of the parent council and the power associated with it. Many times, families who do not attend the school council or parent–teacher interviews are cast as being uninterested in their children's success. However, principals must consider other ways through which families can get involved in the school in an authentic way such as

- day time drop in programs for families to learn more about how they can support students in school
- volunteer reading programs for family members to come in and read to students
- volunteer positions for parents (where income is a barrier, consider paying for police record checks through the school budget)
- evening hours for the library, especially if there is no accessible local library

- first-language reading programs for parents and children
- English as a Second Language classes for adults

All of these allow families not only to have access, but also to develop efficacy in schooling and a capacity to develop a sense of agency authentically within a school.

Conclusion

Leaders are accountable to school boards; however, the power they have affects families, students, and communities. As such, they must carefully consider and reflect upon their construct of leadership. In embracing their role as *power brokers*, principals have the opportunity and responsibility to reconceptualize their positional and authoritative powers inherent in leadership positions. This includes substantive engagement with issues of equity and diversity along with careful consideration of their roles as facilitators of community development. In doing so, such attentive principals will encourage administrative thought and praxis to move towards being service oriented and open to multiple ways of critically and conscientiously deconstructing the power with which leadership mantles are endowed and redistributing it to the stakeholders they are meant to serve.

References

Dantley, M. (1990). The ineffectiveness of effective schools leadership: An analysis of the effective schools movement from a critical perspective. *Journal of Negro Education, 59*(4), 585–598.

Dei, G. (1996). *Anti-racism education: Theory and practice.* Halifax: Fernwood Publishers.

Hallinger, P. (2003). Leading educational change: Reflections on the practice of instructional and transformational leadership. *Cambridge Journal of Education, 33*(3), 329–351.

hooks, b. (2000). *Feminist theory: From margin to center.* Cambridge, MA: South End Press.

Portelli, P. J., Shields, M. C., & LaRocque, L. (2002). Critical practice in elementary schools: Community, voice, and the curriculum of life.

International Journal of Educational Change, 3(2), 93–116.

Ryan, J. (2006). *Inclusive leadership.* San Francisco: Jossey-Bass.

Singh, H. (2010). *Leadership for social justice: From elusive conceptions to arrested developments.* Doctoral Thesis. University of Toronto.

Stewart, J. (2006). Transformational leadership: An evolving concept examined through the works of Burns, Bass, Avolio and Leithwood. *Canadian Journal of Educational Administration and Policy, 54*(1).

Theoharis, G. (2007). Social justice educational leaders and resistance: Toward a theory of social justice leadership. *Educational Administration Quarterly, 43,* 221–258.

Why Should Educational Leaders Be Concerned with Special Education?

Susan C. Bon

Educational leaders work in school systems that serve increasingly diverse communities and student populations. As leaders, their primary function is to ensure that all children have access to meaningful educational opportunities. Yet, their roles as leaders are also defined by complex legal and ethical imperatives (Bon, 2012). Given these dynamics, school leaders must learn to function across tenuous legal and ethical boundaries that are typically at peak conflict when the rights and interests of multiple stakeholders are involved.

Students with disabilities and their parents or guardians represent a growing group of stakeholders whose needs and rights are often dramatically different from their non-disabled peers. At the same time, inclusive learning environments are both the norm and the preferred setting for students with disabilities who benefit from the instructional practices as well as interactions with their non-disabled peers. As a result, school leaders must increase their special education knowledge and skills to promote an educational environment that supports educational opportunities for all students.

Research suggests that educators, particularly school administrators, are inadequately prepared (Sirotnik & Kimball, 1994; Valesky &

Hirth, 1992), and lack sufficient knowledge (Weaver, Landers, Stephens, & Joseph, 2003) to meet the needs of students in special education. At the same time, changes in law and policy, along with increasing demands for accountability, have altered the landscape of schools and shifted the duty to provide effective special education programs and services directly upon principals (McLaughlin & Nolet, 2004). The changing nature and location of special education programming and services have altered the one-size-fits-all model of public schools — and arguably are changing the course of narrowly defined private and charter schools as well. The results of these changes are persistent pressures on educators to focus their attention on special education in order to be effective leaders. In addition, the sheer numbers of IEP meetings, threats of due process hearings, and fear of special education litigation are likewise driving forces behind the central question: Why should educational leaders be concerned with special education?

Legal and Ethical Imperatives

In response, this essay will focus on what I contend are the two primary forces that shape and guide the work of educational leaders. First, the legal duty to educate children is left primarily to the states, which have in turn established education as a mandatory function of local communities. Local school systems achieve this function through state enforcement of compulsory attendance laws, which establish an educational property right for children in K–12 school systems. In conjunction with state efforts, Congress has adopted federal laws aimed specifically at promoting access to education in a non-discriminatory manner (ADA Amendments Act, 2008; Section 504 of the Rehabilitation Act, 1973) and ensuring a free appropriate public education through necessary programs and services individualized to meet the needs of students with disabilities (Individuals with Disabilities Education Act, 2005).

Second, the ethical imperative to educate youth is arguably the most critical responsibility of society because the opportunity to learn is tantamount to the ability to enjoy fully the benefits of a democratic society (Dewey, 1909). As a leader, the ability to pursue these critical ideals fervently and simultaneously is especially important for students with disabilities, who are unlikely and frankly often unable to benefit from a general education system, which was designed to serve the child with average needs and abilities. Thus, educational leaders must be aware of and focused on the unique aspects of special education programs and services in order to meet the instructional needs of students with disabilities.

Although the laws make mandatory and establish enforceable obligations, educational leaders should also recognize that the complex ethical dilemmas in special education require more than strict adherence to laws. Consequently, educational leaders should embrace the ethical imperatives as well as obey the legal mandates. Through careful balancing of both legal and ethical imperatives, educational leaders are more likely to fulfill their critical role of providing educational opportunities for students with disabilities.

Legal Complexity of Special Education

Educational leaders are bound to encounter disputes and litigation regarding the rights and opportunities provided to students with disabilities in education. Given the complexity of the state and federal legal mandates, educational leaders must be actively prepared to oversee the specialized educational needs of students with disabilities. In order to fulfill these responsibilities adequately and effectively, leaders must have at least a rudimentary understanding of special education laws, programs, and services.

Given threats of litigation by parents of students with disabilities, protected under the Individuals with Disabilities Education Act (IDEA) of 2004, local school systems must be confident in their decisions about special education programs, delivery of services, and instruction. Without sufficient understanding of special education laws — particularly the IDEA (2004), Section 504 of the Rehabilitation Act (1973) and ADA Amendments Act (2008) — it will be extremely difficult for educational leaders to balance their competing responsibilities to ensure quality instruction and monitor legal compliance (Bays & Crockett, 2007).

Moral Agency of Special Education Leadership

As moral agents (Fullan, 2001) with significant influence over the lives of students, families, educators, and the greater educational community, educational leaders have tremendous authority to sponsor meaningful educational opportunities for all children. Overseeing the provision of special education programs and services may appear to depend almost exclusively on the legal mandates established by state and federal disability rights laws. Yet, the decisions made by educational leaders about special education eligibility, programs, and services will significantly impact future educational and life opportunities. As such, these critical decisions are "saturated with values and meaning" (Paul, French, & Cranston-Gingras, 2001, p. 1).

In special education particularly, educational leaders make decisions on behalf of students who are vulnerable because of their unique learning styles and accompanying challenges. Strict adherence to the legal mandates without an ethical foundation or understanding of the moral agency necessary to serve these students would continue to disadvantage them in the education environment.

Leadership Response

Encouraging and supporting special education teachers within their classrooms is a crucial responsibility of educational leaders. Without this support, teachers are likely to report low levels of job satisfaction and to experience significant stress as they strive to educate students effectively. As well, educational leaders must be prepared to make staffing decisions, oversee scheduling, and generally ensure that educational programs are meeting the needs of students in special education.

The challenges facing parents, guardians, or family members who care for students with disabilities are different and inarguably more complex than the challenges facing the families of non-disabled children, who do not require specialized instruction, programs, or services as mandated by special education laws. In order to meet the needs of parents and children, an educational leader must create a safe and trusting relationship, which is unlikely to occur if the leader lacks sufficient knowledge and understanding of special education. Finally, trust is most easily cultivated if the parent knows that the principal is aware of and adheres to both the ethical and legal mandates in special education.

Conclusion

Educational leaders are not called upon to be special education experts; instead, they are encouraged to assume responsibility for leading a school focused on meeting both legal and ethical expectations. The knowledge and skills that a school leader brings can dramatically influence the education of all children in the school, and can contribute to a positive working environment for the entire staff. In our inclusive and changing society, there is simply no excuse for a principal to lack the insight and understanding necessary to support learning and promote success for all students.

References

ADA Amendments Act, 42 U.S.C. § 12101 (2008).

Bays, D. A., & Crockett, J. B. (2007). Investigating instructional leadership for special education. *Exceptionality, 15*(3), 143–161.

Bon, S. C. (2012). Examining the crossroads of law, ethics and education leadership. *Journal of School Leadership, 22*, 285-308.

Dewey, J. (1909). *Moral principles in education.* Cambridge, MA: Riverside Press.

Fullan, M. (2001). *Leading in a culture of change.* San Francisco: Jossey-Bass.

Individuals with Disabilities Education Act, 20 U.S.C. §§ 1400–1500 (2004).

McLaughlin, M. J., & Nolet, V. (2004). *What every principal needs to know about special education.* Thousand Oaks, CA: Corwin Press.

Paul, J., French, P., & Cranston-Gingras, A. (2001). Ethics and special education. *Focus on Exceptional Children, 34*(1), 1–16.

Section 504 of the Rehabilitation Act, 29 U.S.C. § 701 (1973).

Sirotnik, K. A., & Kimball, K. (1994). The unspecial place of special education in programs that prepare school administrators. *Journal of School Leadership, 4*, 598-630.

Valesky, T. C., & Hirth, M. A. (1992). Survey of states: Special education knowledge requirements for school administrators. *Exceptional Children, 58,* 399-406.

Weaver, H. R., Landers, M. F., Stephens, T. M., & Joseph, E. A. (2003). *Administering special education programs.* Westport, CT: Praeger Publishers.

Chapter 42

How Can Leaders Support Urban Teachers amidst the Pressures of Neoliberal Education Reforms?

Tricia M. Kress

When the students come into this room, I want them to know this is one safe place that we're all going to get everything that we want out of. And sometimes, that's just asking students to do all the tasks of the day, and they don't have to get any great epiphany from the learning but that they would just understand that in this room it's safe, that they can express themselves, that it's a kind and gentle place within the building. (Carol, 10th grade urban teacher)

I am left with this choice: *dumb it down or forever be wasted potential*. That might sound illogical since you're always told that knowledge is power but coming from where I'm from, knowledge is a burden. (Spock, 11th grade urban student)

Carol and Spock are two very different people. I feel fortunate to have worked with them and gotten to know them while conducting research in their schools in New York City and Boston. Carol is a white, middle-class literacy teacher. She was new to the teaching profession, working in a high surveillance school, and attempting to integrate technology into her classroom despite multiple barriers when I met her (Kress, 2011a). Spock is a lower income young woman of Dominican and Irish descent. She was an especially bright but underachieving high school junior who often felt her intelligence devalued in her failing school in Boston (Kress, 2011b). Although Carol's and Spock's experiences are vastly dissimilar, they harmonize around the need for the cultivation of trust and authenticity in urban schools. For Carol, the school's zero-tolerance policies enforced by live feed video surveillance of students and teachers made risk-taking in the classroom precarious, if not dangerous. For Spock, being smart in a school with a watered down curriculum made her feel as if she had to pretend to not be smart in order to make it through her classes, most of which she found boring and irrelevant to her life.

Carol's and Spock's frustrations about their daily lives in school had very little to do with the act of teaching and learning and much more to do with the impact of school policies and structures on the abilities of teachers and students to teach and to learn. In Carol's case, maintaining order and control in a zero-tolerance environment took precedence over and often prohibited the implementation of curricular innovations like technology integration. In Spock's case, preparing students for high stakes exams by focusing on the memorization of discrete bits of information took precedence over students making connections between the curriculum and their lived realities. In both cases, the socio-cultural and political climate of the school discouraged forms of humanizing education advocated by such authors as Dewey, Noddings, and Freire. The abilities of students and teachers to engage in learning as democratic participation, to develop authentic caring relationships, and to read the word and the world was severely hindered, which created tension and apathy in teachers like Carol and students like Spock, who both desired more from school than simply achieving higher test scores. Cultivating a school culture in which teachers and students can come to know each other, trust each other, connect with each other, and be their authentic selves as they question and learn about the social world together is especially crucial in light of contemporary neoliberal education reform. These "reforms" rely heavily on standardization, high-stakes testing, and punitive sanctions against schools, teachers, and students, all of which encourage distrusting and artificial relationships that hinder authentic teaching and learning.

As Anderson (2009) notes, there is no shortage of leadership literature about the importance of developing trusting relationships in schools. Since educational leaders set the tone for day-to-day life in school buildings, trust between teachers and leaders, and teachers and students, is critical for the successful functioning of school communities (Daly, 2009). However, Anderson (2009) also points out that, in these same bodies of literature, trust is typically seen from a management point of view as a means to ensure greater productivity from workers (i.e., teachers and students). From this perspective, reminiscent of the social efficiency movement of the late 19th and early 20th centuries in the U.S., productivity is measured in test score gains, reflective of human capital theories of education (Johanningmeier & Richardson, 2008). Contemporary education reform in the U.S. follows this same industrial logic, yet with an increasing voracity characteristic of the Darwinian logic of neoliberal capitalism. Education has become a market-driven competition for survival of the fittest — schools and teachers must perform better or become extinct (i.e., closed or replaced by higher performing schools and teachers). As high-stakes tests identify weak or "failing" schools, urban schools like those where Carol and Spock spent their days are targeted with punitive sanctions intended to motivate better performance (Anderson, 2009). Such sanctions include teacher layoffs, school restructuring, curricular reform, and/or school closure. School professionals are too often scapegoated and held accountable for achievement gaps more closely linked to social conditions — like poverty, racial and economic segregation, and discrimination — than they are to what students actually know.

"Trust" in this climate rings hollow as policy put into practice reveals a contradiction: members of the school community need to feel trust to be productive, but they are clearly not trusted by policy makers, which points to inauthenticity at the social and organizational levels.

How can education can be the great equalizer in a society that is increasingly unequal? Education reform bears down on and undermines school professionals' efforts to create authentic and trusting school cultures. As Anderson explains,

> authenticity has to do with viewing human beings as ends in themselves, rather than as means to other ends... In schools, it means that the pedagogical relation, the interaction between teacher and student, is essentially a social relation that requires emotional commitment, caring, and a view that one's students deserve as high a quality education as one's own children receive. (2009, p. 41)

In my research, spaces of trust and authenticity existed but were located "in between" or "outside" of typical school learning structures. For Carol, these occurred during her prep period when students would flock to her classroom to talk with her and eat their lunch while doing schoolwork. For Spock, these were afterschool spaces where she, her teacher, and I read social theory and conducted ethnographic research together. As leaders recognize and reject the hypocrisy of neoliberal logic, they can deflect the weight of policy pressures off teachers and students, and seek out and nurture these tucked away spaces where neoliberal reform has not yet penetrated. By buffering the neoliberal logic that transmogrifies teachers into content dispensers and students into content receivers, and by protecting and growing these spaces of hope, leaders can encourage teachers and students to come to know each other *as humans* engaging in the difficult work of learning together about the world and themselves in relationship.

References

Anderson, G. L. (2009). *Advocacy leadership: Toward a post-reform agenda in education.* New York: Routledge.

Daly, A. (2009). Rigid response in an age of accountability: The potential of leadership and trust. *Educational Administration Quarterly, 45*(2), 168–216.

Johanningmeier, E. V., & Richardson, T. (2008). *Educational research, the national agenda, and education reform: A history.* Charlotte, NC: Information Age.

Kress, T. M. (2011a). Going high tech under high surveillance: Technology integration, zero tolerance, and implications for access and equity. *Radical Teacher, 90,* 15–24.

Kress, T. M. (2011b). Stepping out of the academic brew: Using critical research to break down hierarchies of knowledge production. *International Journal of Qualitative Studies in Education, 23*(3), 267–283.

Afterword

Darrin Griffiths and John P. Portelli

After nearly twenty years in administrative positions in schools, the first author of the Afterword vividly remembers his first few months when his understanding of "leadership" was intentionally good but innocent of the complexities of how our socially constructed world affects schools and their participants. If schools and the people who work in them are to make a difference in the lives of students, then understanding the outside world is paramount. It is easy to fall prey to reading "recipe" leadership books that claim to be the "only" book necessary for "effective schools" and "effective leaders." They tend to be more about management than leadership, and reproduce the mythology of universal quick-fix solutions irrespective of contextual differences.

Of course, educational leadership includes an administrative aspect that implies moral responsibility and fairness. However, just as in any profession, the "recipe" approach to educational leadership eliminates the element of informed judgement and autonomy just as mandatory sentencing eliminates the ability of judges to use their own good judgement in considering each case on its own merits. Educational leadership does not exist in a vacuum; it always operates within a socio-political context. Moreover, the human nature of the project means that we cannot control all the variables, and hence we cannot predict the outcomes. "Best practices" can guide us in our complex work but cannot replace judicious, conscious, critical, and creative educational leadership.

This begs the question: how does educational leadership continue to evolve and improve if there are no straightforward answers? While "constant improvement" is an overused adage, it really speaks to how educational leaders must evolve: moving along the continuum of understanding to deconstruct our socially constructed world. We continue our journey as critical educators seeking to understand how the world operates, while acting in good faith and with openness to new learning.

This development of critical consciousness empowers individuals to combat the negative elements of the system. Experience has taught us that devoting more time to supporting growth in others is the greatest legacy for any educational leader. As we support teachers, they are better able to support students. Teachers who understand the inequities of the system will fight ferociously for their students; once they have witnessed the inequities, they never again see the world in the same way. In other words, educators who are able to deconstruct and understand the system are incredibly powerful, effective, long-term agents of change for all institutions of learning. Facilitating and supporting this awareness in others so that school experiences are indeed equitable for all students is the key concern of educational leadership.

Change begins with school leaders because long-term, substantive progress can never occur without a significant shift in worldviews and practices at the highest levels of power. This book provides educational leaders with both insights and possibilities for practice, outlining numerous ways to deconstruct the system while also supporting and suggesting ways for equitable experiences for students. There is a sense of urgency to improve leadership practices and thus our schools. Given the human predicament there will never be a fool-proof approach that guarantees success; schools are too messy and complex for quick, simplistic solutions.

Thanks to our superb collection of authors, readers can return to this book throughout their careers as they face barriers and address challenges to make their schools more socially just. Our leadership exhibits who we are, and who we are is reflected in our leadership. It is crucial that we know what we stand for and why; we need to make sure that our leadership reflects our values and beliefs. The essays in this collection will help us reflect critically on both our beliefs and our actions. Such critical reflection is but the first step in making all aspects of our schools — and our students' lives — better, much better.

Contributors

Gary L. Anderson is a Professor in the Educational Leadership program at NYU Steinhardt. A former high school teacher and principal, he has published on topics such as critical ethnography, action research, school micro-politics, new policy networks and the new professionalism. His most recent books are *Advocacy Leadership: Toward a Post-Reform Agenda* (2009, Routledge) and *The Action Research Dissertation: A Guide for Students and Faculty, Second Edition* (2014, Sage).

Lawrence Angus is an Adjunct Professor in the Faculty of Education and Arts at Federation University Australia. He is particularly interested in critical approaches to educational policy and management, with particular emphasis on power and politics in organisations. His research focusses on issues of educational reform and leadership, and the assertion, critique, and playing out of reform agendas in sites of educational practice.

Wayne Au is an Associate Professor in the School of Educational Studies at the University of Washington Bothell, and he is an editor for the social justice teaching magazine and publisher, *Rethinking Schools*. Author of numerous books, chapters, and journal article, his research focuses on education policy, critical education theory, multicultural education, and teaching for social justice.

William Ayers, formerly Distinguished Professor of Education and Senior University Scholar at the University of Illinois at Chicago (UIC) has written extensively about social justice and democracy, education and the cultural contexts of schooling, and teaching as an essentially intellectual, ethical, and political enterprise. His books include *A Kind and*

Just Parent; *Teaching toward Freedom*; *Fugitive Days: A Memoir*; *On the Side of the Child*; *Teaching the Personal and the Political*; *To Teach: The Journey, in Comics*; *Teaching toward Democracy*; and *Race Course: Against White Supremacy*.

Heesoon Bai, Professor at Simon Fraser University, teaches educational philosophy, with a focus on ethics and moral education, eco-education, and history of educational theories and ideas. Her scholarship is informed by the integration of Western and Eastern philosophies, and contemplative philosophies and practice. View her website at http://www.sfu.ca/education/faculty-profiles/hbai.html and published works online at http://summit.sfu.ca/collection/204

Ira Bogotch, Professor of Educational Leadership at Florida Atlantic University. His research and teaching interests include critical research methods, leadership for social justice, little "l" leadership theories, and the principalship. He co-edited the *International Handbook of Educational Leadership and Social [In]Justice* (Springer) and his most recent writings have focused on school leadership development in post-Katrina New Orleans and international humanistic leadership within Educational Leaders Without Borders.

Susan C. Bon is an Associate Professor of Education and Law in the Department of Educational Leadership and Policies at the University of South Carolina. Her scholarship and teaching focuses on the impact of law and ethics on education leadership and special education leadership in K-12 schools and higher education programs. She has published nearly forty education law articles and book chapters, is an active leader in national law-related societies, and is dedicated to promoting legal and ethical leadership across the P-20 continuum.

Nicholas C. Burbules is the Gutgsell Professor in the Department of Educational Policy, Organization and Leadership at the University of Illinois, Urbana-Champaign. His primary research focuses on philosophy of education; teaching through dialogue; and technology and education. His current philosophical work focuses primarily on the idea of "situated" philosophy of education, a way of reframing the question of whether philosophy of education is merely a derivative branch of pure philosophy or an "applied" field. Situated philosophy of education begins with real cases and problems and derives philosophical questions from them, rather than beginning with philosophical problems and then using educational cases as examples or illustrations.

Dana Carsley is an elementary school teacher and a Masters student in the Department of Educational and Counselling Psychology at McGill University. She has worked as a teacher and special needs tutor for students at all levels. Her research focuses on classroom interventions to promote mental health, specifically teacher-led mindfulness and stress management programs. She has presented at numerous academic conferences and teacher workshops.

Jeewan Chanicka is the Principal of Aldergrove Public School, a school focused on social justice from full-day kindergarten to grade 8. He has engaged in Equity work for over 20 years. Jeewan can be contacted at jeewanc@gmail.com.

XEMŦOLTW̱ Nick Claxton is from the W̱SÁNEĆ Nation and a PhD. Candidate in Educational Studies in the Department of Curriculum and Instruction at the University of Victoria. Currently Nick is the Indigenous Advisor and Master's Program Coordinator in Indigenous Education at UVIC, where he also teaches courses in Indigenous Education. Nick's research and teaching interests include the revitalization of Indigenous knowledge systems and land/water based practices.

George Dei is Professor of Social Justice Education and Director of the Centre for Integrative Anti-Racism Studies at OISE, University of Toronto. Dei's teaching and research interests are in the areas of Anti-Racism, Minority Schooling, International Development, Anti-Colonial Thought and Indigenous Knowledges Systems.

John B. Diamond is the Hoefs-Bascom Associate Professor in the Department of Educational Leadership and Policy Analysis and a faculty affiliate in the Departments of Afro-American Studies and Educational Policy Studies at the University of Wisconsin – Madison. He studies the relationship between social inequality and educational opportunity examining how educational leadership, policies, and practices shape students' educational opportunities and outcomes. He is co-editor of the book *Distributed Leadership in Practice*.

Mark A. Gooden is Director of the University of Texas at Austin Principalship Program (UTAPP) in the Educational Administration Department. He also serves as an Associate Professor in that department. His research interests include the principalship, issues in urban educational leadership and legal issues in education. His most recent research appears in *Educational Administration Quarterly, Journal of School Leadership, Urban Education, Journal of Research on Leadership in Education, Education and Urban Society, The Journal of Negro Education, The Sage Handbook of African-American Education* and *The Principal's Legal Handbook*.

André P. Grace is Canada Research Chair in Sexual and Gender Minority Studies (Tier 1) and Professor and Director of Research at the Institute for Sexual Minority Studies and Services in the Faculty of Education, University of Alberta. His research includes comparative transnational studies of policies, pedagogies, and practices shaping lifelong learning as critical action, with a major focus on sexual and gender minorities and their issues and concerns regarding social inclusion, cohesion, and justice in education and culture. More information available from: www.ismss.ualberta.ca

Margaret Grogan is Professor and Dean of the College of Educational Studies, Chapman University, California. Originally from Australia she graduated from Washington State University with a Ph.D. in Educational Administration, and then taught educational leadership and policy at the University of Virginia and at the University of Missouri-Columbia. Her current research focuses on women in leadership, gender and education, the moral and ethical dimensions of leadership, and leadership for social justice.

Helen M Gunter is a Professor of Education Policy and Sarah Fielden Professor of Education in The Manchester Institute of Education, University of Manchester, UK. Her research and teaching interests include governance, education policy and school leadership. Her most recent book is, School *Leadership: An Intellectual History of Research and Practice*, published by Bloomsbury Press.

Victoria (Tory) Handford is an Assistant Professor at Thompson Rivers University, and teaches Master's level courses in the Leadership program. Tory has been an elementary School Principal in Waterloo Region, an education officer in the Leadership Development branch of the Ontario Ministry of Education, and a program officer in the Standards of Practice and Accreditation department of the Ontario College of Teachers. She writes about the relationship between trust and leadership, and is currently co-editing a book about the experiences of tenure-track in Canadian faculties of education, among other works. More information at vhandford@tru.ca.

Nancy L. Heath is a James McGill Professor in the Department of Educational and Counselling Psychology at McGill University. Professor Heath has presented at more than 200 conferences and published extensively on issues pertaining to mental health in the schools. She has worked for more than 25 years in partnership with schools on grants, research activities and service delivery to address mental health concerns in the schools.

Kristin Shawn Huggins is an Assistant Professor of Educational Leadership in the Department of Educational Leadership, Sport Studies, and Educational/Counseling Psychology at Washington State University. Her research interests include leadership learning and development and school culture. Her research has been published in the *Journal of School Leadership, International Journal of Leadership Education*, and *Journal of Education for Students Placed at Risk*.

Awad Ibrahim is a Professor in the Faculty of Education of the University of Ottawa. He specializes and publishes widely in Social Foundations, Sociology and Curriculum. Among his latest books is, *The Rhizome of Blackness: A Critical Ethnography of Hip-Hop Culture, Language, Identity and the Politics of Becoming* (Peter Lang, 2014).

Tricia M. Kress is an Associate Professor of Leadership in Education and Graduate Program Director of the Leadership in Urban Schools Ed.D./Ph.D. program at the University of Massachusetts Boston. Her research and teaching interests center on using critical pedagogy and critical qualitative research with teachers and students to improve education in urban schools. She is author or editor of multiple volumes including *Critical Praxis Research: Breathing New Life into Research Methods for Teachers* and *Paulo Freire's Intellectual Roots: Toward Historicity in Praxis* (Winner of the 2014 Society of Professors of Education Book Award) as well as co-series editor of the Sense Publishers book series Imagination and Praxis: Creativity and Criticality in Education and Educational Research.

Randall B. Lindsey is Emeritus Professor, California State University, Los Angeles. He consults on educational issues related to equity and access. He has served as a K-12 teacher and administrator and as a university faculty member – randallblindsey@gmail.com.

Scott Lowrey is an elementary School Principal in Hamilton, Ontario, Canada. He received Canada's Outstanding Principals (COP) recognition in 2005, the inaugural year of the COP program for initiatives relating to early literacy and the creation of a multigenerational continuum of community services encompassing society's youngest to society's most senior. Scott completed his Ed.D. studies (Educational Administration) at OISE, University of Toronto, in 2013. Scott was inducted in the McMaster Alumni Gallery in 2014, and was also a recipient of McMaster University's Lloyd Reed Prize in 1985.

Jacky Lumby is a Professor of Education at the University of Southampton in the UK. Her main research interests are in educational leadership, particularly related to equity and the inclusion/ exclusion of learners and staff. She has researched and published widely on the leadership of schools, vocational colleges and higher education in the UK, Ireland, China and South Africa and has worked with local, regional and national policy makers in relation to developing policy and practice for equity and inclusion.

John MacBeath is Professor Emeritus at the University of Cambridge, held the Chair of Educational Leadership from 2000 to 2013. He served for four years in a an advisory capacity with the Blair Government and the Scottish Action Group on Standards, and has held consultancy positions with OECD, UNESCO, the European Commission and Education International. He has authored 20 books on leadership and school self evaluation and was awarded the OBE for services to education in 1997.

Lejf Moos is a Professor of educational leadership and governance at the Department of Education (DPU), Aarhus University, Copenhagen, Denmark. He has for several years done researched and educated in educational leadership and governance in Danish, Nordic as well as international project. He has published a number of books and articles and has been an editor of the Education Assessment, Evaluation and Accountability journal with Springe and is now the editor of the Springer book series on Educational Governance research.

Pierre Wilbert Orelus is Associate Professor in the Curriculum and Instruction department at New Mexico State University. Professor Orelus has received several awards, including *New Mexico State University Exceptional Achievements in Creative Scholarly Activity Award (2013)*. His research interests include language-accent, race, postcolonial, immigrant, and gender studies. His articles have been published in leading scholarly journals, including *Journal of Black Studies; Journal of Inquiry & Action in Education; Race, Gender, and Class; and Diaspora, Indigenous, and Minority Education*. His most recent books include *Interrogating Critical Pedagogy: The Voices of Educators of Color in the Movement* (with Rochelle Brock, Routledge, 2015) and *Affirming Language Diversity in Schools and Society: Beyond Linguistic Apartheid* (Routledge, 2014).

Katina Pollock is an Associate Professor in the Faculty of Education at Western University, Ontario, Canada and Co-Director for the Knowledge Network for Applied Educational Research in Ontario. Katina teaches in both the initial teacher education program and at the graduate level. Her research explores the intersection of power, access, and engagement in relation to work and learning in the field of education. Recent publications include a special journal issue (School Leadership: Opportunities for Comparative Inquiry) in the Canadian and International Education journal, 2014. (kpolloc7@uwo.ca, twitter: @DrKatinaPollock)

Jason Price is an Associate Professor in the Department of Curriculum and Instruction at the University of Victoria. He is an elected School Trustee in the Saanich District in BC, and a member of UVic Indigenous Education Advisory Board. He teaches courses on educational change and global education, and has taught in community based Indigenous university programs.

John Roberts is a Metis who has retired from Mohawk College in Hamilton, Ontario. He has served as President of the Canadian Metis Council for 11 years, and has written 30 books, mainly textbooks in the areas of communications and Indigenous studies.

James Ryan is a Professor in the Department of Leadership, Higher and Adult Education at the Ontario Institute for Studies in Education. His research interests include leadership, inclusion, micro politics and activism. His latest book, an edited edition with Denise Armstrong, is called *Working (With/out) the System: Educational Leadership, Micropolitics and Social Justice*.

D. Mike Sacken has been a Professor of Education for 35 years, the last 25 at TCU. For the first part of his career he taught and researched educational law, but at TCU, in addition to educational administration, he taught teacher preparation KG-12. His scholarly interests apart from law & education include professional roles, administrator and teacher preparation, and ethical issues in education.

Hairon Salleh is an Assistant Professor at the Policy and Leadership Studies Academic Group, National Institute of Education, Nanyang Technological University. His research and teaching interests center on school leadership and collective teacher learning comprising areas such as distributed leadership, teacher leadership, professional learning communities, teacher professional development and action research. More information available from: http://www.nie.edu.sg/profile/hairon-salleh.

Coleen M. Scully-Stewart, faculty member in the Department of Leadership, Higher and Adult Education, OISE, University for Toronto, where she teaches graduate courses in leadership, policy, change and social justice. She is a former elementary School Principal and co-author of *Principal as Leader of the Equitable School*.

Joan Poliner Shapiro is Professor of Higher Education at Temple University and Co-Director of the New DEEL Community Network. Previously, she served as Associate Dean and Chair of her department at Temple's College of Education, and as President of Temple University's Faculty Senate. Her areas of scholarship are ethics and gender in education, and most recently she co-authored: *Ethical Educational Leadership in Turbulent Times* (2013), 2nd ed., with Steven Jay Gross, and *Ethical Leadership and Decision Making in Education (2011)*, 3rd ed., with Jacqueline Stefkovich.

Carolyn M. Shields, is a Professor of Educational Leadership in the College Of Education at Wayne State University, Detroit, Michigan, where she focuses on critical transformative leadership for inclusive, equitable, and socially-just schools and society. Her publications include 11 authored or edited books and numerous chapters and articles related to transformative leadership, dialogue, and deeply democratic education.

Douglas J. Simpson is an Associate Professor at TCU. During his career, he has taught in the fields of school psychology, curriculum studies, and philosophy of education. His scholarly works examine issues in teacher education, ethical inquiry by P-12 educators, Deweyan and Freirean educational ideals, and development of self in democratic schools.

Herveen Singh is a research Associate with the Centre for Leadership and Diversity, OISE, University of Toronto. Herveen is an Education Consultant. Her area of expertise include educational leadership, organizational development, equity and diversity, teaching quality& assessment and the hiring, recruitment and promotion of employees from designated groups. She conducts equity reviews and professional development training for faculty and management worldwide. Herveen can be contacted at Herveen.Singh@utoronto.ca.

John Smyth is Visiting Professor of Education and Social Justice, University of Huddersfield, UK, was Research Professor of Education, Federation University Australia, and is Emeritus Professor Flinders University of South Australia, and of Federation University Australia. He held the Mitte Endowed Chair in School Improvement, Texas State University and is a former Senior Fulbright Research Scholar, recipient of several awards from the American Educational Research Association, and a Fellow of the Academy for Social Science in Australia. Among his recent books are *Critical educational research: a conversation with the research of John Smyth* (with Down, McInerney & Hatttam, Peter Lang Publishing, 2014). He is the editor/author of 30 books and 200 refereed scholarly papers, and his research interests are in policy sociology, policy ethnography, social justice, and sociology of education. More https://www.hud.ac.uk/ourstaff/profile/index.php?staffuid=sedujs4

Daniel Spikes is an Assistant Professor of Educational Administration at Iowa State University. He is a former K-12 teacher and school administrator. His research interests focus on racial disparities in education and the practices of school districts, schools, and school leaders that serve to perpetuate and/or ameliorate these disparities. Specifically, his research focuses on the following: school leadership, in general, with a specific focus on social justice and anti-racist leadership; pre-service and in-service training of educators on cultural proficiency and/or anti-racism; urban education; social justice; and school tracking policies.

Shirley R. Steinberg, Research Professor of Youth Studies at the University of Calgary is the author and editor of many books in critical pedagogy, urban and youth culture, media/cultural studies, and leadership. The organizer of The International Institute for Critical Pedagogy and Transformative Leadership, she is committed to a global community of educators and community workers engaged in social justice and the situating of power within social and cultural contexts. www.freireproject. org.

Ronald G. Sultana, Professor in the Department of Educational Studies and Director of the Euro-Mediterranean Centre for Education Research, University of Malta. His work focuses on the relationship between education and the world of work, with a particular focus on equity and social justice issues. More information available at www. um.edu.mt/emcer

Jeanne L. Surface received her Ed.D. in Educational Leadership from the University of Wyoming in 2006. She has served in several rural leadership positions in Nebraska and most recently as a Superintendent in a very remote district next to Yellowstone National Park in Wyoming. She is now an Associate Professor at the University of Nebraska at Omaha in Educational Leadership. Jeanne chairs multiple dissertations of future leaders in public schools, teaches School Law, qualitative research methods, and advanced research. Her research interests include rural education and school law. She has been named an Education Star Point leader for the University of Nebraska's Rural Futures Institute. http://ruralfutures.nebraska.edu/. Jeanne can be contacted at: jsurface@unomaha.edu

Charlene Tan is an Associate Professor at the Policy and Leadership Studies Academic Group, National Institute of Education, Nanyang Technological University. A former high school teacher and a philosopher by training, her research interests include philosophy of education, comparative education and critical thinking. She is the author of *Teaching without Indoctrination: Implications for Values Education (2008) and Islamic Education and Indoctrination: The Case in Indonesia* (2011).

Raymond D. Terrell is an Emeritus Professor, College of Education Health and Society, Miami University. He has also served as a professor of educational administration and Dean at California State University, Los Angeles. He began his career as a public school teacher and administrator.

Paul Theobald currently serves as Dean of the School of Education at Buena Vista University in Storm Lake, Iowa. He has published widely in the area of community-based and place-based education. His most recent book, *Education Now: How Re-thinking America's Past Can Change Its Future* (Paradigm, 2009), won the Critic's Choice Award from the American Educational Studies Association. Paul can be contacted at: theobaldp@bvu.edu

Pat Thomson is Professor of Education and Convenor of the Centre for Research in Arts, Education and Literacies (School of Education) and Director of the Centre for Advanced Studies (faculties of Arts and Social Sciences), The University of Nottingham. Her research is primarily focused on school and community change through arts and creative pedagogies; she also researches and teaches doctoral education and academic writing. She can be found blogging on http://patthomson.net and tweeting as @patthomson.

Njoki Wane is a Professor in the Department of Social Justice Education at the OISE, University of Toronto. Until September 2014, she was the Special Advisor on Status of Women at University of Toronto & Director of Centre for Integrative Anti-Racist Research Studies (CIARS). For the last twenty years she has been researching, writing and teaching in the areas of Black feminisms in Canada, African feminisms, African indigenous knowledges, anti-racist education in teacher education, African women and spirituality, and ethno-medicine.

Fei Wang, Is an Assistant Professor in the Department of Educational Studies, Faculty of Education, University of British Columbia (UBC) where he teaches Masters' and Ed.D courses on educational administration, leadership, policy, and organization studies. His research interest focuses on educational administration, subversive and social justice leadership, policy studies, and the work of school principals. Previously, he was a sessional lecturer at the Western University and a research analyst at People for Education.

Kathryn Whitaker is Professor Emeritus at the University of Northern Colorado in Educational Leadership and Policy Studies. Her research interests include principal burnout, principal shortages, school district and university partnerships, and accountability and democratic voice as related to the role of superintendent.

Sue Winton is an Associate Professor in the Faculty of Education at York University in Toronto, Ontario, Canada. Her research examines policy influences and implications of education policy for critical democracy. Previous studies include: critical analyses of safe schools, bullying and character education policies; examination of the emergence and activities of advocacy groups in education; and an investigation of the meanings and enactment of school success and successful school leadership in Ontario schools. She is a former elementary school teacher and has taught in Mexico, Canada, and the USA.

Philip Woods is Professor of Educational Policy, Democracy and Leadership at the University of Hertfordshire, UK, and currently Chair of the British Educational Leadership Management and Administration Society (BELMAS). He is an internationally recognised scholar in the field of educational leadership and policy, with an extensive publication record and a particular focus on questions of democracy, leadership, educational policy and governance, alternative education and entrepreneurialism. Publications include *Transforming Education Policy: Shaping a democratic Future* (Policy Press, 2011).

About the Editors

Darrin Griffiths, who since 1997 has held leadership positions in schools in Toronto and Hamilton, Ontario. Currently he is the principal of Queen Mary School in Hamilton. He is also a part-time Senior Lecturer with Niagara University where he teaches Masters level courses on educational leadership and curriculum. He is the author of *Principals of Inclusion: Practical Strategies to Grow Inclusion in Urban Schools* (2013).

John P. Portelli, Professor in the Department of Social Justice Education and Department of Leadership, Higher and Adult Education, and Co-Director of the Centre for Leadership and Diversity at Ontario Institute for Studies in Education of the University of Toronto. His research and teaching interests include democratic theory and critical pedagogy, equity and social justice issues in educational policy and leadership, and student engagement and 'student at risk'. More information available from: www.john-peter-portelli.com.

CPSIA information can be obtained
at www.ICGtesting.com
Printed in the USA
LVOW01s1733031016
507211LV00035B/1803/P